HEALTH SYSTEMS RESEARCH

Edited by K. Davis and W

Detlef Schwefel   Herbert Zöllner
Peter Potthoff (Eds.)

Costs and Effects of Managing Chronic Psychotic Patients

With 21 Figures and 93 Tables

Springer-Verlag Berlin Heidelberg New York
London Paris Tokyo

Professor Dr. Detlef Schwefel
Gesellschaft für Strahlen- und Umweltforschung mbH München
MEDIS – Institut für Medizinische Informatik und Systemforschung
Ingolstädter Landstraße 1, 8042 Neuherberg
Federal Republic of Germany

Herbert Zöllner, Ph. D.
Regional Officer for Health Economics
World Health Organization, Regional Office for Europe
8, Scherfigsvej, 2100 Copenhagen
Denmark

Dr. Peter Potthoff
Gesellschaft für Strahlen- und Umweltforschung mbH München
MEDIS – Institut für Medizinische Informatik und Systemforschung
Ingolstädter Landstraße 1, 8042 Neuherberg
Federal Republic of Germany

ISBN 3-540-18867-3 Springer-Verlag Berlin Heidelberg New York
ISBN 0-387-18867-3 Springer-Verlag New York Berlin Heidelberg

Library of Congress Cataloging-in-Publication-Data
Costs and effects of managing chronic psychotic patients. (Health systems research) 1. Psychiatric
hospital care – Cost effectiveness. 2. Mentally ill – Care – Cost effectiveness. I. Schwefel, Detlef.
II. Zöllner, Herbert. III. Potthoff, Peter. RA790.5.C675   1988   338.4'33622   88-6564
ISBN 0-387-18867-3 (U.S.)

© Springer-Verlag Berlin Heidelberg 1988
Printed in Germany

The use of general descriptive names, trade marks, etc. in this publication, even if the former are not
especially identified, is not to be taken as a sign that such names, as understood by the Trade Marks and
Merchandise Marks Act, may accordingly be used freely by anyone.

Product Liability: The publisher can give no guarantee for information about drug dosage and application
thereof contained in this book. In every individual case the respective user must check its accuracy by
consulting other pharmaceutical literature.

Typesetting and Bookbinding: Appl, Wemding. Printing: aprinta, Wemding
2119/3145-543210

Preface

Since the early 1970s, delivery of care to people who are considered to suffer from chronic psychotic disturbances has been at a crossroads. In 1983, the European Regional Office of the World Health Organization (WHO), within its health economics programme, encouraged international research on the economic implications of alternative strategies of care for those patients. Originally, it was intended to compare at least two or more strategies of managing chronic psychotics, especially strategies which place different emphasis on inpatient and outpatient care.

Instead of designing a fully coordinated, multinational, multicentre study based on a mutually agreed on study protocol, we decided on the following:
- To meet with researchers interested in the social, psychological, and economic features of health care for chronic psychotic patients
- To stimulate ongoing research projects or to initiate new ones
- To discuss quite different approaches from international and interdisciplinary points of view
- To review and revise the diversified end products of such an open research process

For this purpose, we outlined a broad range of topics which could be included in the study:
- Methodological problems of evaluation in this field
- Social and economic implications of psychiatric deinstitutionalization
- Scenarios of various degrees of deinstitutionalization
- Assessment of (hospital) costs of the treatment for chronic schizophrenic and other psychotic patients
- Public and private costs of the main treatment strategies
- Time-expenditure analyses of chronic psychotic patients

These topics were to be major themes of our study, but as we knew that certainly many other areas of research would also be of interest in a study of the arguments for and approaches to assessing or to strengthening the cost-effectiveness of managing chronic psy-

chotic patients, we were eager to motivate as many study participants as possible to contribute to our common undertaking.

We chose an 'open research strategy' – contrary to a stream-
lined multicentre study – because we believe that the field of study
needs broad exploration first and then quite different approaches
and points of view in terms of units of observation, levels of spatial
aggregation, and types of analyses. It is our prejudice that a bundle
of wild flowers is nicer than a bunch of mechanically produced or
even cloned tulips. Last but not least, we know that we do need
many different arguments in the fight for more efficiency and effectiveness, including the one concerned with more humanity in
the management of chronic patients.

The first drafts of most contributions in this volume were originally presented at our workshop on 'Cost-effectiveness of managing chronic psychotic patients' held in Munich, 16–18 December
1985, and jointly organized by the Gesellschaft für Strahlen- und
Umweltforschung (GSF) and the Regional Office for Europe of
WHO. The two background papers introducing the volume comprise a report on a first WHO meeting, which took place in Mannheim, May 2–4, 1983, and at which we tried to develop terms of reference for our study, as well as the report from our Munich
workshop. The other 13 papers deal, from different viewpoints,
with some problems of cost and effectiveness of (alternative) strategies of psychiatric care. They represent reports spanning a wide
range of nations from many parts of Europe and abroad. Besides
their function of reporting on national particularities, the papers
can be regarded as examples of different approaches to delivering

Table 1. Some characteristics of the 13 chapters in this book

Authors	Units of observation			Level of spatial aggregation			Type of analysis		
	Systems	Institutions	Individuals	National	Regional	Institutional	Theory/ methodology	Descriptive/ cross-sectional	Historical/ longitudinal
Barrelet et al.			×			×		×	
Bridges et al.			×			×			×
Frank et al.	×			×					×
Kastrup et al.			×	×					×
Marinoni et al.			×		×				×
McKechnie et al.		×				×		×	
Ozámiz et al.	×				×			×	
Potthoff et al.			×			×		×	
Sabatini et al.							×		
Walsh et al.	×			×					×
Wiersma et al.			×		×				×
Williams et al.			×		×				×
Yfantopolous		×		×				×	

psychiatric care to the chronically ill and of studies to evaluate the socioeconomic features of this care.

The contributions may be classified according to several dimensions:

- Unit of observation: systems, institutional, and individual approaches
- Level of spatial aggregation: national, regional, and institutional approaches
- Type of analysis: theoretical/methodological, descriptive/cross-sectional, and historical/longitudinal approaches

Since every contribution can fall into more than one of these categories, a classification must be a complex and multidimensional one. A tentative classification can be found in Table 1 of this preface. For the purpose of structuring the book, however, we have chosen an arrangement that follows mainly pragmatic lines. We apologize for this simplification, inevitable as it may be.

The editors of this volume wish to express their thanks to the authors and participants of the workshop, especially for their patience in carrying on the interdisciplinary dialogue between economists, psychiatrists, social scientists, and politicians, and for their constructive contributions to the mutual reviews of the papers.

Munich, April 1988   D. Schwefel
                                                               H. Zöllner
                                                               P. Potthoff

Table of Contents

List of Contributors

Barrelet, L., Dr.
Service de Psychiatrie II, Institutions Universitaires de Psychiatrie
10, chemin du Petit Bel-Air, 1225 Chêne-Bourg, Switzerland

Bender, Wolfram, Priv.-Doz., Dr. Dr.
Ärztlicher Direktor, Bezirkskrankenhaus Haar, 8013 Haar,
Federal Republic of Germany

Bille, Mogens, Dr.
Centralsygehus, 8900 Randers, Denmark

Brenna, Antonio, Prof.
SAGO, Viale Antonio Gramsci, 22, 50132 Firenze, Italy

Bridges, Keith W., Dr.
Department of Psychiatry, Rawnsley Building, Manchester Royal
Infirmary, Oxford Road, Manchester M139BX, United Kingdom

Cabasés, Juan M., Dr.
Gobierno de Navarra, Departamento de Salud,
Ciudadela, 5, 31001 Pamplona-Iruinea, Spain

Dalby, J. Thomas, Ph. D.
Departments of Psychology and Psychiatry, The University of
Calgary and Calgary General Hospital, 841 Centre Ave., East,
Calgary, Alberta T2E OA1, Canada

Ebbli, Daniele, Dr.
Università degli Studi di Pavia, Istituto di Scienze Sanitarie
Applicate, Via A. Bassi, 21, 27100 Pavia, Italy

Elchardus, J. M.
Service Hospitalo-Universitaire de Psychiatrie de l'Enfant et de
l'Adolescent, Centre Hospitalier, Spécialisé du Vinatier,
95, boulevard Pinel, 69677 Bron Cedex, France

Faragher, Brian
Department of Medical Statistics, University Hospital of South
Manchester, Nell Lane, West Didsbury, Manchester M208LR,
United Kingdom

Fischer, Werner, Dr.
Unité d'Investigation Sociologique, Institutions Universitaires de
Psychiatrie, 6, rue du Trente-et-un-Décembre, 1207 Genève,
Switzerland

Frank, Richard G., Ph. D.
The Johns Hopkins University, School of Hygiene and Public
Health, Health Services Research and Development Center,
624 North Broadway, Baltimore, Maryland 21205, USA

Giel, Robert, Prof.
Department of Social Psychiatry of the State University of
Groningen, WHO Collaborating Centre for Research and Training
in Mental Health, Academisch Ziekenhuis, Oostersingel 59,
Postbus 30001, 9700 RB Groningen, The Netherlands

Goldberg, David, Prof.
Department of Psychiatry, University Hospital of South
Manchester, Nell Lane, West Didsbury, Manchester M208LR,
United Kingdom

Goldman, Howard H., M.D., Ph. D.
Mental Health Policy Studies, Department of Psychiatry,
University of Maryland, Baltimore, MD 21201, USA

Grassi, Mario, Dr.
Università degli Studi di Pavia, Istituto di Scienze Sanitarie
Applicate, Via A. Bassi, 21, 27100 Pavia, Italy

Hyde, Clive, Dr.
Department of Psychiatry, University Hospital of South
Manchester, Nell Lane, West Didsbury, Manchester M208LR,
United Kingdom

Jong, Aant de, Dr.
Department of Social Psychiatry of the State University of
Groningen, WHO Collaborating Centre for Research and Training
in Mental Health, Academisch Ziekenhuis, Oostersingel 59,
Postbus 30001, 9700 RB Groningen, The Netherlands

Kastrup, Marianne, M.D., Ph. D.
Psychiatric Department, Frederiksberg Hospital,
2000 Frederiksberg, Denmark

Lave, Judith, R., Ph. D.
School of Public Health, University of Pittsburgh, Pittsburgh,
PA 15261, USA

Leidl, Reiner, Dr.
Medis-Institut der GSF, Ingolstädter Landstr. 1, 8042 Neuherberg,
Federal Republic of Germany

Lowson, Karon
North Western Regional Health Authority, Gateway House,
Piccadilly South, Manchester M607LP, United Kingdom

Marinoni, Alessandra, Prof.
Università degli Studi di Pavia, Istituto di Scienze Sanitarie
Applicate, Via A. Bassi, 21, 27100 Pavia, Italy

McKechnie, A.A., Dr.
Bangour Village Hospital, Broxburn, West Lothian EH526LW,
Scotland

May, J.
Finance Department, Bangour Village Hospital, Broxburn,
West Lothian EH526LW, Scotland

Ozámiz, José, Agustín, Dr.
Eusko Jaurlaritza, Osansunketa eta Kontsumo Saila, Duque de
Wellington, 2, 01011 Vitoria-Gasteiz, Spain

Potthoff, Peter, Dr.
Medis-Institut der GSF, Ingolstädter Landstr. 1, 8042 Neuherberg,
Federal Republic of Germany

Sabatini, Jean, Dr.
Service Médical d'Accueil et d'Urgences, Hôpital Jules Courmont,
Faculté de Médecine Lyon-Nord, 69310 Pierre-Bénite, France

Schwefel, Detlef, Prof.
Medis-Institut der GSF, Ingolstädter Landstr. 1, 8042 Neuherberg,
Federal Republic of Germany

Silva, Santinó, Dr.
Università degli Studie di Pavia, Istituto di Scienze Sanitarie
Applicate, Via A. Bassi, 21, 27100 Pavia, Italy

Slooff, Cees J., Dr.
Department of Social Psychiatry of the State University of
Groningen, WHO Collaborating Centre for Research and Training
in Mental Health, Academisch Ziekenhuis, Oostersingel 59,
Postbus 30001, 9700 RB Groningen, The Netherlands

Sterling, Chris, Dr.
Department of Psychiatry, University Hospital of South
Manchester, Nell Lane, West Didsbury, Manchester M208LR,
United Kingdom

Torre, Eugenio, Prof.
Università degli Studi di Pavia, Istituto di Scienze Sanitarie
Applicate, Via A. Bassi, 21, 27100 Pavia, Italy

Walsh, Dermot, Dr.
The Medico-Social Research Board, An Bord Taighde
Pobal-Liachta, 73 Lower Baggot Street, Dublin 2, Ireland

Wiersma, Durk, Dr.
Department of Social Psychiatry of the State University of
Groningen, WHO Collaborating Centre for Research and Training
in Mental Health, Academisch Ziekenhuis, Oostersingel 59,
Postbus 30001, 9700 RB Groningen, The Netherlands

Williams, Richard, M. B., B. S., MRC Psych., M. Phil., F. R. C. P. (C)
Department of Psychiatry, The University of Calgary and Calgary
General Hospital, 841 Centre Ave., East, Calgary, Alberta
T2E OA1, Canada

Yfantopoulos, John Nic, Dr.
Associate Professor of Health Economics, University of Athens,
12 Sachtouri St., 152 32 Halandri, Athens, Greece

Zöllner, Herbert, Dr.
World Health Organization, Regional Office for Europe,
8, Scherfigsvej, 2100 Copenhagen, Denmark

Background Reports

Studies on the Cost-Effectiveness
of Managing Chronic Psychotic Patients
Report on a WHO Planning Meeting at Mannheim, 2–4 May, 1983

D. Schwefel

Introduction

Incidence. In many European countries, there seems to be an increase in the incidence of psychotic diseases; this appears to be related to an increase in cyclical and/or structural economic problems resulting from the growing recession in Europe, even though there is no definite evidence of the existence of a causal relationship. This leads to further economic consequences: for example, the number of cases of early retirement due to psychotic diseases is also rising, which produces further costs to society. The increase in incidence of psychotic and/or neurotic disorders, presumably caused in part by the economic development and in turn causing economic problems, provokes an analysis of the management of chronic psychotics in terms of health economics.

Strategies. The slogan 'as much outpatient care as possible, as much inpatient care as necessary', and the world-wide fashionable statements aimed at cost-containment indicate the background of current strategies and interventions in the management and treatment of patients diagnosed as chronically psychotic. These 'new' strategies intend to avoid the defects of outdated asylums by providing mental hospitals – concomitantly with extending outpatient and social services – with homes appropriate for human beings and opportunities for work and leisure activities. In view of the economic and political recession, this trend is opposed by increasing efforts to contain costs. Since psychotics are only rarely in a position to articulate their own needs, having only a weak lobby to support them, governments may find it easy to 'experiment' with them, and they really do so: They close down adequate inpatient care facilities, reducing the number of beds, transferring patients with chronic and incurable diseases from mental hospitals to nursing homes or to their families, rather than increasing outpatient care services. Altogether, a tendency towards an increase in outpatient care is evident.

Differences. Trieste is an example of a very rapid – perhaps too rapid – move towards providing chronic psychotics with outpatient care. In Trieste these patients are hospitalized in a mental institution only for a fraction of the time they would be hospitalized in other European cities. This is only one – though extreme – example of the vast differences that exist within Europe.

Implications. Can these experiences be compared? Is an increase in outpatient care not more humane and cost-effective? Or are the costs only transferred from the hospitals to the families, communities, and taxpayers? Will psychotics discharged from the hospital not be found again in the circles of homeless people and city vagrants, without receiving any help? Will they not end up in deteriorated urban areas, in newly emerging 'deviant ghettoes'? Do the savings on the one hand not turn out to be more expensive on the other hand, producing more suffering and less satisfaction of needs?

Background

Slogan. 'Health for all by the year 2000' is a self-imposed, present-day recommendation of a health-care strategy which is supported by all member countries of the World Health Organization, thus also by the European Regional Office of the World Health Organization and its departments.

Mental Health. The priorities set in the area of the department of 'Mental Health' focussed in the past on a description of the mental health care situation in different European regions, and on disability studies carried out in five European centres (Ankara, Groningen, Mannheim, Sofia, Zurich). Although short-term efforts are now primarily concerned with the problems of the elderly and the young, the medium-term emphasis would again be on the care of chronic psychotics, which will be brought to the medical research committee's attention in the meantime.

Health Economics. In the health economics field covered by the European Regional Office of the World Health Organization (WHO), the priorities involve cost control with concomitant assurance of and increase in quality. Besides the problem of care for the elderly, the care for chronic psychotics should now also be investigated in a multinational and multidisciplinary study, which should be performed taking into account the two general WHO guidelines on primary health care and on equity, quality, and justice.

Planning Meeting. These general guidelines were to be supported by a joint multinational and multidisciplinary study, which was designed to be prepared by a planning meeting held in the *Zentralinstitut für die seelische Gesundheit* (Central Institute of Mental Health), Mannheim, Federal Republic of Germany, 2–4 May, 1983. In the studies, at least two or more strategies for managing chronic psychotics were to be compared, strategies which included differing emphasis on inpatient and outpatient care. Nine temporary advisors of the WHO from seven East and West European countries, including five psychiatrists and four economists and social scientists, as well as three representatives of the European Regional Office of the WHO, participated in the planning meeting. Prof. Dr. Dr. H. Häfner was elected chairman and Dr. D. Schwefel was elected rapporteur; Dr. H. Zöllner officiated as secretary.

Former Studies

WHO-EURO. In 21 psychiatric care centres in 16 European countries, cohorts of patients were followed up over a 2-year period in a pilot study on psychiatric care. Each cohort contained about 200 patients who had not had any contact with psychiatric services for the 6-month period preceding their inclusion in the cohort. Besides diagnostic information, sociodemographic data and data on the frequency and duration of the utilization of psychiatric services were collected. The question of how cost aspects could be considered (a posteriori, since the pilot studies are about to be finished) would have to be examined. More detailed data on the type and severity of the disability were collected in five centres – Ankara, Groningen, Mannheim, Sofia, Zurich – in a so-called disability study. But in neither of these cases are data on costs available, although there seem to be more effectiveness indicators in these studies than in the pilot studies.

Ten Horn, Giel. One of the centres Groningen, tried to identify the direct costs (Ten Horn and Giel 1983). Even assessing the institutional costs and, above all, the distribution of overhead costs was extremely difficult, as was assessment of the costs caused by contacts of patients with different and changing staff members.

Mannheim Study. Another psychiatric care centre, Mannheim, carried out a care-pathway analysis in 1983, in which the course of one cohort of patients through eight separate institutions is described. This study was considered to represent an opportunity to examine how to use at least some raw cost values.

Chapalain. In Vendée and Isère, as well as in one sector of Lyon, cohorts were followed up for 3–4 years (Chapalain 1983). In this study, the effectiveness of treatment was measured in terms of psychiatrists' judgments or in terms of the patient's integration into family, society, and vocational situation. On the cost side, only the direct, institutional costs for the health care services were considered but not, for example, the patient's cost of living in his/her family which was either saved, transferred, or imposed. For this reason, the conclusion that inpatient care should be avoided is inconclusive.

Kriedel. On the basis of outpatient care for epileptics, Kriedel (1980) examined cost and effectiveness of alternative forms of care by means of an interesting methodology. While only a brief description of the cost side, which is estimated on the basis of a few assumptions, is given by the author, his most important achievement consists in recording, aggregating, and assessing the programme benefit: health is defined as the fulfilment of a normative role, the assessment of which is performed by means of interviews. On this basis, health can be expressed in terms of a single dimension, which is a year of healthy functioning. In this way, the whole benefit of the programme can be assessed in terms of a single category. Thus, the benefit of the programme can be assessed monetarily by surveys using the concept of willingness to pay.

Goldberg. In addition to measuring different types of costs, Goldberg and his co-workers (Goldberg and Jones 1980; Goldberg et al. 1985) attempted to measure a number of 'soft' costs of psychiatric care and to place them beside a traditional cost-benefit analysis. The different types of costs involve the measurement of social costs. Benefits are described only in terms of cost savings. Types of costs are: the number of days spent in mental hospitals, contacts with outpatient care and social work, costs of administration and insurance, costs of medication, loss of productivity (the patient's wages and taxes). As for the 'soft' costs, the opportunity costs of a family member who is caring for the patient in the family, thus being prevented from doing paid work, as well as the extra household expenses, the patient's cost of living in his family, costs of voluntary social security benefits, and so on, are taken into consideration. In addition, the following factors are identified and assessed: reduction of sociability, the patient's chances of being re-employed, and his personal appearance are taken into account on the cost side, whereas improvement of sociability, heterosexual contacts, constructiveness, realism, structuring of leisure time, and social integration, are taken into account on the benefit side. This multidimensional approach permitted the comparison of the cost-effectiveness of two different psychiatric care centres.

Further Studies. Additional studies, e.g., those by Hirsch et al. (1979) and Fischer (1981), can be found in the appended references.

Some Principles of Economic Evaluation

In the studies just mentioned, the main aspects and main principles of evaluation, especially those of economic evaluation, have been followed more or less completely. In the following, fifteen such aspects will be considered in what is hoped to be a brief and lucid way.

Medicine, Psychiatry in Particular, as a Belief. The major part of health care is based on belief and on experience gained by generations, rather than on 'scientific' knowledge. Cost and benefit of treatments, interventions, and strategies have only very rarely been established. Recommendations concerning treatments are almost always well-phrased beliefs, for which, however, there is rarely any evidence.

Alternatives. For the medical doctor, there may be no alternatives at all in treating a particular patient; he thinks that because of their uniqueness patients cannot be compared with one another, and hence, different treatments cannot be compared with each other either. For the social scientist and for the economist, however, there are at least two levels of comparison:

- Treatment versus no treatment
- Treatment by one doctor (one centre) versus treatment by another doctor (another centre)

In the field of medicine, comparisons of management procedures or treatments are possible only when the treatments may be regarded as alternatives. The basis of any comparison, in any case, is the precise definition and delimitation of the alternatives to be compared.

Costs. All 'relevant' costs are to be measured: current costs, capital or investment costs, public and private costs, costs for the patient, the family, and the community, costs of time, costs for travel, etc., which means that on no account should the costs involved for the hospital be considered exclusively.

Opportunity Costs. The main point of departure of economic evaluation is the concept of opportunity costs: would having done nothing or something completely different not have been more useful and less expensive? Having done nothing or something completely different might have yielded higher benefits or lower costs. The concept of opportunity costs refers back to the basic question of whether there are alternatives.

Costs= Revenues or Expenditures? In economic terms, not all expenditures are costs. Transfer payments, for example, from the health insurance to the patient, are only a shift of money but do not create new values in use or increase the gross national product. Since these payments involve only changes in property rights, their evaluation has to be different from an evaluation of costs which, for alternative use, withdraw resources from society. Furthermore, one should be aware of the fact that there are differences between the industrial management and the political economy points of view, particularly when such categories as spending, expenditure, and costs involved in transfer payments and factor costs are considered.

Average Costs. Economists often analyze the so-called marginal costs rather than the average costs. For example, they deal with the costs involved in treating one additional patient rather than with the average costs of treating a patient, thus considering that changes rather than stock-taking should be focussed on.

Today's Costs for Tomorrow's Costs? Everybody would prefer to have 1000 dollars today rather than in a year, because they would be able to save the money and earn interest. This truism can also be described as the reward of waiting. In economic evaluations, this time preference is taken into account by variations of rates of discount or discountings, which in most cases depend on the current average interest rates.

Costs or Prices, Here or There? Differences in prices developing between regions and in the course of time do not necessarily reflect scarcity differentials, because medications may have been priced too high. Therefore, market prices often are no appropriate basis of comparison. For this reason, economists alter the market prices to be able to reflect costs better. This is also one of the reasons why they use deflations, adjustments of currency exchange rates, and so-called shadow prices, which take into account distortions of prices and differences in productivity in the calculation of costs and benefits; the shadow price of an unemployed person,

therefore, is often rated zero; employing an unemployed person does not withdraw productivity from the economy in another part of the economy.

Is Time Money? An important source of the assessment of costs is the assessment
and evaluation of the time (or the wages) used for certain activities. However, in
this context, indirect activities or uses of time – for example, the time economists
spend thinking about the problem or the time health politicians spend fighting for
the extension of outpatient care – should also be considered.

Benefits. Cost-benefit analyses differ from cost-effectiveness analyses since benefits are measured in monetary units. Whether it is meaningful to perform this kind
of measurement in connection with the question raised here is a controversial
point for economists. An appropriate common denominator of benefit and cost
might also be the use of energy (e.g., measured in joule) – gain of energy and
withdrawal of energy – and not just the money involved.

Does Benefit Equal Cost? Benefits are also saved costs. Costs are benefits forgone.
These equations of negative costs with positive benefits, or of negative benefits
with positive costs, apply only to cost-benefit analysis.

Effectiveness. What is meant by effectiveness, in most cases, is the degree of goal
attainment, which means whether the patient has become healthier, has to suffer
less, and so on. Every (psychiatric treatment or) strategy, however, also has goals
beyond improving the patient's (physical, mental, and social) well-being; in some
projects, more than 300 different goals, or side goals, effects, or side effects, were
counted. Defining and measuring all of them sufficiently would be a difficult task.
Therefore, any cost-effectiveness analysis can be only partial – a reason why, in
this field, the economist depends on the help of the psychiatrist, psychologist, and
sociologist.

Cost-Effectiveness Analysis. An analysis of cost-efectiveness is thus the attempt to
identify, measure, and balance essential costs as well as effectiveness parameters.
What cannot be avoided in this procedure is the neglect of certain (indirect) costs
and benefits (which may be the most important ones for certain interest groups).
What is always needed to correct these shortcomings is a systems analysis which
explores implications. Without such an analysis, a cost-effectiveness analysis,
however precise it is, may turn out to be irrelevant.

Individual. Economic evaluation is based on the paradigm of the individual who
decides and evaluates autonomously. In the case of the chronic psychotics, one is
presented with the problem of who is to decide and evaluate for them; one is presented, to an increased extent, with the problem of interindividual comparison
and the external evaluation of human lives.

Value Judgements. Any evaluation contains a great number of value judgements as
well as other judgements for which different judgements could certainly have been
made instead. To make them explicit and modifiable is a precondition or intended
by-product of economic evaluations.

Summary. Cost-effectiveness analyses are nothing but a compilation of aspects to be considered in any evaluation. What becomes particularly conspicuous in this context is that evaluations, of necessity, have to be multidisciplinary if on the one hand economic costs and on the other hand social, health-related, or mental health-related benefits are to be assessed.

Neglected and/or Concealed Aspects

When the principles of economic evaluations and the former studies are compared, a number of neglected and/or concealed aspects or aspects just worth mentioning become visible, aspects which are important in the context of a study on the cost-effectiveness of managing chronic psychotics.

Costs

Opportunity Costs. Costs are benefits forgone. What is important, therefore, is not only an accounting of expenses, which is an essential prerequisite, but also the assessment of opportunity costs. This procedure can be performed by means of a comparison with other conceivable uses of resources.

Types of Costs, Places of Costs, Times of Costs. As far as the accounting is concerned, one first has to deal with the types of costs for any measure taken: capital costs, current costs, which include personnel costs, non-personnel costs, which include travel expenses, maintenance costs, etc. What should be considered are not only the costs of medical care but also the differences in costs of living as well as the general overhead costs involved for different kinds of bureaucracies. These types of costs may be present wherever costs arise: hospital, outpatient care, family, community, single's household, etc. By identifying the times when costs emerge, for example, by means of time-budget analyses, it is possible to get information on the sequence in which the costs occur as well as on shifts in costs.

Level of Costs. Concerning the types, places, and times of costs, the level of costs or amounts of money which – due to scarcity – would be involved are to be assessed. In performing this task, comparisons of costs will have to be made on the basis of discounted costs, shadow prices, etc., which tend to neutralize as well as to make explicit the distortions that occur on account of interventions, administered prices, differing systems of budgeting and accounting (even within one country), modalities of financing, systems of economic incentives, and transfer payments. Procedures of evaluation have to be elucidated so that one is able to revise estimates of costs if, for example, it is found that no more than assessments and calculations of partial costs have been performed. The same applies to the solution to the problems of attributing outcome to input, for example, in the case of staff meetings or manager activities.

Indirect Costs and Further Aspects. What must be considered, furthermore, are the indirect costs involved in nonoptimal treatment, lack of compliance, the higher suicide incidence of psychotics treated on an outpatient basis, unemployment of personnel after reduction in hospital beds, and unavailability of the psychotics and their caretakers to the national economy, to mention only a few parameters of indirect costs. On what level of measurement costs should be assessed, with expert estimates on the basis of the Delphi or Refa methods as extremes, is a methodological problem to be considered elsewhere. What has to be stated from a pragmatic point of view is that previous studies on chronic psychotics have often neglected the assessment of the costs involved in outpatient care, as well as the costs involved for the family. In particular, they have neglected the fact that, as a rule, it is the female family members who have to care for the patient and are thus prevented from pursuing a paid occupation. Further details, e. g., on marginal costs or factor costs, are dealt with in the literature (see, e. g., Glass and Goldberg 1977; Kriedel 1980; Drummond 1980, 1981).

Effectiveness
Scales. For chronic psychotic diseases the following criteria – which vary for different psychiatric schools, however – are viewed as measures of effectiveness:

- Improvement in the patient's ability "to cope with his/her disability"
- Reduction in or alleviation of illness episodes
- Reduction in symptoms of hospitalism
- Reduction in social handicaps
- Increase in the fulfilment of social roles or reduction in functional impairments
- Reduction in deviant behaviour
- Production of social, vocational, and societal (re-)integration
- Making (social) quality of life possible
- Producing insight into the nature of the illness
- Stabilization of emotional balance
- Reduction in the severity of the disease or in the pressure produced by suffering

These measures apply only if improvement constitutes a goal of care at all, if the goal is not merely the protection of the patient from himself/herself and the protection of others from the patient and the prevention of deterioration, if care means more than the inclusion of the patient and the exclusion of the community.

For such rather 'intangible', 'soft' areas of the measurement of disability, a large number of psychometric scales have been suggested. Some of them have been subjected – according to scientific standards – to tests of reliability and validity by means of item and factor analyses and standardized on the basis of normal populations; but this applies only to very few scales. The identification of social preferences which are to be assigned to the illness conditions defined by the scales remains to be performed. This is particularly important to cost-effectiveness analysis, meaning that this concerns the problems of index construction. Such scales, however, reduce the process of mental 'illness' to characteristics of the individual, which may be regarded as problematical.

Indicators. In contrast, what is predominantly available are (often uncontrolled) doctor's ratings that are not very reliable; arbitrary symptomatology (although often oriented towards WHO recommendations); the use of such available service indicators as the readmission or relapse rate (the severity of illness is sometimes tautologically measured in terms of service utilization), length of patient's stay in hospital, diversity of treatment, etc,; the use of available data on lost years of active life, lost work days, early retirement, or assessment of transitional probabilities between states of illness; the use of certain items arbitrarily selected from the scales.

Effect for Whom? What is left out of consideration in most cases is the fact that one has to deal with effectiveness diffusion or effectiveness externalities (which may, of course, also be regarded as costs) when reductions in the quality of life, etc., have to be assessed for the affected family members and for further participants of the social environment so that a complete balance can be made.

Research Objectives

Research Objectives. The adequacy of cost and benefit assessment can be evaluated only when the research goals are known. Representatives of various medical and social science disciplines view as scientific even the 'preliminary stages' of experimentation, which are reliable descriptions, exploratory comparisons, evidence of plausibility, or presumptive evidence. Besides such internal research objectives, external ones, which include the societal use of science, also have to be considered: support of treatments, support of policies or criticism of policies (by demonstrating their unintended implications).

Research for Whom? These external research goals refer to the fact that the emphasis of research may differ according to which target group is primarily focussed on. If the focus is on the patient as a whole person, life, suffering, and survival will be the main topics; if the emphasis is on medicine, it is the production functions which have to be identified, while the allocation of patients and resources has to be stressed if the community or state is made the reference point of research.

Privacy and Data Protection. Side goals or effects of research and the possible misuse of research are points which support data protection: this may be particularly true of the field of mental illness. From the viewpoint of internal research goals, certain regulations concerning data protection have become barriers to research. One of these regulations concerns the informed consent of the person involved, which could hardly be obtained from paranoid schizophrenics, for example. These barriers might be reduced through the involvement of custodians, the use of probabilistic assignments, or similar ways and means. In any case, data protection refers to a real dilemma between legitimate research interests and legitimate personal interests.

Research Methodology

Only a few aspects of research methodology and related problems were mentioned in the planning meeting. They will be illustrated in the following sections.

Comparisons. Comparisons are the basis of science, even if the medical profession may at times dismiss them as fata morganas. However, reliable descriptions, standardizations, exclusion of what is a priori not comparable (e.g., good versus bad treatment, alternatives which actually are not alternatives) do not by themselves guarantee the scientific acceptability of a comparison, though exploration can be enriched even at this early stage (e.g., by false conclusions).

Homogeneity/Heterogeneity. The test for homogeneity or heterogeneity (of populations, regions, etc.) is a measure of the justification of comparisons, though it materializes – by means of circular reasoning – by comparing the (not) comparable. This refers to the necessity of performing explorations before the test. Randomization does not make this test superfluous; rather, this test is able to indicate the adequacy of the randomization.

Variability/Constancy. In cost-effectiveness comparisons, costs can be held constant and effectiveness altered, or effectiveness can be held constant and costs altered. What can also be held constant is treatment or any other background variable. This is only a special variant of controlling for homogeneity and heterogeneity.

Further Aspects of Methodology. As for these, the relevant literature has to be referred to.

Influences of the Broader System and the Environment

Premature Attributions. In some cases the results of studies – as can be shown by the former studies presented above – are set up as absolutes. Changes in effectiveness are attributed to psychiatric strategies, without testing for intervening variables, though these strategies may be only concurrent, and one has to look for the causation elsewhere, or a general 'secular' trend may be found beyond all specific care activities. This very frequent fallacy has to be assumed to exist as long as it has not been tested or explored, as long as the environment and the surroundings of care are described in terms of policies, competing and/or coexistent services, structures of supply, etc.; systems analyses and (external) system comparisons are therefore essential.

Exaggerated Differentiation. The fallacy opposite to premature generalization or attribution is the one associated with exaggerated differentiation, which in the extreme case ascribes uniqueness and incomparability to any and every activity and patient. This fallacy is a relative one: depending on the interests involved in possible uses of the assertion, high or low differentiation may be appropriate. Above all, this applies to the identification of subpopulations; in this case one equally deals with a special application of the homogeneity/heterogeneity problem.

Subpopulations. Cost-benefit or cost-effectiveness relationships may be influenced by specific characteristics of the subpopulations of chronic psychotics. These in fluences may be connected with:

- The patients' careers through the mental institutions as a crucial factor in form-
  ing the patients (who may have been in inpatient care – instead of outpatient
  care – from the beginning)
- Psychotics not in need of psychiatric care
- Psychotics with illness episodes of more than average intensity
- Psychotics treated (only) partly on an outpatient basis

Such subpopulations also have to be identified within the group of patients who have left the care system (dropouts):

- Cured patients
- Migrated patients (who have moved to other regions or to other care systems)
- Patients who are insufficiently or not at all cared for
  Leaving out of consideration subpopulations which are heterogeneous between
  and homogeneous within themselves can also lead to severe fallacies.

Research Options
Experiments. The procedure often regarded as the *non plus ultra* of research is the experiment, or the randomized clinical double-blind trial. Yet to choose it exclu-sively is erroneous and scarcely feasible, if acceptable at all on ethical grounds. Natural experiments, as contrasted to the type of experiment just mentioned, are carried out by lawmakers, politicians, therapists. Comparisons can be made on the basis of such quasi experiments, which are more natural than controlled experi-ments. After all, the question of whether experiments may be a ground for general application is a controversial one from the point of view of the theory of science, because randomization is not a guarantee of a reasonable amount of heterogeneity as well as homogeneity; because what alone can be analyzed are chains of close (time) relationships; and because scientific discoveries are not often promoted by this type of experiment – rather, they may be prevented by its exclusiveness.

Exploration/Testing. Experiments manipulate known relationships, i.e. relation-ships which have already been discovered; hence, first of all, relationships have to be discovered: the search for implications, side effects, repercussions in terms of a large-scale systems analysis, and description of heterogeneities and homogeneities – this search is the prerequisite to a comparison of groups which are heteroge-neous between and homogeneous within themselves. In the field of epidemiologi-cal psychiatry exploration still is a basic and crucial method; the age of discover-ies is not yet over.

Explicit/Implicit Research. Exploratory research designs often use the black-box approach, because exact sequences of causation are not known or may be chang-ing; these sequences of causation remain implicit, and they are made explicit only as assumptions on intervening variables. Hypothesis-testing research does not always make all relationships explicit; black-box approaches can be found frequently also in this context, though sometimes it is not admitted that they are used.

Clinical/Epidemiological Research. Sometimes studies prematurely generalize their findings to populations, though these refer only to subpopulations – e.g. those treated clinically. Depending on the formulation of the question, not only the demand for treatment but also the need for treatment is important; the latter can be assessed only on the basis of epidemiological research.

Prospective/Retrospective Studies. If one compares medical and economic research approaches, it becomes evident that the prospective study is sometimes considered to be the better method. However, aspects of adequacy should also be mentioned in this context: prospective studies can investigate only short time sequences, while long-term time-series analyses are typical of questions examined in political economics since long-term time lags between risk factors and mortality can often be found. Furthermore, combinations of prospective and retrospective study approaches, such as the nonconcurrent prospective design, which may examine time sequences of, let us assume, minus 3 to plus 3 years, are also possible.

Research Methods

Data and Indicators. Whether data and indicators are sufficiently specific and precise, and what level of measurement they refer to are questions that can be argued about for a long time: a simple set of data or indicators is appropriate when other data – e.g. on severity of illness – are available on a corresponding selective and low level of measurement. What certainly has to be preferred are case registers, which sometimes, however, make research obsolete (yesterday's diagnoses!) or prevent it while or because they are compiled, and lead to unjustified attributions of validity.

Magnitudes/Statistics. To the question concerning the number of cases to be observed, there can be only a relative answer. In this context only the following criteria can be mentioned: desired statistical assertions or tests, increase in quality relative to a census data collection as compared with sampling, possibility of disproportional subpopulation enlargements, research efforts involved, data protection or privacy. A small study may sometimes be more predictive than a large scale one.

Goals and Target Group

Research Goals

General Research Goals. The objective of the study to be designed consists in identifying, describing, measuring, and/or comparing the various implications entailed in differing (components of) strategies and those entailed in differing supply patterns involved in outpatient and/or inpatient psychiatric care. What should be considered in this context are the costs, effects, and/or benefits, not only to the patients but also to the family, the community, and society at large. Moreover, new questions should be raised, new dimensions should be opened, curiosity should be aroused, and awareness should be produced, in order to recommend and propagate the most cost-effective strategy. However, the study and its results are not designed to be forced upon the member countries; rather, the study should be carried out in these countries' own centres, adjusted to their needs but remaining multinational.

Cost-Effective Studies. Likewise, the study itself should satisfy criteria of cost-effectiveness. This means that by examining the existing literature and by supplementing available studies, for example, by adding an economic analysis to already completed or ongoing (cohort) studies, one could possibly avoid replication of already existing studies. Furthermore, studies should be started where particularly interesting aspects can be investigated, where political and social commitment is found, or where the evaluation of the strategies chosen seems to be indicated – in short, where the necessity and economic efficiency are coexistent.

Procedure. The aim is to identify and present relevant and hopefully innovative research in this broad area of costs and effects of managing chronic psychotics; ideally the aim would be a relevant planning of research, which may yield results within several years and which at first would compile a joint protocol outlining the research focusses (e.g. also providing a 'how-to' book on the costs involved), with some methodological details and general terms of reference for the experts in research methodology and economics who should be involved in any case, and for the counselling psychiatrists, psychologists, social workers, etc. Whether a 'productive' or 'collective' type of study – i.e. collecting relevant and diverse studies or producing one highly standardized multinationally coordinated study – is more reasonable seems to be disputable; more feasible is the first aim.

Scientific Goals. Since the scientific goals of the study on the cost-effectiveness of managing chronic psychotics have a wide scope and should be achieved in a short period of time, effects pertaining to a reconciliation of medicine, economy, and the theory of science may be expected only to a limited extent. However, in this context medicine should also conceive of itself as a social science.

Target Group
Features. The target group is the chronic psychotics (and their social environment). They have to be distinguished from the addicts, the mentally retarded, the neurotics, and the persons with personality disorders. The psychotics may be characterized by their symptoms: distortions of perception, delusions, bizarre ideas, exaggerated fantasies, hallucinations, poor adjustment to reality, withdrawal from social contacts. The combinations in which these symptoms occur and their severity may vary with the diagnostic subtype. Those subtypes diagnosed as chronic will, with a high probability, suffer relapses again and again, which makes them dependent on care. Their impairment is threefold:

- Nearly permanent impairment
- Severe disability in terms of impairment of individual functioning
- Severe handicap in social and economic terms

The chronic psychotics do not constitute a homogeneous group. According to the International Classification of Diseases (ICD), the following subgroups can be distinguished:

- Organic psychoses with a change in the morphology of the brain
- Schizophrenic psychoses, for which no organic change is known
- Affective psychoses with elated and/or depressed mood
- Other psychoses

Whether senile psychoses belong to geriatrics or psychogeriatrics is a special field of psychiatry is a controversial question.

Besides appling 'psychiatric' designations, one should also describe the social deficits of psychotic people, which are not only characteristic of this illness. The deviations in social behaviour shown by the psychotics as compared with the behaviour shown by the 'normal' and 'healthy' population would have to be analyzed in detail, with special reference to their relation to specific cultural settings. In this context it is not the symptomatology that is important. Although alleviating symptoms may be the patient's and doctor's principal concern, this may turn out to be socially irrelevant.

Data. Social value judgments, concealment of diagnoses, and multimorbidity make it difficult to give precise data on incidence and prevalence. For schizophrenia, the incidence is estimated at 0.15-2.5 per 1000, and the point prevalence is estimated at 2-5 per 1000. The mortality data, which are particularly invalid because of multimorbidity in the elderly, may hardly be used as a reference point.

Schizophrenia as a Tracer? In view of the heterogeneity of psychotic disorders, research purposes require a good indicator or tracer or subpopulation. Schizophrenia seems to meet this requirement, for the following reasons:

1. Relatively unambiguous diagnosis (although diagnoses may vary from country to country)
2. Relative validity of diagnosis (e.g. by means of psychiatric scales)
3. Relative consensus on management (which is sometimes assumed to exist)
4. Differing institutional arrangements of strategies for management (14% versus 92% inpatient care in different European regions)
5. Availability of data and information (in spite of a general shortage)
6. Sufficient frequency (with an incidence rate ranging from 0.15 to 2.5 per 1000)
7. Economic significance (about 50% of all hospitalized mental patients are diagnosed as schizophrenic)
8. Great importance to, or strain on, the family and the social environment
9. Long duration of illness (varying for the different subtypes of schizophrenia)
10. Accessibility for research groups (via research centres)

In this context, the fact that schizophrenic characteristics vary with the specific cultures in which they occur may be viewed as a problem.

Homogenization Before or After the Fact? For the purpose of getting a sufficiently homogeneous group of schizophrenics one could exclude age-specific (e.g. 20-45 years old), care-specific (e.g. patients with less than 1 year of hospitalization), management-specific (e.g. patients receiving special medication), severity-specific (e.g. agitated or aggressive schizophrenics in acute episodes and in need of full day and night attention), or other specific subgroups. Whether such an exclusion should be carried out before, i.e. when the subpopulations to be studied are selected, or after, i.e. when the statistical analysis of the subpopulations is performed, is a question not of principle but of money and methodology. As a general rule, a relatively large cohort should be preferred.

Goals of Management and Treatment

The governing goals of treatment and care depend on the viewpoints assumed by those who are involved in and affected by the care system.

Patient. From the patient's viewpoint, the goal may consist in preventing disability and/or handicaps or in increasing the chance of being able to play, independent of others, subjectively satisfying social roles, as well as in preventing patients from endangering themselves and others. However, statements on goals of management are difficult to make from the psychotics' point of view, since they often show utterly bizarre preference systems, which is tautological; this refers to the dialectical relationship between 'subjective' and 'objective' definition and to the real and different implications entailed in these two views – psychotic versus 'normal' – and their confrontation. Furthermore, from a certain point during hospitalization and onwards, psychotics are often afraid of being reintegrated into society. Another essential goal from the patient's point of view is a change in the social reality rather than in their own social competence. This applies, for example, to patients who have developed delusional systems, who maintain that they have to fulfil a mission or to save the world. But if the individual and collective care goals cannot be deduced from authentic statements made by the psychotics themselves (some psychotics, for example, have adopted the view that their fellow patients and not they themselves are crazy), who knows then what their viewpoint is? The psychiatrists? Health may turn out not to be a goal of care and management for psychotics at all.

Family. The family may find an improvement in the patient's functioning and his/her reintegration essential, but especially in times of economic crises, they may also desire to place the patient in a mental hospital to reduce efforts and expenditures, as well as to regain a 'normally' functioning family life. Reintegration may also pose a threat to the unstable psychodynamic equilibrium of the family.

Therapists. For the doctor, nurse, and social worker the goal will not be cost containment or sudden discharge from the hospital, but rather the development and application of effective management and treatment with an optimal combination of the type, timing, and intensity of drugs and other kinds of therapeutic assistance (administered by therapists with differing training backgrounds as well as by their aides). Sometimes a problem arises from the therapist's inability to fulfil his function as a 'healer' in cases of incurable illness, which may cause conflict. Last, but not least, therapeutic goals may vary with the different psychiatric schools: curing, alleviating, protecting, etc.

Scientists. The scientists are interested not only in describing and analyzing care, but also in optimizing care, for example, with respect to an optimal allocation of patients, to developing cost-effective management models, to improving the supply models of care. The possibility of studying 'monstrosities' may sometimes also constitute a motive.

Care Institutions. The goals of care institutions may be different from those adopted by the therapists working in these institutions.

State. The goals pursued by the state in managing chronic psychotics may involve avoiding complaints and dissatisfaction which might be voiced by the press; sometimes, however, they also include cost-containment in places where the least opposition is to be expected. In contrast, a slogan like 'health for all by the year 2000' may be revived if the content is also a concern voiced by the electorate.

Five Research Issues

The general question of the cost-effectiveness of managing chronic psychotics includes many special questions. Before looking at some of these special questions, however, one should in the first place consider whether it is justified at all to raise the basic question of cost-effectiveness, since it assumes cheaper or more effective alternatives to exist, not just the one and only unparalleled, need-adjusted treatment or particular management method. In the second place, this question is based on the assumption that not only the testing of hypotheses by means of randomized clinical double-blind trials should be regarded as scientific, but also the exploratory search for implications, side effects, and 'intangible' effects. The special questions can be assigned to five research issues.

Special Patient and Target Groups (Exploration)
Questions. What are the economic problems associated with undiscovered and/or untreated cases of chronic psychosis, or with an increasing dropout rate due to overly rapid change from inpatient to outpatient care, or with uncoordinated and/or paternalistic treatment provided by the doctor, who leaves family- and community-related conditions out of account? Exploratory empirical studies may elucidate these questions by defining and denominating problems, even if they cannot quantify their scope. Who are the groups most affected by unbalanced strategies of change or by the absence of such strategies? The deinstitutionalized? The discharged? The psychotics without families? Those psychotics already at a social

disadvantage? The family? The welfare organizations? The social workers? The city vagrants' milieu? For these problems as well, social research, exploratory and empirical, seems to be preferable in order to make it possible to identify problem groups.

Definition. The problems to be identified refer to the effects and side effects of management and treatments, strategies, or changes in supply; the groups most affected by them may be the members of the family of the schizophrenics who are treated on an outpatient basis, or the deinstitutionalized single schizophrenics without families. Identifying problems and most-affected groups is a voyage of discovery for which only rough plans can be made.

Aims. Identifying, describing, and explaining social problems resulting from changes, or from changes which fail to come about, or identifying the groups most affected by them is intended to draw our attention to concealed or negative costs. The identification of problems and of most-affected groups is a prerequisite for the identification of relevant costs, a prerequisite which is also included in all the other research designs.

Indicator System. See *Regional Differences,* below; if necessary, 'soft' indicators have to be included to a greater extent.

Procedure. Participant observations, structured interviews, depth interviews, other oral interviews, discussion procedures, analysis of contributions from the press and literature, etc.; each of these methods will serve as a complement or corrective to the other.

Regional Differences (Macrostudies)
Questions. Why do psychiatric services in Europe differ to such a large extent from one country to the other, and what are the economic and social consequences of these differences, provided that cause and effect can be separated from one another? One way of answering this question consists in describing and subsequently comparing extremely different regions or mental health care centres by carrying out macrostudies.

Definition. Macrostudies refer to the comparison of indicator systems and aim at describing essential parameters of psychiatric care. They can be performed (a) as time-series comparisons (in one centre) and/or (b) as cross-sectional comparisons (different centres). Cross-sectional comparisons may also occur as comparisons of extremes (e.g. Trieste versus Belgrade), i.e. as comparisons of centres with extremely different structures of supply.

Aims. Carrying out macrostudies is particularly rewarding when time-related changes have occurred, and/or when there are differences between centres worth being explained. By means of macrostudies, intervening variables can be identified, which help to 'explain' such time- or place-related differences. For this reason, a clear indicator system is needed on the one hand, and a feeling for presumptive evidence on the other.

Indicator System. The principal elements of the indicator system are:

- Population: age, sex, employment, migration, unemployment, criminality, social integration, etc.
- Community: policies, financing system, sources of employment, economic situation, welfare services, degree of organization, regional integration, etc.
- Mortality and morbidity: according to ICD, with special reference to multimorbidity
- Health services: indicators of supply and demand for inpatient care, primary health care, social services, etc.
- Psychiatric services: supply- and demand-related indicators, utilization of capacity, length of institutionalization, use of medication with reference to particular medicaments, etc.
- Costs: current costs, capital costs, time-related costs, family-related costs, etc.

Procedure. Critical analysis of the former WHO pilot regional studies with reference to comparability, interpretation, etc. Use of methodologically acceptable, possibly comparable macrostudy designs in some regions.

Patterns and Pathways of Care (Cohort Studies)
Questions. Are there different patterns and pathways of recruitment and care even within one care centre, and what are the economic and social implications these entail? Are these differences to be explained in terms of underutilization or in terms of different case mixes? Or in terms of differing applications of diagnoses? Such questions can be answered on the basis of a cohort study, for example.

Definition. Follow-up over a certain period of time of a group defined by diagnosis. Depending on the specific formulation of the question, the cohorts have to be homogenized, for example, by:

- Excluding schizophrenics suffering from the schizo-affective type of schizophrenia
- Excluding multimorbid schizophrenics
- Including only schizophrenics with the first occurrence of their illness
- Including schizophrenics who have been in inpatient treatment for less than a year
- Including schizophrenics who have suffered from the disorder for 3–5 years

There are three aspects to be considered when such a homogenization is performed:

1. Any such selection involves distortions with respect to chronicity, institutionalization, etc.
2. It has to be determined whether psychopathological changes may be expected or not.
3. Subpopulations which are clearly defined and differentiated on analytical grounds are often too small for a statistical analysis to be reasonable.

These aspects might be a reason for specifying cohorts ex post facto, for example, in a study on all schizophrenics ranging in age from 20 to 45 years.

Aims. Cohort studies, being census-like surveys, offer the opportunity of finding and explaining homogeneities, heterogeneities, and distributions of utilizations and pathways of care, because sometimes only 10% of the patients may be assumed to receive a pathway of care other than the usual one – an assumption which still has to be substantiated, however.

Indicator system. Essential indicators are (a) outcome measures for patients and their families, particularly activities, time budgets (shopping, washing, travelling, working, etc.), impairments in functioning, satisfaction, emotional stability, social integration (in family, neighbourhood, educational and vocational situation, etc.), symptoms; (b) indicators of supply and utilization: time, type, place of care with determination of costs. Beyond this, one has to search for intervening variables and systemic influences.

Procedure. Path analyses and/or cluster analyses may be methodological aids in evaluation, for example, in determining the different pathways. If pathways are different in spite of equal need, a full comparative cost-effectiveness analysis should follow. Therefore, costs have to be assessed on a patient-specific basis.

Psychiatric Treatment (Experiments or Quasi-experiments)

Questions. Is the cost-effectiveness rate better when outpatient rather than inpatient care is intensified? When a diversified strategy rather than a simple one is applied? When differing locations, forms, and dosages of medication are involved? When no treatment rather than treatment is applied? When the patient is seen by a general practitioner rather than by a psychiatrist? When long-term care rather than repeated short-term care is applied? Does the cost-effectiveness rate vary with different psychiatric schools? Or with differing structures of supply involved in different health-care systems? Or do such differences only reflect differences between 'good' and 'bad' treatment (or between fashions)? These questions could typically be answered on the basis of matched-pair comparisons, but also occasionally on the basis of randomized clinical trials.

Definition. For performing treatment comparisons, mixed-pair design comparisons or randomized clinical experiments may be employed; but what can also be used are model scenarios, which hypothetically demonstrate the implications of different treatments. A crucial point in this context is that comparable groups are compared by application of rules of assuring comparability, i.e. homogenization, randomization.

Aims. (Quasi-)Experimental treatment comparison studies aim at testing the effectiveness and the undesired side effects of a treatment in question, such as orally administered versus injected medication, care at home or in hospital, no treatment versus treatment, or certain mixed forms of treatment. If several treatments turn out to be effective, cost-effectiveness analyses may be added; if only one treatment proves to be effective, cost-effectiveness analyses transcending the sectors studied (e.g. on treatment versus prevention) should be added.

Indicator system. Outcome, activity, and cost measures, as well as intervening variables.

Procedure. See available textbooks.

Optimal Solutions (Optimization)
Questions. Are there optimal pathways, treatments, strategies and their sequences in psychiatric care, with different elements of care (outpatient care, protected homes, inpatient admissions, etc.) in terms of improving cost-effectiveness? How can primary, secondary, and tertiary prevention be optimally employed? These questions will not be answered with reference to any norms but by use of numerical optimization procedures, with effectiveness being the target function and cost parameters being the constraints on the basis of sensitivity-tested standards for social medical care.

Definition and Aims. Identifying and recommending the optimal sequence of treatment steps and places and of primary, secondary, and tertiary prevention, as well as performing the optimal allocation of patients and setting the most cost-effective priorities is what constitutes the meaning and aim of cost-effectiveness analyses. In optimization procedures, operations research and applied political economics work together, proceeding from a static approach to a dynamic one.

Indicator System and Procedure. The principal data include outcome measures, production functions, and cost measures; if the need arises, further constraints can be operationalized. For the modelling of sequences, Markov chains or similar methods can be applied.

Advantages and Disadvantages of Different Research Designs
In selecting from among the research approaches mentioned one may apply the following criteria for decision-making, which include not only arguments pertaining to measurement theory and research strategies but also pragmatic considerations.

- *Reliability:* Reliability is a prerequisite of all the research approaches, but is has only rarely been tested for special indicators and items.
- *Validity:* Validity is a prerequisite of all the research approaches but can best be guaranteed in problem studies.
- *Relevance:* Examining relevance constitutes the meaning and purpose of problem studies.
- *Long periods of time* can best be covered by macrostudies (retrospectively) or by non-concurrent prospective cohort studies.
- *Large populations:* The type of study supported by this point are macrostudies and – to a lesser extent – full cohort studies; depending on the formulation of the question, problem studies may also cover total populations.

- *Flexibility:* The studies which can be evaluated with the greatest flexibility are the cohort studies in which no prior selection was performed; nearly complete flexibility is involved in the definitional phase of the problem studies.
- *Comparability:* Macrostudies and treatment-comparison studies are procedures in which comparability is involved to a relatively large extent, while this characteristic is least present in problem studies.
- *Closeness to the construct:* This is another point in support of problem studies.
- *Utilization of case registers:* Case registers can be used in all the research approaches.
- *Costs:* The least costs are involved in macrostudies and problem studies; higher costs are involved in cohort studies, and even higher ones in treatment-comparison studies; in optimality studies the costs depend on the research focus chosen.
- *Internationality:* Macrostudies aim at an exchange of international experiences, such as those of Sofia and Verona, for example; cohort studies can be carried out most easily in places where data protection constitutes a relatively small hindrance to research (e.g. in Eastern Europe).
- *Availability of tested tools:* There are a number of tested scales on functional impairments available which may support cohort and treatment-comparison studies.
- *Duration of studies:* The longest time span is involved in prospective cohort studies, but treatment-comparison studies are also of relatively long duration.
- *Actuality:* Involved to the greatest extent in macrostudies, cohort studies, and problem studies.
- *Multifunctionality:* Involved to the greatest extent in macrostudies, cohort studies, and problem studies, because the indicator systems can be extended at will or a great variety of evaluation designs may be used.
- *Political attractiveness:* To the greatest extent involved in international comparisons and problem studies, while optimality or treatment-comparison studies may have an undesired binding effect for health politicians.
- *Scientific standards:* At first sight, comparisons and treatment studies follow higher scientific standards than seem to be involved in other types of study, although the latter are necessary prerequisites for performing the former.

These evaluative criteria show that there is no design among the different research approaches which would deserve to be given priority. In view of the considerable prerequisites for research in terms of preparation, infrastructure, time lags of effects, etc., special attention should be paid to exploratory studies and to the collection of innovative arguments and approaches to assessing and strengthening cost-effectiveness of managing chronic psychotic patients rather than to sophisticated new studies.

Dimensions of Research

The study should have a threefold aim, in relation to the five research issues mentioned above regarding chronically schizophrenic patients.

Review of Completed and Ongoing Research

This part of the study will identify, review critically and summarize completed research studies, ongoing research activities, and definite proposals for future research. The review of each project will include its scope (objectives, rationale, issues tackled), methodology (economic, epidemiological, and statistical methods employed) and any findings (for health and related action, education and training, and future research).

Rehabilitation of Completed Research

This part of the study will take up any completed research that lacks an adequate health-economics component. Some researchers, for example, might not have included cost information at all; others might have disregarded costs to the family, the community, and society; still others might have used expenditure and average cost figures when opportunity and marginal cost concepts would have been appropriate.

Where feasible and useful, the study will attempt to rehabilitate these research projects retrospectively by adding economic aspects and information, by recalculating the research findings within the cost-effectiveness (cost-benefit or other appropriate economic) framework, and by reformulating any implications for health and social policy.

Redirection of Ongoing and Planned Research

This part of the study will run in parallel with the rehabilitation of completed research. Contact will be made with institutes that have current research activities in this field or have recently developed detailed research proposals. The aim is again to include economic questions and information whenever appropriate.

In addition, it is hoped that some study participants may find it possible to initiate original research themselves, although these projects need not be finalized within the time frame of the study.

Organization of the Study

Prerequisites. Studies on the cost-effectiveness of treating chronic psychotics cannot be carried out in all the centres. The prerequisites for conducting them are (a) political and social interest, (b) the meeting of minimal requirements for scientific research, and (c) availability of a case register (which is an arguable point).

Minimal Requirements Concerning Staff and Equipment. Concerning scientific staff and equipment, the following minimal requirements – which may be modified according to the concrete objective of research – should be met: an expert in research methods and one economist, with the following experts as possible advisors for specific tasks:

- Psychiatrists: assessment, treatment, access to the hospital
- Psychologists: testing of psychometric scales and items

- Sociologists: identification of problems and groups
- Biostatisticians: statistical evaluation designs
- Computer scientists: hardware and software
- Social workers: outpatient care for patients

Access to patients and access to other health services – primary health care, welfare organizations, etc. – are further essential prerequisites.

Reference Group. The team from the Federal Republic of Germany serves as the reference group; it will be supported by advice from the WHO department of health economics in Copenhagen.

Participants

Temporary Advisers
Dr. L. Barrelet, Carouge-Geneva, Switzerland
Ms. M.-T. Chapalain, Paris, France
Professor C. Christozov, Sofia, Bulgaria
Professor R. Giel, Groningen, Netherlands
Professor H. Häfner, Mannheim, Federal Republic of Germany
Ms. G. ten Horn, Groningen, Netherlands
Professor A. Maynard, York, United Kingdom
Dr. D. Schwefel, Neuherberg, Federal Republic of Germany
Dr. D. Walsh, Dublin, Ireland

WHO Regional Office for Europe
Mr. J. U. Hannibal, Technical Officer for Mental Health
Dr. J. H. Henderson, Regional Officer for Mental Health
Dr. H. Zöllner, Regional Officer for Health Economics

WHO Headquarters
Dr. W. Gulbinat, Division of Mental Health

Note

This report on "Studies on the Cost-Effectiveness of Managing Chronic Psychotics" summarizes the essential points which were formulated during a WHO planning meeting, and it outlines or even construes the connections between these points. Moreover, such a report must add as well as omit information. The rapporteur begs to be excused for distortions arising from these additions or omissions.

For their suggestions, the rapporteur thanks his colleagues Peter Potthoff, Reiner Leidl, and Annerose Hechler. Finally, he acknowledges the translation into English provided by Annerose Hechler.

References

Akehurst RL, Holtermann S (1978) Application of cost-benefit analysis to programmes for the prevention of mental handicap. Ciba Found Symp 59: 173-191

Arnold H (1977) Aufwand und Erfolg der Suchtkrankenbehandlung. Münchner Med Wochenschr 119 (38): 1201

Awad AG, Durost HB, Gray J, Kugelmass M, Smith C (1980) Psychiatric audits. The Ontario scene. Can J Psychiatry 25 (2): 155-162

Bank R, Schore R (1982) Medical information systems: a historical overview. Int J Ment Health 10 (4): 6-16

Baugher D (1981) Summary: developing a successfull measurement program. In: Baugher D (ed) New directions for program evaluation: measuring effectiveness no 11. Jossey-Bass, San Francisco, pp 101-105

Belmont L (1981) The development of a questionnaire to screen for severe mental retardation in developing countries. Int J Ment Health 10 (1): 85-99

Bennett D, Morris I (1983) Deinstitutionalization in the United Kingdom. Int J Ment Health 11 (4): 5-23

Bernard J (1979) Cost-benefit analysis and mental retardation center funding. Ment Retard 17 (3): 156-157

Biefang S (ed) (1980) Evaluationsforschung in der Psychiatrie: Fragestellungen und Methoden. Enke, Stuttgart

Blair P (1975) Mental handicap provision. Health Soc Serv J 84, 4437: 1004-1005

Brand M, Menzl A, Escher M, Horisberger B (1975) Vom Elektroschock zum Antidepressivum: Eine Kosten-Nutzen-Analyse. Pathomorphosis - Krankheit im Wandel, vol 2. Pharma Information, Basel

Brand M, Menzl A, Escher M, Horisberger B (1975) Kosten-Nutzen-Analyse Antidepressiva. Springer, Berlin Heidelberg New York

Bruckenberger E (1976) Konflikt zwischen Einzel- und Gesamtnutzen im Gesundheitswesen. Das Krankenhaus 68 (1): 8-14

Budman SH, Feldman J, Bennett MJ (1979) Adult mental health services in a health maintenance organization. Am J Psychiatry 136 (4A): 392-395

Bühringer G, Hahlweg K (1986) Kosten-Nutzen-Aspekte psychologischer Behandlung. Psychologische Rundschau 37: 1-19

Burns BJ, Regier DA, Goldberg ID, Kessler LG (1979) Future directions in primary care/mental health research. Int J Ment Health 8 (2): 130-140

Bursten B, Fontana AF, Dowds BN, Geach B (1980) Ward policy and therapeutic outcome. II. Ratings of patient behavior. Hosp Community Psychiatry 31 (1): 33-37

Cannon NL, McGuire TG, Dickey B (1985) Capital costs in economic program evaluation: the case of mental health services. In: Catterall JS (ed) New directions for program evaluation: economic evaluation of public programs, no 26. Jossey-Bass, San Francisco, pp 69-82

Centerwall BS, Criqui MH (1978) Prevention of the Wernicke-Korsakoff syndrome: a cost-benefit analysis. N Engl J Med 299 (6): 285-289

Chapalain M-T (1978) Perinatality: French cost-benefit studies and decisions on handicap and prevention. Ciba Found Symp 59: 193-206

Chapalain M-T (1983) Cost-efficiency estimates in psychiatry. Unpublished paper.

Choate R, Smith A, Cardillo JE, Thompson L (1981) Training in the use of goal-attainment scaling. Community Ment Health J 17 (2): 171-181

Cicchinelli LF, Binner PR, Halpern J (1978) Output value analysis of an alcoholism treatment program. J Stud Alcohol 39 (3): 435-447

Clark A, Friedman MJ (1982) The relative importance of treatment outcomes, a delphi group weighting in mental health. Evaluation Review 6 (1): 79-93

Clarke GJ (1979) In defense of deinstitutionalization. Milbank Memorial Fund Quarterly 57 (4): 461-479

Coates DB, Kendall LM, Macurdy EA, Goodacre RH (1976) Evaluating hospital and home treatment for psychiatric patients. Can Ment Health 24 (1): 28-33

Coe RM (ed) (1970) Planned change in the hospital. Case studies of organizational innovations. Praeger, New York

Delaney JA, Seidman E, Willis G (1978) Crisis intervention and the prevention of institutionalization: an interrupted time series analysis. Am J Community Psychol 6 (1): 33–45

Deutscher Bundestag: Auszug aus dem Bericht über die Lage der Psychiatrie in der Bundesrepublik Deutschland – zur psychiatrischen und psychotherapeutisch/psychosomatischen Versorgung der Bevölkerung. Bundestagsdrucksache 7/4200. Bonn

Dittman DA, Smith KR (1979) Consideration of benefits and costs: a conceptual framework for the health planner. Health Care Manage Rev 4 (4): 45–63

Doelker RE jr (1979) A multi-program cost analysis and planning model for social service programs. Administration in Social Work 3 (4): 477–488

Dressler DM (1981) Clinical services within a general hospital department of psychiatry: conceptual issues and operational guidelines. Gen Hosp Psychiatry 3 (4): 310–314

Drummond MF (1980) Principles of economic appraisal in health care. Oxford Medical Publications, Oxford

Drummond MF (1981) Studies in economic appraisal in health care. Oxford Medical Publications, Oxford

Eastaugh SR, Hatcher ME (1982) Improving compliance among hypertensives: a triage criterion with cost-benefit implications. Med Care 20 (10): 1001–1017

Endicott J, Herz MI, Gibbon M (1978) Brief versus standard hospitalization: the differential costs. Am J Psychiatry 135 (6): 707–712

Fenton FR, Tessier L, Contandriopoulos AP, Nguyen H (1982) A comparative trial of home and hospital psychiatric treatment: financial costs. Can J Psychiatry 27 (3): 177–187

Fieve RR (1979) The lithium clinic for treatment and prevention of manic depression: a cost-benefit approach. Egyptian J Psychiatry 2 (2): 166–190

Filstead WJ, Shadish WR, Crandell JS, Altman DB, Gottlieb DB, Visotsky JL (1982) Developing a multidimensional clinical rating scale: evaluating mental health services. Evaluation Rev 6 (4): 559–576

Fischer W (1981) La crise économique et ses effêts sur la population psychiatrique. Med Hyg 39: 3117–3122

Flatz VG (1978) Kosten-Nutzen-Analyse der Prävention des Morbus Down durch pränatale Diagnostik in der Frühschwangerschaft. Fortschr Med 96 (24): 1255–1256, 1295

Frank R (1981) Cost-benefit analysis in mental health services: a review of the literature. Administration in Mental Health 8 (3): 161–176

Frank PJ, Klein S, Jacobs J (1982) Cost-benefit analysis of a behavioral program for geriatric inpatients. Hosp Community Psychiatry 33 (5): 374–377

Fryers T (1981) Problems in screening for mental retardation in developing countries. Int J Ment Health 10 (1): 64–75

Gaspari KC (1983) The use and misuse of cost-effectiveness analysis. Soc Sci Med 17 (15): 1043–1046

Ginsberg G, Marks I (1977) Costs and benefits of behavioural psychotherapy: a pilot study of neurotics treated by nurse-therapists. Psychol Med 7 (4): 685–700

Glass NJ, Goldberg D (1977) Cost-benefit analysis and the evaluation of psychiatric services. Psychol Med 7 (4): 701–707

Glatzel J (1976) Zur Lage der Psychiatrie in der Bundesrepublik: Eine unkonventionelle, aber notwendige Betrachtung. Soz Fortschr 25 (4/5): 83–86

Goldberg DP, Bridges K, Cooper W, et al. (1985) Douglas House: a new type of hostel ward for chronic psychotic patients. Br J Psychiatry 147: 383–388

Goldberg D, Jones R (1980) The costs and benefits of psychiatric care. In: Robins LN, et al. (eds) The social consequences of psychiatrical illness. Brunner/Mazel, New York, pp 55–70

Gregory D, Jones RK, Rundell OH, Stanitis T, Stanhope P (1981) Feasibility of an alcoholism health insurance benefit. Curr Alcohol 8: 195–202

Gregory D, Rundell OH (1981) A model for service delivery research and evaluation: management implications for alcohol, drug abuse and mental health organizations. Curr Alcohol 8: 119–136

Guillette W, Crowley B, Savitz SA, Goldberg FD (1978) Day hospitalization as a cost-effective alternative to inpatient care: a pilot study. Hosp Community Psychiatry 29 (8): 525–527

Gustavson K-H (1981) The epidemiology of severe mental retardation in Sweden. Int J Ment Health 10 (1): 37–46

Häfner H, an der Heiden W (1982) Evaluation gemeindenaher Versorgung psychisch Kranker. Arch Psychiatrie Nervenkrankheiten 232: 71–95

Häfner H, an der Heiden W (1983) The impact of a changing system of care on patterns of utilization by schizophrenics. Soc Psychiatry 18: 153–160

Hall W, Goldstein G, Andrews G, et al. (1984) Estimating the economic costs of schizophrenia. Paper: School of Psychiatry, Prince Henry Hospital, Little Bay, Australia

Harding TW, Busnello EA, et al. (1983) The WHO collaborative study on strategies for extending mental health care. III. Evaluative design and illustrative results. Am J Psychiatry 140 (11): 1481–1485

Harding TW, Climent CE, et al. (1983) The WHO collaborative study on strategies for extending mental health care. II. The development of new research methods. Am J Psychiatry 140 (11): 1474–1480

Hasan Z, Aziz H (1981) Report on a population survey of mental retardation in Pakistan. Int J Ment Health 10 (1): 23–27

Hellinger FJ (1980) Cost-benefit analysis of health care: past applications and future prospects. Inquiry 27 (3): 204–215

Herzman P (1983) The economic costs of mental illness in Sweden 1975. Acta Psychiatr Scand 68: 359–367

Hirsch SR, Platt S, Knights A, Weyman A (1979) Shortening hospital stay for psychiatric care: effect on patients and their families. Br Med J 1: 442–446

Hoeper EW, Nycz GR, Cleary PD, Regier DA, Goldberg ID (1979) Estimated prevalence of RDC mental disorder in primary medical care. Int J Ment Health 8 (2): 6–15

Hohl J (1983) Gespräche mit Angehörigen psychiatrischer Patienten. (Diss) Werkstattschriften zur Sozialpsychiatrie, vol 36. Psychiatrie-Verlag, Rehburg-Loccum

Isaac MK, Kapur RL (1980) A cost-effectiveness analysis of three different methods of psychiatric case finding in the general population. Br J Psychiatry 137: 540–546

Jerrell JM (1982) Evaluating a management and organization development effort in mental health agencies. Evaluation and Program Planning 5: 169–179

Jones R, Goldberg D, Hughes B (1980) A comparison of two different services treating schizophrenia: a cost-benefit approach. Psychol Med 10 (3): 493–505

Kapur RL, Isaac M (1978) An inexpensive method for detecting psychosis and epilepsy in the general population. Lancet 2: 1089

Kazdin AE, Wilson GT (1978) Criteria for evaluating psychotherapy. Arch Gen Psychiatry 35 (4): 407–416

Kirshner LA (1982) Length of stay of psychiatric patients. A critical review and discussion. J Nerv Ment Dis 170 (1): 27–33

Köhler FC (1984) Der Hausarzt und die Betreuung chronisch Kranker. Z Ärztl Fortbild (Jena) 78 (12): 465–469

Kriedel T (1980) Effizienzanalysen bei Gesundheitsprojekten: Diskussion und Anwendung auf Epilepsieambulanzen. Medizinische Informatik und Statistik, vol 23. Springer, Berlin Heidelberg New York

Kunze H (1981) Psychiatrische Übergangseinrichtungen und Heime – Chronisch psychisch Kranke und Behinderte im Abseits der Psychiatrie-Reform. In: Bundesministerium für Arbeit und Sozialordnung (ed) Wissenschaftlicher Preis: Gesundheitsökonomie 1978/79 und 1979/80. Forschungsbericht Gesundheitsforschung, vol 46. BMA, Bonn, pp 149–173

Lamberg L (1978) Spending money saves money, epilepsy study shows. Am Med News 21 (13) [Suppl]: 6

Laska EM, Siegel C, Bank R (1982) Management information systems in mental health. Int J Ment Health 10 (4): 33–53

Layde PM, von Allmen SD, Oakley GP jr (1979) Congenital hypothyroidism control programs. A cost-benefit analysis. JAMA 241 (21): 2290–2292

Lehmkuhl D, Faehnrich E, Kruckenberg P, et al. (1980) Planungsgrundlagen für eine gemeindenahe psychiatrische Versorgung Charlottenburgs. Daten, Analysen, Untersuchungen zur Frage der sektorisierten Psychiatrie in einem Berliner Bezirk. Werkstattschriften zur Sozialpsychiatrie, vol 27. Psychiatrie-Verlag, Rehburg-Loccum

Leu R (1978) Nutzen-Kosten-Analyse der Behandlung von Alkoholkranken. Wirtschaft und Recht 30: 376–399

Levine MS, Weiner OD, Carone PF (1978) Monitoring inpatient length of stay in a community mental health center. J Nerv Ment Dis 166 (9): 655–660

Lewis SB, Barnhart FD, Gossett JT, Phillips VA (1975) Follow-up of adolescents treated in a psychiatric hospital: operational solutions to some methodological problems of clinical research. Am J Orthopsychiatry 45 (5): 813–824

Linn MW, Caffey EM jr, Klett CJ, Hogarty GE, Lamb HR (1979) Day treatment and psychotropic drugs in the aftercare of schizophrenic patients. A Veterans Administration cooperative study. Arch Gen Psychiatry 36 (10): 1055–1066

London P, Klerman GL (1982) Evaluating psychotherapy. Am J Psychiatry 139 (9): 709–717

Longabaugh R, Delmonico F, Epstein N (1981) Evaluation and the psychiatric hospital. Nat Assoc Private Psychiatric Hospitals 12 (4): 167–171

Mandell W (1979) A critical overview of evaluations of alcoholism treatment. Alcoholism (NY) 3 (4): 315–323

Marconi J (1980) La eficiencia del programa integral de salud mental: perspectivas asistenciales, docentes y de investigación. Rev Neuropsiquiatrica 43 (1): 39–54

Mason JC, Louka JL, Burmer GC, Scher M (1982) The efficiency of partial hospitalization: a review of the literature. Int J Partial Hospitalization 1 (3): 251–269

McGlothlin WH, Anglin MD (1981) Shutting off methadone. Costs and benefits. Arch Gen Psychiatry 38 (8): 885–892

McGuire TG, Weisbrod BA (1981) Perspectives on the economics of mental health. J Human Resources 16 (4): 494–500

McPheeters HH (1980) Measurement of mental health program outcomes. New Directions for Program Evaluation 6: 53–63

Miller GH, Willer B (1977) Information systems for evaluation and feedback in mental health organizations. In: Rutman L (ed) Evaluation research methods: a basic guide. Sage, Beverly Hills, pp 199–215

Mooney GH (1979) Economic approaches to alternative patterns of health care. J Epidemiol Community Health 33: 48–58

Mosher LR (1980) Community residential treatment for schizophrenia: two-year follow-up. Int J Rehabil Res 3 (3): 393–395

Muller CF, Caton CLM (1983) Economic costs of schizophrenia: a postdischarge study. Med Care 21 (1): 92–104

Murthy RS, Wig NN (1983) The WHO collaborative study on strategies for extending mental health care. IV. A training approach to enhancing the availability of mental health manpower in a developing country. Am J Psychiatry 140 (11): 1486–1490

Mushkin SJ (1977) Evaluation of health policies and actions. Soc Sci Med 11: 8–9, 491–499

Narayanan HS (1981) A study of the prevalence of mental retardation in Southern India. Int J Ment Health 10 (1): 28–36

Normand CH, McConville K (1984) A marginal budget analysis of services for the mentally ill in Northern Ireland. Paper presented to the ESRC/NPHT Health Economists Study Group, Aberdeen, July 3–4

Penk WE, Charles HL, Van Hoose TA (1978) Comparative effectiveness of day hospital and inpatient psychiatric treatment. J Consult Clin Psychol 46 (1): 94–101

Ploeger A, Schleicher V (1977) Medizin-soziologische Analysen zur Effizienz psychiatrischer Konsiliartätigkeit. Arzt und Krankenhaus 10: 24–30

Prognos AG (ed) (1982) Konzeption für die wissenschaftliche Begleitung des Modellprogramms Psychiatrie. Cologne

Prognos AG (ed) (1984) Modellprogramm Psychiatrie: regionales Psychiatriebudget (1. Intermediary report). Basel

Regier DA, Kessler LG, Burns BJ, Goldberg ID (1979) The need for a psychosocial classification system in primary-care settings. Int J Ment Health 8 (2): 16–29

Richardson BA, Smith DC, Hargreaves JA (1981) A 5-year clinical evaluation of the effectiveness of a fissure sealant in mentally retarded Canadian children. Community Dentistry and Oral Epidemiology 9 (4): 170–174

Rose SM (1979) Deciphering deinstitutionalization: complexities in policy and program analysis. Milbank Memorial Fund Quarterly 57 (4): 429–460

Rosen A, Proctor EK (1981) Distinctions between treatment outcomes and their implications for treatment evaluation. J Consult Clin Psychol 49 (3): 418–425

Rubin J (1982) Cost measurement and cost data in mental health settings. Hosp Community Psychiatry 33 (9): 750–754

Rundell OH, Paredes A (1979) Benefit-cost methodology in the evaluation of therapeutic services for alcoholism. Alcoholism (NY) 3 (4): 324–333

Rundell OH, Jones RK, Gregory D (1981) Practical benefit-cost analysis for alcoholism programs. Alcoholism (NY) 5 (4): 497–508

Sabatini J (1983) Valeur et structure de la consommation médicale en soins psychiatriques. J Economie Méd 1 (3): 151–159

Sadovnick AD, Baird PA (1981) A cost-benefit analysis of prenatal detection of Down syndrome and neural tube defects in older mothers. Am J Med Genet 10 (4): 367–378

Sartorius N, Harding TW (1983) The WHO collaborative study on strategies for extending mental health care. I. The genesis of the study. Am J Psychiatry 140 (11): 1470–1473

Schainblatt AH (1980) What happens to the clients? Community Mental Health J 16 (4): 331–342

Schmid S (1978) Freiheit heilt. Bericht über die demokratische Psychiatrie in Italien. Wagenbach, Berlin

Scull AT (1980) Die Anstalten öffnen? Decarceration der Irren und Häftlinge. Campus, Frankfurt

Shapiro J, Sank LI, Shaffer CS, Donovan DC (1982) Cost-effectiveness of individual vs. group cognitive behavior therapy for problems of depression and anxiety in an HMO population. J Clin Psychol 38 (3): 674–677

Sheffet AM, Kakumanu PV, Lavenhar MA, Feuerman M (1982) Treatment benefit functions for a drug-abuse rehabilitation treatment system. Soc Sci Med 16: 2109–2116

Simpson MG (1976) Health. Operational Research Quarterly 27 (1): 209–219

Singer NM, Bloom HS (1977) A cost-effectiveness analysis of patuxent institution. Bull Am Acad Psychiatry Law 5 (2): 161–170

Steiner KC, Smith HA (1973) Application of cost-benefit analysis to a PKU screening program. Inquiry 10 (4): 34–40

Steinmeyer H-D (1980) Rechtliche Überlegungen zu einer Reform der psychiatrischen Versorgung. Soz Fortschr 29 (5): 112–117

Stolz P (1974) Psychopharmaka – volkswirtschaftlich analysiert. Eine Nutzen-Kosten-Analyse der Verwendung von Tranquilizern in der Bundesrepublik Deutschland im Jahre 1972. In: Bernholz P, Bombach G, Frey RL (eds) Basler sozialökonomische Studien, 4. Schulthess, Zürich

Straw RB (1983) Deinstitutionalization in mental health. A meta-analysis. Evaluation Stud Rev Annu 8: 253–278

Sturiano V, Korts D, Hanbury R, Cohen M, Jackson G, Stimmel B (1980) The effectiveness of psychometric testing to identify alcoholics in a narcotic-dependent population. In: Galantor M (ed) Currents in alcoholism, vol 8. Recent advances in research and treatment. Grune and Stratton, New York, pp 147-154

Swint JM, Decker M, Lairson DR (1978) The economic returns to employment-based alcoholism programs: a methodology. J Stud Alcohol 39 (9): 1633–1639

Swint JM, Shapiro JM, Corson VL, Reynolds LW, Thomas GH, Kazazian HH jr (1979) The economic returns to community and hospital screening programs for a genetic disease. Prev Med 8 (4): 463–470

Ten Horn GHMM, Giel R (1984) The feasibility of cost-benefit studies of mental health care: an attempt with a Dutch case register. Acta Psychiatr Scand 69: 80–87

Thompson MS, Fortess EE (1980) Cost-effectiveness analysis in health program evaluation. Evaluation Rev 4 (4): 549–568

Thompson RH, Stanford G, Wilson JM (1981) Child life in hospitals. Theory and practice. Thomas, Springfield

Uhlenhuth EH (1982) Buspirone: a clinical review of a new, non-benzodiazepine anxiolytic. J Clin Psychiatry 43 (12, Pt 2): 109–116

Volkert JJ (1979) MIS-based client outcome evaluation: a multi-measure approach. Addict Dis 3 (4): 491–504

Wagner M (1977) Kosten-Nutzen-Rechnung zu den Reform-Empfehlungen der Psychiatrie-Enquete-Kommission. Soz Fortschr 26 (1): 9–18

Wald I, Zdzienicka E (1981) Simple neurological and clinical means of diagnosing severe mental retardation. Studies in Poland. Int J Ment Health 10 (1): 47 55

Warner KE, Hutton RC (1980) Cost-benefit and cost-effectiveness analysis in health care – growth and composition of the literature. Med Care 18 (11): 1069-1084

Weeden R, Burchell A (1982) Alcohol and disease: economic aspects. Br Med Bull 38 (1): 9-11

Weisbrod BA (1981) Benefit-cost analysis of a controlled experiment: treating the mentally ill. J Human Res 16 (4): 523-548

Weisbrod BA, Test MA, Stein LI (1980) Alternative to mental hospital treatment. II. Economic benefit-cost analysis. Arch Gen Psychiatry 37 (4): 400-405

Weiss KJ, Dubin WR (1982) Partial hospitalization: state of the art. Hosp Community Psychiatry 33 (11): 923-938

Windle C, Flaherty EW (1981) Emerging evaluation methods in mental health services. In: Smith N (ed) New directions for program evaluation: federal efforts to develop new evaluation methods, no 12. Jossey-Bass, San Francisco, pp 57-75

Wing JK, Cooper JE, Sartorius N (1982) Die Erfassung und Klassifikation psychiatrischer Symptome. Beltz, Weinheim

Wing JK, Häfner H (1973) Roots of evaluation. The epidemiological basis for planning psychiatric services. Proc International Symposium Mannheim Juli 26-29, 1972. Oxford University Press, London

Wing L, Wing JK, Hailey A, Bahn AK, Smith HE, Balduin JA (1967) The use of psychiatric services in three urban areas: an international case register study. Sozialpsychiatrie 2: 158-167

Wooldridge RJ, Bernhard JA (1981) Evaluating mental health service systems: a case in retrospect. In: Wooldridge RJ (ed) New directions for program evaluation: evaluation of complex systems, no 10. Jossey-Bass, San Francisco, pp 77-94

World Health Organization (ed) (1976) Cost/benefit analysis in mental health services – report on a working group. The Hague, June 21-25, 1976. WHO, ICP/MNH 006 11

World Health Organization (ed) (1983) WHO Collaborating Centre Groningen, Annual Report, Groningen

Summary Report of the WHO Meeting 'Cost-Effectiveness of Managing Chronic Psychotic Patients', Munich, 16–18 December, 1985

R. Leidl

Scope and Purpose of the Meeting

The cost-effectiveness of managing chronic psychotics is – among other issues such as the care for the elderly – one part of the health-economics programme of the World Health Organization (WHO) on the economic evaluation of health strategies, which in turn is one of three health-economics programmes intended to support the Health for All by the Year 2000 Strategy. The work of the study group on the cost-effectiveness of managing chronic psychotics was preceded by a planning meeting in Mannheim in 1983. At the Mannheim meeting, five major issues (special patient and target groups, regional differences, patterns and pathways of care, psychiatric treatment, and optimal solutions) were agreed upon as fields of research for a multinational study group. Chronic schizophrenia was suggested as a tracer diagnosis for cost-effectiveness analysis. No optimal research design suitable for all studies could be found, and thus the collection of diversified exploratory studies was favoured.

Research groups were identified, studies were stimulated, and the group was coordinated by Detlef Schwefel of the MEDIS Institute (WHO Collaborating Center for Health Planning and Health Economics), in close cooperation with the WHO Regional Office for Europe. The Munich meeting, which is summarized in this report, was organized for a presentation and discussion of contributions produced by the study group members. Criteria for a further review of the papers and possibilities of future studies were discussed, and the publication of the papers was agreed upon. The Munich meeting was attended by an international and multidisciplinary group comprising 22 participants from 13 countries. About half of the participants were psychiatrists, while the other half had their professional background in social sciences or economics.

Papers Presented and Discussion

Fifteen papers were presented and discussed at the meeting. These contributions, most of them earlier versions of papers compiled in this book, are briefly reported in the following section.

D. Walsh (Dublin): Measurement of the Cost-Effectiveness of Managing Chronic Psychotics in the Irish Context

This paper gave an historically based overview of the development of mental health services in Ireland, particularly in regard to its implications for cost and effectiveness. Special attention was paid to the high hospitalization rates and to the unemployment situation. The data available and the outlines of an Irish cost-effectiveness study were presented.

In the discussion, the constant share of mental health expenditures within the (growing) health-care budget was clarified. Unemployment, intangible suffering and the use of family time were identified as major determinants of the 'human costs' of care. The integration of the quality of care in cost comparisons of inpatient and outpatient services was raised as an important question.

A. Ozámiz and J. Cabasés (Bilbao): Economic Analysis of Alternative Patterns of Psychiatric Treatment and Management of Chronic Psychotics in the Basque Country

The paper presented calculations of direct costs for 26 treatment units for psychiatric care in the Basque Country. Cost estimates were conducted for a random sample of patients selected from a psychiatric case register. With hospital cost data for inpatient care and calculations in terms of 'work units' for outpatient contacts, average costs were calculated and cost relations between the treatment alternatives were established.

In the discussion, it was clarified that average time estimates were used as the basis of the 'work units', and that calculations referred to public expenditures (however, information on the patient's income situation is also available in the study). The additional inclusion of treatment effectiveness was suggested.

C. Christozov (Sofia): Economic Aspects of Managing Chronic Psychiatric Patients in Different Kinds of Institutions in Bulgaria

The paper described different types of extramural care (family care and family patronage), intramural care (psychiatric hospitals and homes for the mentally disabled), and care in semi-hospital institutions (day hospitals, etc.) for psychiatric patients in the Bulgarian system. Cost categories, problems of (costing) the different types of care, and approaches for effectiveness calculations were introduced, and cost comparisons between different institutions were considered.

In the discussion, the effectiveness of occupational therapy (in 'sheltered workshops') was pointed out.

R. Williams (Alberta): Cost-Effectiveness of Health Care Delivery to Chronic Psychotics in Southern Alberta, Canada

The paper introduced the health care system for psychiatric patients in Alberta, and presented the evaluative work of an interdisciplinary study group. This comprised a regional epidemiological study on schizophrenia, a questionnaire for patients' relatives on the impact of disorders on the families, and preliminary results of a study on the efficacy of an outpatient medication group.

In the discussion, the surprisingly low number of readmissions was explained by the high intensity of personnel in the hospitals, good outpatient monitoring, and a high density of physicians rather than by age effects, for example. As to some questionnaires of patients, reliability problems of patients' reports were mentioned. From their subjective feeling, the most problematic group of patients was found to be those who were unemployed and depressive.

J. Yfantopoulos (Athens): The Cost of Hospital Psychiatric Care in Greece
Starting from considerations on some defaults in the care of psychiatric patients, some epidemiological data were presented and the current situation of hospital services, personnel and financing of the care of the mentally ill in Greece were described. For an analysis of the direct costs of hospital care, methodological problems of cost measures (as average versus marginal costs, or the shape of the cost curves) were discussed, and empirical results (econometric estimates of alternative cost curves per patient day depending on bed occupancy or hospital size in beds) were shown.

The discussion went into details of the methodology and the relevance of estimating least-cost combinations by cost curves. It was suggested to include case mix measures and to increase the number of observations, to take into account the interrelations with outpatient care, and to integrate effectiveness measures.

D. Goldberg, K. Bridges, et al. (Manchester): The Description and Cost-Benefit Evaluation of a Hostel Ward for Chronic Psychotic Patients
From a 2-year study, the paper presented clinical assessments (including, e. g., diagnostic scales or the use of social facilities) and economic evaluations (such as professional time costing, an index of 'constructive' use of time, average costs per day for the National Health Insurance) of two groups of patients, one of them in a hostel ward (Douglas House), the other one in a hospital ward. The two groups were standardized according to diagnosis, duration of illness, psychological impairment, age, sex, and problem behaviour. The study concluded that treatment in a hostel ward is cheaper and more beneficial to patients. The results were limited by the lack of a comparison with a large psychiatric hospital.

In the discussion, it was clarified that administrative costs were included for both groups, that costs of the study were included only in case of a clinical involvement, and that the hostel is a long-term project. The standardization of the two groups compared did not take into account combinations of standardization variables (like age, sex, or the size of patient families).

M. De Munshi and S. Maitra (Calcutta): Chronic Suffering and Cost-Effectiveness
The paper reported a longitudinal study of 45 patients in a private day clinic in Calcutta, comparing patients before and during the study. Effectiveness was measured by an aggregate index of a multidimensional scale. Cost calculations were limited to direct treatment expenditures but disaggregated for different types of cost. Several relations between effectiveness dimensions were presented, and conclusions for less expensive treatment styles were drawn.

In the discussion, it was mentioned that most patients in the study had better chances of recovering than similar patients in Western countries. Also, the aggregation process for the index of the multidimensional scale (which applied an average calculation of means) was debated.

A. McKechnie (Broxburn): The Cost of Long-Term Psychoses in a Scottish Psychiatric Hospital

Within the framework of the British National Health Service, the paper discussed general management budgets (comparing the developments of psychiatric and other hospital budgets), clinical costing data (where types of costs within hospitals were compared and major cost determinants debated), activity data (aggregate indices of inpatient and outpatient hospital utilization; institutional costs per capita of population) and data on the outcome and quality of services (those needed most badly were listed).

In the discussion, it was suggested to control changes in (weekly) working hours in longitudinal comparisons of personnel costs.

P. Jauhar (Glasgow): Microcomputer-Mediated Auditing of Clinical Care

The paper introduced a computer-based clinical monitoring system (Glasgow Eastern Psychiatric Auditing System) for the control and evaluation of the treatment of acute psychiatric patients. The system included data on initial contacts, discharges, depot neuroleptic therapy, and lithium therapy but did not use any cost data.

Most of the discussion was devoted to problems of the confidentiality of the patients' data files. Further, it was suggested to compare the costs of the information system with increases in patients' compliance and with side effects of drug therapy.

D. Schwefel, P. Potthoff, R. Leidl, and W. Bender (Munich): Time-Budget Analyses for Chronic Psychotic Patients. A Pilot Study

The paper introduced an explorative approach towards the development of a patient-based indicator system of costs and effectiveness measures. The approach was primarily related to the analysis of time budgets of chronic psychotic patients. Empirical methods suited for different settings of psychiatric care were presented, empirical work and the results of the pilot study were discussed. With data collected from patients, relatives, and personnel, the analysis covered daily routines, activities, institutional care, therapies, drugs, living conditions, incomes and expenditures of chronic (non-paranoid) schizophrenics in inpatient and outpatient settings.

In the discussion, the use of control groups was suggested. Regarding questionnaires as a data source, reliability and validity of the answers were debated, and problems of adequately attributing figures reported for household income and expenditures to the patient were mentioned.

L. Barrelet and W. Fischer (Geneva): Management of Schizophrenia: Cost-Benefit, Time Budget, Better Treatment? Which Time Frame Are We in?

After an introduction to the course, stages, and outcomes of schizophrenia, the paper described the social environment (demographic characteristics, labor situation, education and professional background) and the therapeutic patterns for a cohort of chronic schizophrenics. For a group of young patients, a time-budget analysis focussed on interpersonal contact times. Additionally, the benefits of treatment (connected with hospitalization; related to working capacity, to the course of symptoms, to interpersonal relationships, to the quality of life, to individual independence) were discussed, and a cost analysis estimating direct and indirect costs was presented. In a conclusion, it was suggested to promote the patients' wage earning capabilities, and to improve the treatment modalities.

In the discussion, it was found that the valuation of time should distinguish between the time of care and the time other persons just spent with patients, and that the frequency of contacts does not reflect their length and intensity. It was suggested to give an overview (table) of the dimensions used, to point out the reference group, and to consider transfer payments.

D. Wiersma (Groningen): Schizophrenia: Results of a Cohort Study with Respect to Cost-Accounting Problems of Patterns of Mental Health Care in Relation to Course of Illness

The paper presented calculations of the costs of care for different patterns of care and the courses of illness for a cohort of new schizophrenic patients over the first 3 years of their disease; this was referred to as an incidence approach. Especially day- and community-centered types of care were compared with inpatient care. Patient data were taken from a former WHO screening study. Admissions, hospital days, outpatient contacts and aggregates thereof were used to describe the patterns of care. Average costing was applied to evaluate the costs. The course and the outcome of the illness was described and costed, and costs and effects of treatment alternatives were combined. However, an assessment of the relative effectiveness of patterns of care was not feasible, and more qualitative analysis seemed necessary.

In the discussion, it was emphasized that the mortality of the sample analyzed was high, and that some of the patients' professional contacts outside the study might have been hidden from the researchers. The progress of the disability status of the patients in the cohort was not looked upon optimistically.

A. Marinoni, E. Torre, and A. Brenna (Pavia): The Effect of the Dehospitalization Law on Chronic Psychotic Patients in Italy: A Tentative Cost-Effectiveness Evaluation

The paper presented a longitudinal economic and social evaluation of a cohort of schizophrenic or paranoid patients under the influence of the Italian deinstitutionalization movement. The information was based on case registers and three questionnaires administered to patients and relatives. Multivariate statistical techniques were applied to the analysis of the data. Some preliminary results showed that noninstitutionalized patients were found to be less costly to public funds than institutionalized ones, while among the noninstitutionalized those with more contacts with the services implied higher expenditures (in monetary as well as nonmonetary terms) but also showed more social autonomy and fewer mental disturbances.

In the discussion, it was suggested to integrate more variables on education, the employment situation, and migrations of the patients. It was found that the study also reveals benefits from psychiatric (out)patients to their families (like support in house-keeping) as well as costs to the families for hospitalization; also, the emotional situation of the family was considered. Concerning suicide, it was pointed out that it is not a good indicator of effectiveness for short periods of time.

J. Sabatini and J. M. Elchardus (Lyon): Methodological Problems in Comparing the Cost-Effectiveness of Different Mental Health Institutions

The paper presented several methodological considerations on cost-effectiveness analyses. It covered the evolution of treatment facilities, professional resistance to assessment programmes, the types of costs, the different diagnoses, the dimensions of effectiveness, standardization requirements, and the patients' careers.

In the discussion, it was suggested to supplement the paper with empirical results. For costing procedures, it was debated whether they could be standardized (as some clinical instruments are) or whether their specific application depended on the interest of the researcher. The question of which social situation could favour or motivate cost-effectiveness analyses was raised.

M. Bille (Randers): Psychiatrists and Politicians. A Personal Experience

The paper introduced difficulties in the relationship and understanding between psychiatrists, whose perspective is oriented towards the care of their patients, and politicians, who are to determine the framework for care and the allocation of funds. In the struggle for a share of the funds, comparative disadvantages of psychiatry against other fields of health care were stressed, as well as disadvantages of chronic diseases against nonchronic diseases.

The discussion focussed on how psychiatry – as psychotics do not have any lobby, or because psychiatric diseases imply only low mortalities – could be strengthened in the competitive health-care market and on how results of the study could be made better known to politicians and exercise more influence on them. As major issues, the publication of more information, especially data on disabilities, on the cost of mental disorders, and on retrospective monitoring (e. g., of programme-budgeting approaches) was suggested.

Criteria for a Review of the Papers

The presentation and discussion of papers was supplemented by working groups. Criteria by which the papers should be checked were developed in three groups and then discussed and agreed upon in a plenary session. The discussion raised the following questions, which can be regarded as a check list for research contributions in this field.

Target Group, Purpose, and Problem of the Paper

- Is information support given to politicians or to the scientific (economic and clinical) community by the study-group papers, are they easy to understand by the target group (for their interdisciplinarity, a glossary might be useful), and are they relevant to decision-making?
- What are the basic objectives of the paper (description, development of methods, empirical results), and what does it try to evaluate, what to compare?

- In particular, what types of care are compared: inpatient and outpatient care, psychiatric and social work, hospital/community or family services?
- Can the approach be applied to a spectrum of services?

Methods Used
- Is an interdisciplinary approach (sociological, economic, clinical) used?
- Are there methodological constraints – e.g., on the statistical interpretability of the results – that should be made explicit?
- Is a list of the operational criteria given in the paper (what costs or effects are operationalized and compared between different institutions or types of care)?
- What aspects of cost-effectiveness analyses are dealt with?

Data and Field of Application
- Are the data sources and variables clarified and their limitations explained in the paper (e.g., is the patient population which is analyzed defined in terms of institutions or regions)?
- Is background material on mental health services provided?
- Is information on socioeconomic factors (e.g., work opportunities, family support) provided?

Outcome of the Papers
- What are the results and (policy) conclusions of the paper; can they be transferred to the situations in other countries?
- Are there suggestions for future research work (for a modification of the instruments used, or for an alteration of the research design or research issues)?
- Can the paper be improved by the editorial review of an interdisciplinary board?

Discussion on Future Studies

In the plenary meeting issues of future studies (e.g. which type of studies should be strengthened, where could starting points for further multinational research be found, and what studies are considered reasonable and feasible) were discussed. The following suggestions were made for research priorities:

- Comparisons of inputs (costs or expenditures) and outputs (e.g. outcomes in terms of mortality or morbidity) within the health services, i.e. an analysis of the proportion of psychiatric and other health service budgets (e.g. for cancer or heart disease)
- Comparisons with the community as a whole (also taking non-health services into account)
- Analyses of the regional organization of psychiatric services
- Studies of the public/private mix in mental health services
- Analyses of the proportion between inpatient and outpatient budgets
- Changing institutional factilities for psychiatric care, changing philosophies of psychiatric illness, and changing therapeutic goals

- A comparison between societies with expanding and contracting psychiatric services
- Studies on the choice between two policies: either a low level of care for many patients or intensive care for a few patients
- Studies in which psychiatrists and economists have to work together, e.g. in the evaluation of the new institutionalism
- More detailed work on the different types of interventions in the patients' life by different types of care
- Long-term studies on the control of (time-)lagged effects
- Methodological developments towards a research model of evaluating psychiatric services, e.g. community services

Special attention was paid to the problem of health status measurement in the cost-effectiveness analyses. Future work should comprise:

- Studies using alternatives to diagnostic labelling, especially measures for a classification of impairments, disabilities and handicaps (which, for example, could follow the WHO concept of satisfactory health); these measures can then be used either in the standardization of patient populations or as measures of the effectiveness of care
- Studies on mental health status measurement integrating sociological aspects (functional/dysfunctional approaches), clinical aspects (mortality or morbidity measures), and economic aspects (probabilities of changing health status and related costs)
- No more developments of additional health indices, but rather an agreement on the basic indexing techniques, whereas the indexes should also be instruments oriented towards decision-making

Results of the Meeting

The study group planned the publication of the papers, which finally resulted in the present book. Most of the papers were carefully reviewed and revised, and one was included that was not presented in the Munich meeting.

National Approaches

Management of the Cost-Effectiveness
of Managing Chronic Psychotic Persons in Ireland

D. Walsh

Introduction and Justification for this Research

Public Health and Economic Implications of Chronic Psychosis

There are in Ireland[1] approximately 40 psychiatric hospitals and units, of which one quarter are private and the remainder public. They provide 14500 beds, 30% of all hospital beds in the country, and in 1983 there were 28000 admissions to these beds, of which 30% were returned as first admissions. The cost of running these hospitals in 1982, together with their outpatient services, was £ 120000000, out of a total net noncapital cost of the health services generally of £ 950000000, representing just over 8% of the gross national product and of which £ 860000000 was contributed directly by the exchequer. Capital expenditure on psychiatric hospitals in 1982 was just short of £ 3000000, the major part of which came from health boards or local governmental sources, only £ 35000 being supplied by voluntary bodies. Much of this expenditure was concerned with chronic psychotic patients, among whom schizophrenics were by far the largest group, constituting 50% of resident patients and a quarter of psychiatric hospital admissions. The extent to which chronic psychotics required nonhospital psychiatric services varied from place to place but, on average, at any one point in time approximately half of the schizophrenic patients in care are being managed as inpatients, with the other half in alternative forms of care. There can be little doubt, then, that mental illness is a major public health problem in Ireland and this, surely, is sufficient justification for what may broadly be called 'health service research' into the most efficient and effective way of delivering mental health care.

---

[1] "Ireland" refers to the 26 counties of the island, and excludes the 6 counties which constitute (in international usage) Northern Ireland, which remains a part of the United Kingdom

Planning for the Future

Ireland has the unenviable record of having proportionally more patients psychiatrically hospitalised than any other country in Europe (Walsh 1968). That some
political disquiet has been occasioned by the generally unsatisfactory nature of
mental health care was formally acknowledged by the setting up in 1961 of a
Commission of Inquiry on Mental Illness, whose brief was to review the existing
services and recommend what improvements were necessary (Department of
Health 1966). Although the Commission's recommendations included the undertaking of research into the social aspects of psychiatric illness and the reasons underlying the high hospitalisation rate, inquiry into the cost aspects of providing
services was not mentioned. The Commission predicted that if its recommendations to provide alternatives to hospital care were realised the 21 000 psychiatric
beds existing in 1961 would be reduced to 8000 by 1981. In fact, by that year there
were still almost twice the predicted number in use. The Irish hospitalisation rate
of about 4.5 per thousand of population was more than twice that of England,
France or Denmark. It was hardly surprising, then, that on reviewing the situation
the Minister for Health in that year (1981) set up a Working Party

to examine the main components, both institutional and community, of the psychiatric services; to
assess the existing services, to clarify their objectives and to draw up planning guidelines for future development of the service with due regard to cost implications; to carry out such studies and
to take part in such consultations as are necessary to assist this examination (Department of
Health 1984).

The phrase "with due regard to cost implications" is of interest in the brief and, indeed, Chap. 14 of the report is entitled "Organisation and Management", Chap. 15
"Cost Implications", and Chap. 16 "Planning and Evaluation" (Department of
Health 1984). Although there was no explicit mention of specifically health ser-
vice-oriented research, there are strong implications of the necessity of this type of
work in these three chapters. For example, the first recommendation is that substantial deinstitutionalisation of psychiatric patients should take place and alternative methods of care be provided for them in the community, and it was recommended that this process should be monitored and evaluated and that some
estimate of the cost-effectiveness of the process should be undertaken.

Utility and Objectives of Health Services Research In Ireland

In the worst sense of the word, the delivery of psychiatric care in Ireland, and to
some extent everywhere, has been empirical. The nineteenth-century attitude to
dealing with psychiatric illness was unambiguous and clear cut. It was felt that the
mentally ill needed to be institutionalised both for their own good and for the
good of society. That was the policy of containment, and in Ireland extensive asylum building was undertaken, often after an assessment of need including community surveys of the numbers of mentally ill, so that by 1900 virtually all the mental-

ly ill were in asylums and the objectives of the policy had been fulfilled. However, treatment and discharge were also important, if sometimes secondary, goals of policy, even if few treatments were specific and if success, partial or complete, was not exactly frequent.

With the coming of the twentieth century and the realisation that containment was not always necessary and that treatment could be provided outside the hospital, the emphasis shifted from institutional to community care. Nevertheless, the administrative and managerial traditions of the institution continued to dictate attitudes and sometimes practices well into the second half of the twentieth century. When change came about it was often empirical, often ideologically rather than scientifically determined, and it is only in the past 15 years or so that a scientific approach to the provision of mental health care has become evident. Even so, it has not been easy to induce economists, administrators or health care professionals to interest themselves in the health services research field and so the amount of work that has been done has been strikingly small. Therefore, the utility of studies of the kind proposed in this paper must necessarily have an educational and heuristic value so that health care providers will become more questioning, more scientifically minded and more aware of the cost implications of alternative approaches for care delivery.

To some extent, the recent recession and the decrease in monies available for health care have disciplined minds and moved them in the direction of thinking about value for money in the health field. Despite the fact that mental health and the care of the mentally ill do not have high political visibility, more interest has been taken in the care of the mentally ill by politicians in Ireland during the past year than in the whole of the preceeding quarter century. The matter has been politicised by the Cabinet's decision to reduce the Minister for Health's allocation of budgetary resources when the Minister presented his estimates for his department. He has resolved to expedite the implementation of the recommendations of Planning for the Future to ensure that these recommendations do not suffer the same fate as those of the Commission of Inquiry on Mental Illness in 1981. To speed things up he has announced his intention to close two health board psychiatric hospitals by the end of 1986 and has indicated to the health boards involved that no further funding will be available for these hospitals. Instead, the monies formerly paid to maintain them will go to the provision of community care.

Constraints on Alternatives to Hospitalisation and the Introduction of Health Services Research

The great utility of the nineteenth- and early twentieth-century approach to mental illness in Ireland was that the policy of total institutionalisation had come to completion by 1900, at which time 0.5% of the nation's citizens were in psychiatric hospitals. There they remained for half a century or more. The building of these great institutions had given considerable employment to architects and engineers at a time when, as now, jobs were hard to come by in poverty-stricken Ireland. The indirect benefits, therefore, of mental illness in the Irish community were considerable. These were to continue, and to such an extent that towns like Ballinasloe in Co. Galway counted among its 6000 population 2000 mentally ill people and at least another 500 individuals directly employed in looking after them. Indirect benefits to many of the merchants and other persons who partly lived off a hospital in one way or another contributed greatly to the local economy.

Jobs as attendants in mental hospitals were strongly contested and often ran in families. More particularly, in the twentieth century the attendant or nursing profession had so strongly come to protest its own interests that the institutions were run for the benefit of the staff as much as for the patients. Thus, rostering, in particular, was so arranged that it allowed for many attendants or nurses to develop alternative businesses, run farms or mind children. This, a benefit to a small number of people, was of course a cost to many unemployed who were thus deprived of jobs and effectively widened the gap between rich and poor. These practices in Irish mental hospitals continued until staff members went on strike in an attempt to resist change. Management refused to yield, and as a result a national forum representing central government, local health administration and the trades union to negotiate change in the contentious areas of staff rostering, promotion by seniority and integration of the sexes in nursing activities has been set up.

The current organisation of psychiatric care in Ireland is based on broad catchment responsibility, whereby hospitals are the focus of services to populations which vary from 50000 to 200000. Increasingly, the catchment populations are becoming "sectorised" so that a relationship between service teams and the population service has come about. This goes some way towards ensuring a continuity of care that was lacking previously. The growth of general hospital units has not always helped the situation, in that some, but not all, general hospital units function so that they serve specific types of patients rather than defined communities. In Ireland there is also a substantial private psychiatric sector in which, because it is predominantly institutional based, there is a more limited range of options open to the clinical decision-maker. In addition, particular ideologies which support institutionalisation – such as orientation towards intensive and costly inpatient treatment for alcoholism in the absence of convincing evidence that this is any more cost-effective than cheaper outpatient alternatives – increase bed days and therefore costs.

Information Systems

There are in Ireland well-established information systems in the mental health services. The National Psychiatric Inpatient Reporting System supplies a wealth of detail concerning the activities of residential hospitals and units. Activities of psychiatric services outside hospitals are available in some detail for 10% of the Irish population through the mechanism of two psychiatric case registers. Unfortunately, very little information is available on the management of psychiatric patients outside the specialised mental health services, for example, in primary health care settings.

Whereas patient movement data within the psychiatric service are readily available through the case registers, as already mentioned, budgetary or accounting data are not so conveniently procured. In fact, it is notoriously difficult in Ireland to cost single items of service, such as outpatient visits, in the psychiatric service either because budgetary and accounting data are grouped for an individual hospital service as a whole, without distinguishing the recipients of wages or differentiating between those who work in the hospital and outside the hospital, or because data are given for groups of psychiatric services massed together.

Costs

If basic data are available on patients' utilisation of psychiatric services – and they are – and on the nature of patients and their illnesses, then the remaining data that are needed relate to costs. Generally, in work of this kind costs are referred to as direct and indirect. Direct costs concern the monies spent on the care and treatment of the patients, with treatment costs generally covered by the mental health service and maintenance costs paid by the social welfare or welfare payments made to the patient. In Ireland these can be broadly quantified, but, as stated earlier, difficulties arise when gross treatment costs have to be proportioned to specific categories of patients, such as chronic psychotics. Some difficulty arises in proportioning costs to various forms of treatment. Welfare payment costs are, of course, easily ascertained.

Indirect costs concern material and human costs. Indirect costs relate first to the patient and second to his or her family. Among the material of indirect costs are the loss to the patient of potential earnings because of his inability to obtain and hold employment. Given the individual's former training and earning experience it may be simple enough to compute these costs. However, it must be realised that one person's misfortune is another person's advantage and in the current recessionary period patients' inability to work may provide an opportunity cost for someone else who otherwise would be unemployed but is now able to take the patient's job. Therefore, there is sometimes the cost to an individual patient which may not be a cost to society. Likewise, the welfare payments to a patient may simply replace unemployment assistance given to an individual who, now having taken the patient's job, would otherwise have been unemployed.

In like manner the cost to family members may not be a significant burden to society. Thus, a family may forgo earnings because someone has to give up work to look after a patient who is maintained at home rather than in hospital. However, this may provide the opportunity for someone else in the labour force to obtain employment through the vacancy created.

The human costs again involve both the patient and his family and, of course, are less easily measured. The effectiveness of treatment may improve the patient in two ways: first in terms of his subjective well-being and second in the functional sense of being able to return to work and earn money (thus incidentally displacing someone from employment), and also of reducing the suffering cost to his family by his being less of a nuisance or burden at home. The clinical state of the patient including his subjective sense of well-being, is now readily measurable and comparable by means of standardised clinical examinations which can be objectively quantified and compared over time. The human suffering to the family is less easily quantified but this can be done. Though it is difficult to say so, suicide by a schizophrenic who has failed to respond to treatment and is a considerable burden to himself and to others and to the health services may count as a benefit, exemplifying that in certain circumstances death may be an acceptable outcome.

Among other specific issues relative to cost-effective studies in the Irish context is the very high level of unemployment, which makes it extremely difficult for persons who have mental illness to be returned to full open employment. Indeed, given that some psychiatric patients with residual impairment will not function at an efficient level in industrial or other employment, so that the job can be better performed by a person not mentally ill, it becomes difficult to advocate the employment of one who may be a cost to the national economy even though his employment would figure as a benefit in terms of an evaluation of the psychiatric service.

Comparative and Control Studies

Macrostudies – the Economic Cost of Mental Illness and of Schizophrenia in Ireland
No comprehensive data are available on the cost of mental illness generally or schizophrenia specifically in Ireland. As a beginning, then, an exercise such as that undertaken recently for Australia by Andrews et al. (1985) needs to be replicated for Ireland. Among the questions to be addressed in such a study are: What are the direct costs of mental illness or schizophrenia? What are the indirect costs, and how are they to be measured? The methodological approach to be adopted will have to consider whether the prevalence approach, in which the costs and losses are assigned to the years in which they occur, or the incidence approach, where costs arising are computed from the year in which the illness begins, is to be employed. If such an exercise were to be carried out in Ireland the basic morbidity data to be obtained are readily available. One of the difficulties to be encountered is the variation in costs during an uncertain and fluctuating economic future which influences substantially the prospects of employment for the mentally ill as well as for the general population. Because of the change in the nature of psychiatric services and the movement towards community care which will undoubtedly occur, it is difficult to ascertain precisely indirect costs and/or benefits resulting from changes in the employment of health professionals that community care will bring about. In Ireland there are 6000 psychiatric nurses, many of whom are employed in carrying out a simple custodial function that is uninteresting and is below the level of their general intelligence and education. Movement towards a predominantly community service will undoubtedly result in nonrecruitment or unemployment of nurses and therefore will be a cost to the national economy in that so many more people will be supported by public funds. On the other hand the psychiatric service will function at lower cost. Overall, the welfare payments will be only half as costly as nurse salaries so there will be a net benefit to society.

Cost-Effective/Cost-Benefit Comparisons of Alternative Forms of Care of Chronic Psychotics

A study of this kind is very much needed in Ireland because one of the objections to the implementation of Planning for the Future has been that the community-care approach may cost far more than the psychiatric hospital approach. The truth of the matter is that nobody knows, since comparative costings have never been effected. That is why such a study is particularly important. There are some areas of the country which are ideally suited for it. For example, there is in one western county a traditional mental hospital, with little by way of community services, which continues to provide psychiatric care for its own catchment area within that county. In the other part of the county a new general hospital unit has been established for some years now and is providing community-based care for the other parts of the county. A ready-made situation exists here for a multi-disciplinary cost-effective/cost-benefit analysis of the community versus the institutional approach. An approach has been made to the health board responsible for the county in which these two services operate in an attempt to set up a study, but unfortunately the administration has not agreed to cooperate in the project. This illustrates the considerable administrative and political difficulties faced in undertaking work of this kind when a central organisation is dependent on the cooperation of local administrations. Since the recession and the reduction in health budgets supplied to local health administrations or health boards by the central government in Ireland, there has been a certain amount of friction between the two administrations which has not helped the promotion of studies of this kind. Ultimately, the greatest value of such a study may not be in its scientific content but in the fact that it enjoins self-criticism in those who provide service and thereby induces change.

Cost-Effectiveness of Personnel Utilisation in the Delivery of Mental Health Care

In a multidisciplinary type of service such as mental health services usually are, there is often a lack of definition and a blurring of functional role boundaries which raise questions as to which type of personnel is the most useful, the most effective and the cheapest in performing specific acts of treatment. For this reason there is substantial need for outcome studies of treatment of similar conditions by different levels of personnel. This is important because psychiatrists, for example, cost twice as much as nurses or social workers in hourly rates of pay. Yet much of the psychiatrists' time is spent in dealing with neurotic illnesses and substance-abuse disorders, where there is little evidence that their input is more efficacious than that of other professionals. Indeed, the comparison of self-help or informal systems of care with the formal statutorily provided systems of care in terms of cost and effectiveness is equally important.

Diverse Issues

Much time is given in Ireland to alcohol counselling and, again, the outcome has not been evaluated. There is also the current practice of community nursing from a hospital base which means considerable cost because of travelling expenses paid for long journeys in rural areas. Indeed, a day may be spent travelling to visit two or three patients, and this does point out that a community-based approach is not homogeneously constituted but involves several different items of service, each of which can be compared with one another in terms of costs and benefits. The community-located service will also have closer links with general practice and primary care, thus leading to earlier referral and more effective treatment. This will decrease morbidity and operate as a benefit.

Finally, the day-centre movement is a growing one, and at a time of high unemployment it is common to find people who have little quantifiable illness attending psychiatric day centres – they do not in fact meet the criteria for "caseness". The costs and benefits of their coming to day centres rather than staying at home, unemployed, with their families needs to be investigated.

References

1. Walsh D (1968) Hospitalised psychiatric morbidity in the Republic of Ireland. Br J Psychiatry 114 (506): 11–14
2. Department of Health (1966) Commission of Inquiry on Mental Illness. Stationery Office, Dublin
3. Department of Health (1984) The psychiatric services – planning for the future. Stationery Office, Dublin
4. Andrews G, Hall W, Goldstein G, Lapsley H, Bartels R, Silove D (1985) The economic costs of schizophrenia. Arch Gen Psychiatry 42: 537–543

Social and Economic Policies in the Mental Health Sector in Greece

J. N. Yfantopoulos

Introduction

During the past two or three decades there has been a growing interest among social scientists in investigation of the social organization, control, and functioning of alternative forms of psychiatric care. A wider approach has been promoted, which is based on the search for an interdisciplinary methodology. The complexity of sociopsychiatric problems confronted by the modern societies could not be solved by the medical profession alone, or by the administrators, planners, psychologists, economists, and other social scientists. The inexplicity of the social problems and the increasing need for reforms require harmonic collaboration between the above professions.

The examination of institutional psychiatry is not a new subject in social sciences. Foucault (1971) described the situation in the early European asylums of the seventeenth and eighteenth centuries. Digby (1983) presented the economic and social situations of the York Asylum, one of the early mental hospitals in England. J. A. Talbot (1978), in his book *Death of the Asylum,* analyzed the predominant forces which have influenced the history of the public mental hospitals.

Since the middle of the 1950s we have witnessed impressive changes in the European mental health systems (Mangen 1985), i. e. the gradual decline of the traditional asylum with more than 2000 beds and the birth of community mental centers as well as mental hostels. The expansion of psychiatric services in general hospitals has also been observed. A psychotic patient who would have been institutionalized in the 1950s would have stayed in a public hospital for an average of 20 years; in 1975 the inpatient treatment of a psychotic patient lasted for an average of 9 months.

In Greece, although in the scientific psychiatric domain there have been a number of articles (see Stefanis and Madianos 1981) describing the need for reform of the institutionalized, highly problematic psychiatric sector, the whole interplay between psychiatry, social values and socioeconomic policies has not been investigated.

In March 1983 the European Commission established a committee to study the possibilities for reforming the medical, social, and vocational rehabilitation aspects of the Greek mental institutions. The committee produced a report which noted:

It is broadly accepted that psychiatric care is totally inadequate. The manner of dealing with psychiatric patients is often close to the limits of the denial of the most basic notions of human digni-
ty. Radical reform is needed to change this intolerable situation. (EEC 1984, p 7)

The situation in the Greek public psychiatric hospitals is tragic. (EEC 1984, p 18)

The above critiques state the need for immediate reform of the Greek psychiatric
sector. Since some measures are already implemented, it should be emphasised
that the planned changes should not be viewed in isolation from the social and
economic system. The potential for decreasing the number of days of treatment
for chronic psychiatric patients requires the development of other forms of social
and welfare services. Deinstitutionalization also requires reallocation of the scarce
resources available. The opportunity costs of alternative forms of care should be
studied and some concrete proposals should be formalized on the future development of the services. Hence, a socioeconomic approach should be adopted, aiming at the analysis of the historical factors that have influenced the development of
the system and attempting to identify the relationship between the social, political
and fiscal forces. Also needed is an analysis of the role of the medical profession
and their attitudes as health care providers in conjunction with the organizational
structure of the institutions.

   This paper is restricted to a rather small area of the economics of the mental
health sector and attempts to shed some light on the economic performance of
public psychiatric hospitals. The first part presents a general overview of the
Greek mental health system. Since social policy deals with the social, economic,
and political problems, emphasis is given to the legislative acts adopted by different governments. Some initial estimates of the governmental 5-year plan are presented in order to give a notion of the policy-making intentions. The second part
concentrates on the economic aspect of psychiatric hospitals, presenting initially
some methodological problems of measuring costs and benefits of alternative
procedures. Some econometric cost functions are used in order to study the economics of scale of the psychiatric hospitals, as well as the main parameters which
influence cost. Finally, some proposals are made for a better organization and a
cost-effective utilization of the resources.

An Overview of the Greek Mental Health System

When describing the Greek mental health services system, it is important to ac-
knowledge the changing patterns of the whole health sector, and special reference
should be made to the recently established (Law no. 1397, 1983) National Health
Service System (NHS). The main aims of the Greek NHS are to provide comprehensive service free at the time of use, to reduce regional and social inequalities
(see Yfantopoulos 1985a), and to promote primary health care services. The current situation and the proposed reforms of the mental health sector will be considered under this general framework of the Greek NHS.

   In Greece, as in many other European countries (see Mangen 1985; McKechnie 1985), the main trend has been to the provision of psychiatric services at large,

overcrowded mental hospitals. Despite the policies proposed by WHO (1953, 1976), such as institutions with fewer than 1000 beds and community-oriented services, various delays or even diversifications have been observed among European countries in implementing these commonly accepted principles. Greece is a country with chronic delays in the implementation of social policies, uneven distribution of mental health resources between regions, ineffective planning, and low-quality services provided in old asylum buildings dating from the nineteenth century. These conditions established gradually the stigma of social isolation of the mentally ill and decreased the value of human beings.

Studying more closely the evolution of psychiatric services in Greece during the past decade (see Table 1), we can clearly see the impressive increase in the number of private psychiatric hospitals (by 10.9%) and private psychiatric beds (by 63.3%) and the corresponding zero growth or even negative growth (-3.1%) regarding the number of public hospitals and beds. If we take into account the amount of services provided and if we use the annual hospital discharges as a crude indicator, we can see (Table 1) that despite the zero or negative growth in the public sector the services there provided were five times more than in the private sector. If we permit for some other parameters of hospital performance, such as average length of stay and occupancy rate, we find that the total amount of public services has been much greater than that of privately administered services. It should be noted that this extra service provided by the public sector came at the expense of significant quality reductions creating an inhumane environment. The private sector (see Tables 2 and 3) has specialized in the provision of services in small hospitals with a capacity of 90 beds whereas of the nine public hospitals,

Table 1. The evolution of the greek psychiatric sector (National Statistical Service of Greece)

Hospitals	1970	1982	Changes in%
Public	9	9	0.0
Private	46	51	10.9
Voluntary	3	3	0.0
Total	58	63	8.6
Beds			
Public	7528	7292	− 3.1
Private	2838	4634	63.3
Voluntary	1063	1047	− 1.5
Total	11429	12973	13.5
Personnel			
Doctors	323	675	109.0
Nurses	1472	2422	64.5
Discharges			
Public	4709	8609	82.8
Private	13593	15822	16.4
Voluntary	686	539	−21.4
Total	18988	24970	31.5

Table 2. Public-private mix in the Greek psychiatric sector (National Statistical Service of Greece)

	Hospitals	Beds	Doctors	Nurses	
				Qualified	Non-qualified
Public	9	7250	293	280	1063
Voluntary	3	1054	39	17	131
Private	49	4589	304	153	815
Total	61	12893	636	450	2009

Table 3. Distribution of psychiatric resources by number of hospital beds, 1981 (National Statistical Service of Greece)

Capacity range (beds)	No. of hospitals	No. of beds	Psychiatric medical personnel	Psychiatric nurses	
				Qualified	Nonqualified
11–20	3	60	3	5	4
21–40	10	338	28	15	61
41–100	21	1381	126	37	252
101–300	18	3118	215	147	478
301–1000	7	3712	159	125	500
1001–3000	2	4286	105	121	714
Total	61	12895	636	450	2009

Table 4. Age-specific deaths reported in public psychiatric hospitals in Greece, 1980 (Ministry of Health and Welfare)

Age-Group (years)	Males	Females	Total	Percent of total
0–15	5	7	12	2.4
16–50	26	7	33	6.6
51–65	47	22	69	13.9
+65	167	216	383	77.1
Total	245	252	497	100.0

two have a capacity of more than 1000 beds (Dafni, Leros) and the rest of them range between 300 and 1000 beds. The ratio of doctors per bed is three times higher in the private sector, revealing the better quality of services; however, with regard to nursing the same superiority does not exist. This may be attributed to the vast increase in the number of doctors and the relatively much smaller increase in the number of nursing personnel (see Table 1). The private sector has been better able to attract the new type of psychiatrist and to offer their services in a smaller hospital, is better organized, and offers better employment conditions. The qualified nurses are concentrated in small private hospitals (100–300 beds), and the large asylums remain with relatively fewer medical and qualified nursing personnel (see Table 3). One of the greatest problems of the medical and nursing personnel working in public psychiatric hospitals (see Figs. 1 and 2) was the great number of mainly chronic psychotic cases. In the public hospitals, one doctor corresponded on the average to 141 patients (see Fig. 1) and one nurse to 13 patients (see Fig. 2); at the same time significant discrepancies exist between the different public hospitals, which reveals the lack of any health planning. Although there are no available indicators on the type of psychiatric needs and demands for public services, one can ascertain that a relatively large number of chronic psychotics live in the public hospitals until they die. From the data collected on age-specific deaths in various public psychiatric hospitals (see Table 4) it was found that 497 patients (about 5.7% of the total of treated patients) died in 1980 in public psychiatric hospitals, 77% of these being more than 65 years old.

The majority of deaths were reported in Dafni and Leros, where the two largest asylums in Greece are located. The situations in these two hospitals were described by the EEC committee as "unique, calling for special attention". More specifically, the EEC report states:

In Leros the problems extend well beyond the walls of the institution and affect the whole island. The EEC team's impression is that the use of Leros for years, perhaps even centuries, as a dumping ground for the unwanted – lepers, convicts, political exiles, and now handicapped children and the psychiatric patients – has led to a deterioration of the entire life style and culture of the island. (EEC 1984, p. 56)

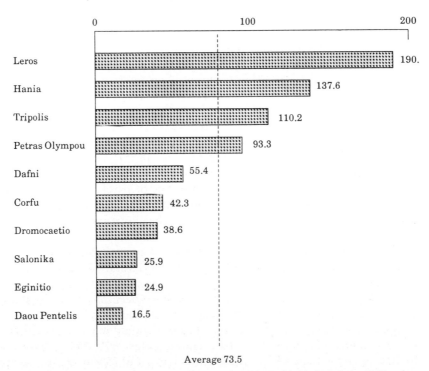

Average 73.5

Fig. 1. Number of mental patients per clinical doctor in public psychiatric hospitals, 1983

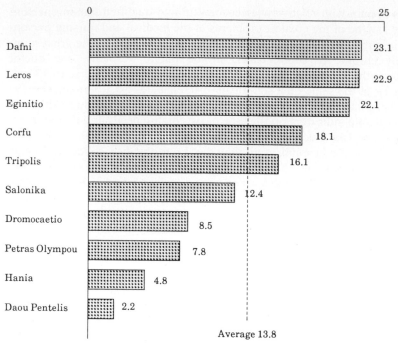

Average 13.8

Fig. 2.   Number of mental patients per nursing personnel in public psychiatric hospitals, 1983

Regional Distribution of Resources

In order to assess the regional distribution of resources we should have some indicators of regional needs (see Yfantopoulos 1979; Culyer 1976). Systematic efforts to analyze the regional prevalence and incidence of mental illness have been carried out during the past few years (Haughton 1979; Madianos 1983). A study (Madianos 1983) covering private and public mental institutions in Greece in 1978 reported that the number of new patients was 18557, i.e., 185 cases per 100000 population. Of these, 54.2% were diagnosed as suffering from "organic psychotic syndrome and schizophrenic or alternative type of psychosis". In a more detailed study which covered 33 of the 51 counties in Greece it was found that 24.1% of women and 11.1% of men presented some of the above syndromes at some time in their life.

With regard to the regional distribution of mental illness (see Table 5), the study points out that Athens, Crete, Epiros, and Central Greece are the areas with the highest prevalence of disease. By considering the regional distribution of resources (see Table 6), we can see that there have been other historical and social reasons which have influenced the regional distribution of neuropsychiatrist and hospital beds. The same trend with regard to regional inequalities exists in terms of the remaining health services (see Yfantopoulos 1979, 1985). Sixty percent of the neuropsychiatrists, 49% of the hospital beds, and 39% of the psychiatric institutions are concentrated in the Athens area. Central Greece, Epirus and Thrace,

Table 5. Regional mental health status: mentally handicapped and mentally ill persons in Greece (Haughton 1979)

Region	No. of psychiatric patients	
	High estimate	Low estimate
Athens	454391	220659
Central Greece	178998	87236
Peloponnesus	171401	83016
Ionian islands	32188	15833
Epirus	62154	29834
Thessaly	115686	55455
Macedonia	332225	159423
Thrace	57918	27192
Agean islands	52893	25797
Crete	79471	38492
Total	1537325	742937

Table 6. Regional distribution of psychiatric resources and personnel, 1981 (National Statistical Service of Greece)

Region	Hospitals	Beds	Neuropsychiatrists
Athens	24	6329	461
Central Greece	1	40	7
Peloponnesus	3	517	23
Ionian islands	1	416	6
Epirus	–	–	11
Thessaly	10	650	26
Macedonia	17	2615	190
Thrace	–	–	16
Aegean islands	1	1836	10
Crete	4	490	15
Total	61	12893	765

which have increased prevalence of disease, are badly served; in Epirus and Thrace there are no institutions whereas in Central Greece there is just one hospital of 40 beds, and the whole area is covered by just seven neuropsychiatrists. The institutionalization of the psychiatric services and the poor quality of public asylums, combined with the complete lack of any regional planning programmes results in overcrowding of Athens hospitals. Also the flourishing expansion of the psychiatric sector has led to a high concentration of services.

Legislation

Policy-making is related rather to political than to rigourous scientific plans. Politicians all over the world since the 1950s have declared the need for adopting nationwide public policies in order to improve the mental health services. In the U.S.A., John F.Kennedy stated in 1963 that "a national mental health program" would be supported by his government in order "to assist in the inauguration of a wholly new emphasis and approach to care for the mentally ill."

In European countries many reforms have taken place (Mangen 1985) in the socialpsychiatric sector, and various legislative acts were promoted for the reorganization of mental health services towards primary care and community-based systems.

In Greece the legislation has been formalized in a way that it compulsorily admits all patients into psychiatric hospitals. As it has been described by the EEC study group, the Greek legislation "is cumbersome and outdated" because it leads to easy access to asylums and blocks many attempts to get a patient out (EEC 1984).

Before making any criticism of the current system, it is worth considering briefly the main legislative acts retrospectively and indentifying the main factors which have influenced the formation of different policies. It is also worth viewing the extent of various attempts for reforms at different times. Many pieces of legislation became impressive historical texts without achieving the stated objectives (see Yfantopoulos 1985). At least three important laws that have determined the psychiatric policies should be mentioned.

Law MB Passed in 1862

On May 19, 1862, in the kingdom of Greece, newly established after the Turkish occupation, one of the most humane and revolutionary laws was enacted, referring to "the establishment of mental hospitals". Because of its importance we will consider it at length. It consists of 30 articles and is divided into four major parts.

The first part delineates the objectives of mental hospitals and states that "all of them are under the supreme administrative powers of the Greek government." The second part defines under what legal and social conditions a person might be admitted to a psychiatric hospital and sets forth the obligations of the local administration as well as of medical personnel with regard to provision of care. The third part covers the management of and responsibility for the property and assets of psychiatric patients during their hospitalization.

The fourth part deals with the organization, administration and financing of the mental hospitals. Since one of the objectives of this paper is the analysis of the financial aspect of the psychiatric sector, it is worth pursuing this topic further. Article 35 states that the hospital expenditures as well as the cost of treatment will be paid by the patient or his relatives. In case of a poor mentally handicapped person, the province is responsible for covering the expenses.

Article 37 refers to the financial aspects of the mental hospitals and states that hospital revenues will be covered by patient contributions as well as by other insurances and third-party sources. In the case that a mental hospital presents a deficit, this will be covered by the government out of the social budget funds.

It is rather remarkable to see at such early times, when the rest of Greece was going through a period of renovation, such comprehensive and humane legislation. Since 1862 Greece has gone through severe political, social and economic changes which have had a significant impact on the formation and the evolution of the Greek welfare state. Despite the increased pressures for satisfying the social needs of the mentally ill, this law was in effect until 1973.

Law 104, Passed in 1973

The significant aim of this legislation was to replace the anachronistic law M B and at the same time to introduce a rather ambitious new plan for the psychiatric sector in Greece. It was also an effort to keep up with the new reforms envisaged in the southern European countries and, more specifically, in the Italian psychiatric system.

Articles 6 and 7 of this law promote the establishment of psychiatric units in the general hospitals with a capacity of more than 200 beds. In addition, child psychiatric wards of more than 50 beds would be created in children's hospitals. Unfortunately, this never took place. Compulsory psychiatric care continued to be provided by the psychiatric hospitals as well as by the large asylums of Leros, Dafnis, Chania, Salonika, Corfu and Tripolis, enhancing even more the social stigma of madness. With regard to the continuity of psychiatric care, article 12 states that once a psychiatric patient is discharged the relatives should take care of him. If they refuse they will be sentenced to prison for up to 6 months. Again, this article has not been implemented, and instead of being discharged most psychiatric patients remain in the psychiatric hospitals as chronic cases.

Some efforts for improving the whole situation were attempted later in 1978 by legislative act L2B/52445, but the psychiatric sector remained fragmented, without any rehabilitation of primary-care programmes.

Law 1397, Passed in 1983

In September 1983 a law was passed introducing a new philosophy in the Greek health sector aiming at the establishment of a National Health System. The first article of this legislation states that services will be provided to people regardless of their financial, social and occupational position, by means of a single decentralized national health system, under which it shall be the responsibility of the state to provide health care for the whole population. Article 21 of this law refers to the psychiatric sector and states the organizational structure as well, as a way of providing mental health services. The notions of psychosocial care, primary care and rehabilitation are introduced unter the new philosophy.

Article 21 states that mental health care is to be provided by a triad of institutions: (a) The mental health care centers, (b) the psychiatric units in several hospitals, and (c) the special psychiatric hospitals.

The mental health care centers will offer primary and community care, health education, and preventive care and will contribute to the rehabilitation and social integration of the patients. The psychiatric units of general hospitals will provide short-term treatment and refer the chronic cases to the special psychiatric hospitals. The special psychiatric hospitals, according to the 1397 legislation, will be reorganized, aiming at the rehabilitation and "deinstitutionalization of the patients."

A psychiatric committee was established by the Central Health Council, undertaking the responsibility for planning, organization and development of this triad of mental health services. From this historical overview it can be seen that although Greece was quite innovative in terms of legislation in the middle of the nineteenth century, very little was accomplished after that. Law no. 1397 may bring a new era in the development of psychiatric services in Greece. In fact, a 5-year plan has been drawn up and a considerable part of this plan will be financed by the European Economic Community, which will provide financial support of up to 60 million ECU "for reforming the system of medical, social and vocational rehabilitation of persons in psychiatric institutions in Greece."

The Five-Year Plan

The prime objectives of the 5-year plan are to reduce regional and social inequalities, improve the organizational structure of the system, introduce primary and rehabilitation services, and decentralize the functioning and the decision-making process of the health care system. In order to achieve these objectives Greece will be divided into "mental health regions" which will also constitute a part of the so-called health regions. According to the geographical structure, the epidemiological, demographic, and other social aspects of the different counties, 33 community psychiatric sectors will be created, which will offer a broad spectrum of community and other psychiatric services to adults as well as to children and adolescents. The services provided by the primary and secondary health care institutions are shown in Fig.3. In some areas where, due to the geographical situation, the accessibility of mental health services becomes problematic, mobile psychiatric units will be established. It has been planned that these units will work in the areas of Evros, Phokida, Rhodes, the Cyclades, the Sporades, the Aegean Islands and Evia-Central Greece.

Since law no.1397 deals with the triad of mental health care centers, psychiatric units in general hospitals and special psychiatric hospitals, we will describe the 5-year plan in terms of these three dimensions.

Primary Care at Mental Health Care Centers

The Mental Health Care Centers (see Fig.3) offer a great spectrum of primary mental health services to the population. They represent the first contact of the patient with the psychiatric hospital, (secondary care). Within the organizational level of primary health care we should distinguish between three basic forms of institutions. The first is the community mental health center (CMHC), the second is the psychiatric hostel, and the third is the mobile unit. The services to be provided by all of these units are:

- Diagnosis
- Emergency care
- Day and night care
- Short-term therapy
- Psychotherapeutic services
- Hostel care
- Continuity of care-follow-up of chronic patients
- Health education
- Rehabilitation

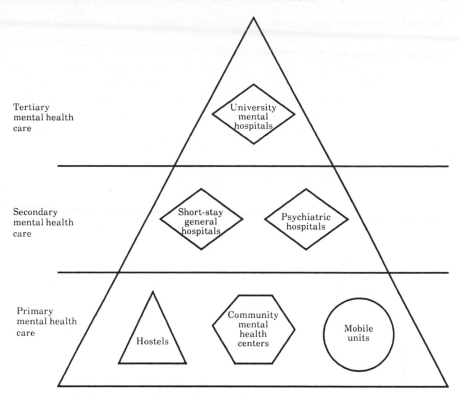

Fig. 3. Organizational structure of mental health services

Table 7. Number of primary care centers, primary mental health care plan (Ministry of Health and Welfare)

Area	1983	Medium-term 1984–1988	Long-term 1989–1993	Total
Athens	3	4	8	15
Salonika	1	1	2	4
Rest of Greece	–	15	15	30
Total	4	20	25	49

Currently, there are four CMHC, three of which are in the Athens area and one in Thessaloniki. These centers are planned to cover the psychiatric needs of a population ranging from 100 to 200000 people. The primary mental-care plan (see Table 7) is divided into a medium-term plan for 1984–1988 and a long-term plan for 1989–1993. In both of these plans emphasis is placed on the regionalization of the services. Hence, 15 of 20 CMHC will be constructed in urban and rural areas other than Athens and Salonika under the medium-term plan, and another 15 of 25 will be constructed in the same areas under the long-term plan.

Hospital (Secondary and Tertiary) Psychiatric Care

Hospital care (see Fig. 3) will be provided by two types of institutions: the psychiatric units in general hospitals and special psychiatric hospitals. Although psychiatric units in general hospitals were proposed by law no. 104 in 1973, nothing really was accomplished until recently. The medium-term plan stipulates the creation of 28 psychiatric units in various general hospitals, and each of these units is to have a capacity of 10–20 beds. In total, the creation of 598 beds is planned, regionally distributed in such a way as to reduce the existing inequalities.

The units will provide a wide range of secondary services, and their main goal is to reduce the average length of stay of chronic cases by means of intensive care. The unit will provide services on a 24-h basis and will admit patients referred by CMHC, the police, the local authorities, the family and the family doctor. Outpatient home services will be provided, which will also specialize in community psychiatry. It is expected that the establishment and the effective operation of these psychiatric units will gradually substitute the long-term ineffective services of the existing asylums. Also, the expected high quality of services provided by these units will establish a competitive environment with the private sector.

Special Psychiatric Hospitals

In 1982 there existed in Greece ten public psychiatric hospitals with a total capacity of 8486 beds. Three of these hospitals, in Dafni, Leros and Salonika, had a capacity of more than 1000 beds. As mentioned above, since 1953 WHO has promoted the idea of reducing the number of beds in psychiatric hospitals to an acceptable level of 600. Since one of the objectives of law no. 1397 is the deinstitutionalization of the existing asylums, it is forecasted that by the end of the medium-term plan the number of psychiatric beds will be reduced not only in absolute terms (by 19.4%; see Table 8) but also in relative terms, by a gradual reduction in the number of beds in all large hospitals. There will also be established in the northern part of Greece three new psychiatric hospitals, one in the eastern Macedonia-Thrace region (200 beds), one in the western Macedonia region (200 beds), and the last in Thessaly (200 beds). In terms of regional (and size) distribution of hospitals, a more even distribution should be achieved by the new legislation. The coefficient of variation[1] which shows the proportional inequality will be reduced from 95% in 1982 to 88% in 1988. Hence, under this plan, not an immediate but a gradual improvement is expected in the regional equality of the psychiatric services.

---

[1] The coefficient of variation (c. v.) is defined by the ratio of standard deviation (s. d.) over the arithmetic mean ($\bar{x}$):

$$c.v. = \frac{s.d.}{\bar{x}} \times 100$$

Table 8. Five-year plan regarding the number of public psychiatric beds in Greece

Psychiatric hospitals	Beds		Changes in %
	1982	1988	
Dafni	2750	1700	− 38.2
Dromocaetio	880	940	+ 6.8
Eginitio	100	100	0.0
Salonika	1000	750	− 25.0
Leros	1905	1600	− 16.0
Tripolis	420	360	− 14.3
Corfu	416	360	− 13.5
Petras Olympou	500	450	− 10.0
Hania	415	400	− 3.6
Daou Pentelis (children)	100	200	+200.0
Total	8486	6860	− 19.2
Three new ones planned (200 beds each)		600	
	8486	7460	− 12.1

Source: Ministry of Health and Welfare

Table 9. Budgetary forecasts for the 5-year plan of the Greek public psychiatric sector: public expenditures on capital outlays in millions of ECU, 1984 prices (Ministry of Health and Welfare)

	1984	1985	1986	1987	1988	Total
Primary care						
Centers for mental health and mental hostels	0.75	8.75	5.5	–	–	15.000
Secondary care						
Short-term treatment in general hospitals	1.125	2.875	4.3125	4.750	1.9375	15.000
New psychiatric hospitals	0.625	4.125	7.500	7.750	6.250	26.250
Existing psychiatric hospitals	8.750	15.625	20.000	20.000	18.125	82.500
Total	11.250	31.375	37.3125	32.500	26.3125	138.750

Social Budget Forecast of Psychiatric Expenditures on Capital Outlays

For the medium-term psychiatric plan (1984–1988) a 5-year budget was formalized by the Ministry of Health and Welfare, aiming at the improvement of the existing infrastructure of psychiatric services. As mentioned above, the medium-term psychiatric plan is developed in three basic dimensions covering (a) primary mental health care centers and hostels, (b) psychiatric units in general hospitals, and (c) special psychiatric hospitals. By considering the allocation of money (see Table 9) to the above sectors we can see that secondary care absorbs the largest share of capital outlays. The term is used for the amount of expenditures devoted (a) to the study of a project, (b) to the construction of buildings, and (c) to the purchase of equipment. The time trend of total expenditures shows that in 1985 a radical increase of 179% was achieved in comparison with the year 1984. In the subsequent year (1986) an increase in the budget of 18.9% was expected, and then in 1987 a gradual reduction in the rate of growth by 19%. In the first period of the medium-term plan a clear priority is given to the primary health sector; in the last 2–3 years priority is given to improvements in existing institutions as well as to the construction of three new psychiatric hospitals.

If the data represent the real allocation of funds, and if there is consistency in the stated objectives, then if not by the end of 1988 at least by 1990 some basic improvements in the quality of psychiatric services can be expected. However, it should be noted that reforms are achieved not only by the construction or reconstruction of a psychiatric hospital but also by the persistent education and training of personnel. Hence, in conjunction with the improvements in buildings, the concept of providing psychiatric services should also change. This is a difficult process because it cannot be achieved as an automatic alteration in the asylums: The deficient educational programmes and the serious lack of skills of the existing personnel must be reconsidered. The personnel working in the psychiatric fields should be educated and trained in the recent achievements of psychiatry, psychology and the social sciences. Then the 5-year plan will accomplish its objectives.

The Economics of the Public Psychiatric Hospitals in Greece

According to a study carried out by the Center for Planning and Economic Research (KEPE 1979), public health expenditures devoted to the psychiatric sector in 1978 accounted for about 10% of the total public health expenditures. Another study carried out in 1982 for the European Economic Community (EEC 1984) estimated that the above percentage had remained the same. The public expenditure on health care (including social security expenses), in a conservative estimation, reached roughly 10 billion drachmas in 1982. A considerable amount of the expenditures for mental health care are for private psychiatric services, but there are unfortunately no data available on this. Since the existing macroeconomic figures are of questionable validity, and given that the purpose of this article is not to make a macroanalysis of the Greek psychiatric sector but to reach some concrete social proposals, we will restrict ourselves to the economics of the public psychiatric hospitals. As mentioned above, there are ten psychiatric hospitals in Greece. The main questions regarding the economic performance of these hospitals can be summarized as follows:

1. Do the Greek psychiatric hospitals show a financial deficit?
2. Who finances these deficits and how?
3. Should we have large or small hospitals?
4. Is there any evidence for returns to scale?
5. What is the impact of the occupancy rate on hospital costs?

6. What is the impact of the length of stay in psychiatric hospitals?
7. If the turnover of patients increases, how will this affect the cost aspect of the hospitals?

The above list does not exhaust this topic. It only tries to tackle the above issue in a more technical way. However, before attempting to answer these questions we should mention that various attempts have been made in the literature (Fein 1959; WHO 1976, 1978; Wright and Hay-Cox 1985) to evaluate the cost-benefit side of psychiatric care. Various cost-benefit, cost-effectiveness, or programme-management techniques have been developed for assessing the cost of psychiatric care as well as the cost of alternative types of treatment.

Since there are no data on the cost of primary care and the cost of private psychiatric hospitals we will focus on the measurement of cost of public psychiatric hospitals. In the econometrics literature different types of cost functions have been used (Johnston 1960; Yfantopoulos 1986). Also, various statistical cost studies have used time series or cross-sectional data in order to estimate long-term average cost functions or the least-cost combination of recourses for a short period, usually 1 year. Four basic formulas of average cost functions were used:

1. Linear $\quad\quad\quad\quad C = a + bx + u$
2. Logarithmic $\quad\quad C = aX^b u$ or $\log C = \log a + b \log X + u$
3. Semi-logarithmic $\quad \log C = a + bx + u$
4. Quadratic $\quad\quad\quad C = a + b_1 x + b_2 x^2 + u$

where C = average cost, i.e., cost per patient, or cost per patient day

$\quad\quad\quad x$ = vector of inputs, i.e. beds, doctors, nurses, drugs
$\quad\quad\quad u$ = disturbance term
$\quad\quad\quad a, b$ estimated parameters

Each of the above formulas is based on different mathematical principles and gives different results. It is worth experimenting with different formulas in order to achieve the best possible fit.

However, even having selected the best mathematical model, we should not forget that there are still some interpretational problems with a number of restrictions, for instance:

1. There are often significant deficiencies or inaccuracies in the collected data.
2. Econometric cost studies are based on data available after a time period, whereas traditional economic theory is based on preceding relationships.
3. Econometric cost studies are based on the accounting data of a time period, whereas economic theory is based on various notions of opportunity costs.
4. Usually, we assume that there will be no changes in other factors such as technology prices and quality of care; however, these factors very rarely remain unchanged.

In the face of these problems, one may question whether the econometric exercise can give us realistic answers to the stated questions or if it is of any use at all. Despite the above restrictions, economic theory does provide some indications of the resource allocations; for instance, it is useful to estimate the cost elasticities of different parameters (see Fig. 4) and see which hospitals could be identified to the left of point A, which reveals the lowest average cost combination of resources. In point A the average cost (AC) is identical with the marginal cost (MC).

$$MC = AC$$

Furthermore, it is interesting to study the relationship between the marginal and average cost because different types of conclusions can be reached and, therefore, different types of proposals for financing the psychiatric hospitals could be formulated.

Methodology

The parameter which shows the interrelationship between marginal and average cost is cost elasticity (e_i). The cost elasticity shows the percentage impact on cost from a percentage increment of one input. The marginal cost shows the incremental increase in cost due to an incremental increase in one of the inputs. For instance, in the linear formula MC is constant and given by:

$$MC = \frac{\partial c}{\partial x} = b$$

Average cost shows the ratio of cost over one input e.g.:

$$AC = \frac{c}{x} = \frac{a + bx}{x} = \frac{a}{x} + b$$

And the cost elasticity is defined by the ratio:

$$e_i = MC/AC$$

By further analyzing this relationship we are able to identify three important policy proposal cases:

$$e_i = 1 \Rightarrow MC = AC \text{ point A}$$

Case A
The first case refers to point A (see Fig. 4) where marginal cost is equal to average cost and, hence, elasticity is equal to 1)

$$e = 1 \Rightarrow MC = AC \text{ point A}$$

If the objective of the government policy is to achieve a least-cost combination of resources for the psychiatric hospitals, then it is preferable to pursue point A.

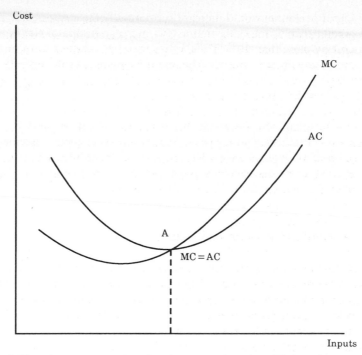

Fig. 4. Marginal-cost *(MC)* and average-cost *(AC)* functions. A, Point of equilibrium, lest-cost combination

Case B

In the public sector there are many inefficiences arising from less-than-optimal utilization of resources, lack of an effective organizational structure, and lack of managerial abilities of the administrative personnel. Hence, it is rather rare to achieve point A. Most of the hospitals will be either to the left of point A or to the right of it. Here we will examine the consequences for the hospitals which are identified to the left of point A. In this case, elasticity will be less than 1. This implies that a 10% increase of an input will affect the cost by less than 10%. Thus, it is beneficial to the economic unit to expand its economic activity by increasing the output or the services provided (e.g. psychiatric care). If this is the case then

$$e < 1 \Rightarrow MC < AC$$

It is beneficial for the Greek government to provide the hospitals which are identified to the left of point A with the appropriate incentives to be more efficient, to better utilizate their resources, and to increase their activity.

Case C

Case C refers to the hospitals which are identified to the right of point A. By over-utilizing their resources these hospitals bypass the optimal point A and reach an economic performance where further utilization of their resources and further hiring of personnel would increase substantially the cost of care. The cost elasticity is greater than 1, implying that a 10% increase in one of the inputs would increase cost by more than 10%. Thus, it becomes very expensive to hire further personnel or use any other resources. The marginal cost gradually exceeds the average cost:

$$e > 1 \Rightarrow MC > AC$$

For hospitals which are identified to the right of point A it would be beneficial from an economic policy point of view to reduce their capacities, because they will achieve more at less cost. Once we have analyzed the policy implications of different values of the elasticity parameter, it is worth pursuing an estimation of the above parameter for different types of inputs.

Economic Background and Data

Before attempting any econometric exercise we should provide some information on the financial situation of the Greek public psychiatric hospitals.

An analysis of the yearly sheets of these hospitals shows one common feature: there are significant deficits. In order to compare these deficits we have to bring all the hospitals to some comparable basis. We divide the annual expenditures and revenues for the year 1983 by the number of treated patients. The reader should be extremely careful with any of these exercises, because there are significant differences in the quality, intensity and type of care provided by these institutions. However, for the purpose of this exercise, which aims at a more general description of the economics of the psychiatric hospitals, some comparisons may be permitted. Table 10 presents the expenditures and revenues per patient for the public psychi-

Table 10. The economics of public psychiatric hospitals in Greece, 1983 in drachmas (Ministry of Health and Welfare)

Psychiatric hospital	Expenditures per patient	Revenues per patient	Deficits per patient
Dafni	136,445	41,023	− 95,422
Salonika[a]	181,866	56,674	− 125,192
Corfu	348,325	178,312	− 170,013
Hania	394,432	104,987	− 289,445
Leros	303,585	87,458	− 216,127
Daou Pentelis (children)	865,523	310,174	− 555,349
Petras Olympou	250,988	111,939	− 139,049
Tripolis	152,442	45,640	− 106,802
Dromocaetio	232,137	155,213	− 76,924
Eginitio	95,376	29,607	− 65,769

[a] 1982 data

atric hospitals. The highest deficits in absolute terms have been observed in the Daou Pentelis children's hospital, Hania, Leros, and Corfu where the insurance organizations or the alternative (excepting public) sources of financing have to cover a small part of the expenses. The government has to pay 555000 drachmas per patient at the Daou Pentelis children's hospital, 290000 drachmas per patient in Hania, 216000 drachmas per patient in Leros, and about 170000 drachmas per patient in Corfu. If we take a more general view of the hospitals we see that the revenues received from the alternative sources of finance, not including government funds, cover only 30% of the total expenditures. The rest has to be covered by direct subsidies provided by the Ministry of Health and Welfare. This simple arithmetic points out the need for a more rigorous analysis of how public money should be allocated and what criteria should be used.

Econometric Results

The reader should be aware of the limited amount of information available on the cost of psychiatric hospitals, which inevitably influences the results of economic analysis. The econometric models which will be used for testing the various hypotheses with regard to returns to scale, occupancy rate, and average length of stay are also bound to be limited. We will use simple models, taking every independent variable above, i.e. beds, occupancy rate, average length of stay, and turnover, and then estimating the impact of these variables on the dependent variable. We could use two dependent variables, one for the cost per patient and another for the cost per patient day. With all the econometric models it was found that the cost per patient day is much more sensitive to changes of the various inputs and

Table 11. Returns to scale in the Greek public psychiatric hospitals: forecasted cost per patient day for various sizes of psychiatric hospitals in drachmas

	Econometric model used			
No. of beds	Linear	Double logarithmic	Semi- logarithmic	Quadratic
50	2112	4094	1850	3031
200	2018	2265	1760	2550
300	1955	1905	1703	2255
500	1830	1532	1594	1730
750	1673	1288	1467	1192
1000	1516	1139	1350	787
1500	1202	958	1143	374
1750	1045	897	1052	366
2000	888	847	969	490
Correlation coefficient (r)	-0.49	-0.71	-0.50	0.73
Coefficient of determination (R^2)	0.24	0.52	0.25	0.53

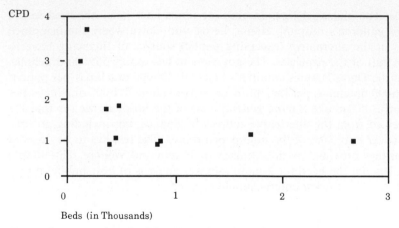

Fig. 5. Cost per patient day *(CPD)* in various sizes of mental hospitals

provides better statistical results, as can be judged by the R^2 coefficient of determination. For this reason, in the rest of the analysis we will use cost per patient day as a dependent variable.

Classic economic theory predicts U-shaped average cost curves, but various researchers such as Mann and Yett (1968) and Lave and Lave (1970) have provided justifications for L-shaped average cost curves. Given the lack of a consensus in the economic and econometric literature, we will provide estimates of various functional forms.

Size of Psychiatric Hospitals

Using linear, logarithmic, semi-logarithmic, and quadratic cost functions we attempted to investigate the hypothesis of returns to scale in the Greek public psychiatric sector. All the estimated econometric models provided statistically significant fits, but the best results, as can be judged by the value of the coefficient of determination R^2, were obtained with the double logarithmic and quadratic forms (see Table 11). However, all the functional forms showed that significant returns to scale exist, i.e. cost per patient decreases as the size of the hospital increases. A visual impresison of the economics of scale is given in the Fig. 5.

In an attempt to estimate the least-cost combination of resources we solved the quadratic form (see Fig. 6).

$$CPD = 3\,202,206 - 3474\,B + 0.001\,B^2$$
$$\quad\quad\quad (5.07)\quad\quad (2.43)\quad (2.05)$$

$R^2 = 0.525$
$r = 0.725$
$F = 3.87$
$DW = 1.85$

Where CPD is cost per patient day, B number of beds, and $(\cdot)$ t ratios.

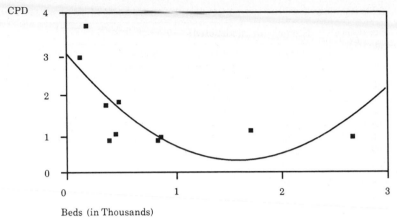

CPD

Beds (in Thousands)

Fig. 6. Quadratic cost functions for public psychiatric hospitals. Cost per patient day *(CPD)* according to hospital size

By taking the first derivative and solving the equation we obtained the least-cost combination of resources at a capacity of 1735 beds. But the whole analysis is influenced by the two large hospitals of Leros and Dafni; if we exclude them and run the same quadratic regression, then the least-cost combination of resources is estimated at 650 beds. This finding is consistent with the 5-year plan estimates (see Table 8), where the average size of the psychiatric hospitals has been forecasted to be about 620 beds. The estimated returns to scale for the Greek psychiatric hospitals may be supported on economic grounds, but that does not mean at all that we should adopt larger asylums in the future. There are other, social rather than economic, arguments like quality of care or humane environment which should also be taken into account. Economically efficient by no means implies that it is also feasible in terms of effective, good-quality psychiatric care. Despite this possible contradiction there will be second-best solutions, which will satisfy both psychiatric effectiveness and efficiency. It is much more important to adopt a managerial and an operational process in a smaller hospital than to establish large inhumane asylums.

Occupancy Rate
An exercise similiar to the above was carried out for the occupancy rate, and it was also found by the use of different models that the higher the occupancy rate, the lower the cost of psychiatric care (see Table 12). Again, the best statistical fit was achieved for the double logarithmic estimation ($R^2 = 0.52$). The general message which the alternative estimations provide is that significant gains could be achieved for the psychiatric hospitals of Hania, Daou Pentelis, and Petras Olympou where the occupancy is less than 90%, but high occupancy should not be achieved at the cost of quality care. Effective management and operation of the psychiatric clinics would improve the functioning of services, increase occupancy, and decrease the inefficient utilization of resources.

Table 12. Forecasted cost per patient day for various levels of occupancy in drachmas

Occupancy rate (%)	Econometric model used			
	Linear	Double logarithmic	Semi-logarithmic	Quadratic
60	4,991	13,395	9,086	8,628
70	3,918	5,876	5,040	5,490
80	2,845	2,878	2,795	3,159
85	2,309	2,081	2,082	2,296
90	1,772	1,533	1,550	1,634
95	1,236	1,148	1,155	1,174
100	699	873	860	916
Correlation coefficient (r)	−0.68	−0.72	−0.72	
Coefficient of determination (R^2)	0.46	0.52	0.52	

Average Length of Stay

The average stay in Greek psychiatric hospitals is very long, reaching 365 days in Corfu, 250 days in Petras Olympou, 240 days in Dromocaetio, 233 days in Daou Pentelis, and 230 days in Leros. The only exception to the rule, that the higher the average length of stay the higher the costs of care per day, is Eginitio. It is beneficial from an economic point of view to adopt operational policies aiming at the reduction of the average length of stay. This reduction would not only decrease the cost of psychiatric care but also increase the services provided per bed, i.e. the turnover. Different econometric estimates (see Yfantopoulos 1986) have pointed out the higher the patient turnover, the lower the cost of care. The proposed reforms of psychiatric care, such as provision of services by hostels and general hospitals, would reduce significantly the length of stay and consequently bring significant economic benefits to society.

Estimation of Elasticities

In the theoretical section, when we discussed the notion of cost elasticity, it was illustrated that empirical estimates on the value of this parameter are useful for policy implications. Given the limited amount of information and the econometric problems involved (see Johnston 1960), we attempted the estimation of elasticities for hospital size, occupancy rate, and average length of stay (see Table 13). If the data used reflect the real functioning of the Greek psychiatric sector, then it can be said that different values of elasticities provide different policy proposals.

If the elasticity (e_i) is greater than 1:

$$e > 1 \Longrightarrow MC > AC$$

this implies that significant economic benefits can be achieved by enlarging the production capacity of the psychiatric hospitals. The value of occupancy elasticity

Table 13. Estimation of cost elasticities

Independent variables	Dependent variable: cost per patient day	
	Linear estimation	Double-logarithmic estimation
Beds	−0.31	−0.42
Occupancy rate	−6.00	−5.35
Average length of stay	−0.45	−0.36

was found to be greater than 1 (see Table 13), and based on this finding we may propose that some hospitals such as those in Daou Pentelis, Hania, and Petras Olympou may gain significant economic benefits by increasing their occupancy rates.

If the elasticity (e_i) is less than 1:

$$e < 1 \Longrightarrow MC > AC$$

then the hospitals are overutilizing their inputs in an inefficient way. The elasticities of hospital beds and the average length of stay were found to be less than 1 (see Table 13). The policy which could be proposed based on this finding is to reduce both hospital size and the average length of stay. The development of short-stay hospitals and hostels proposed by the 5-year plan would reduce the hospital size and the average length of stay and finally achieve a more efficient and humane environment in the psychiatric sector.

Conclusions

A proper analysis of the psychiatric sector requires a historically sound retrospective which investigates the clinical, sociological, and economic climates at different times and articulates the relationship of early asylums with the medical, social, political, and fiscal forces. This paper was designed on these principles.

The first part provided an overview of the Greek mental health system by analyzing the recent evolution of public and private psychiatric services. The public sector tends to provide services in large psychiatric hospitals which show a historical continuity with the early asylums, whereas the private sector has specialized in the provision of services in smaller hospitals. There is a significant lack of outpatient, community, and rehabilitation services; this is satisfied by the public sector, which, however, shows great discrepancies in the quality of services. Significant regional inequalities also exist in the distribution of resources. Since the objective of this paper is the analysis of social and economic policies, a critical appraisal of legislative acts passed since 1862 was made and emphasis was placed on recent reforms as in the proposed 5-year plan for 1984–1988.

The second part attempted to illuminate, by the use of various economic and econometric techniques, the analogy between the stated objectives of the 5-year plan and their economic rationale. It was found that the Greek hospitals present great deficits, which may be attributed to the lack of clinical management as well as to the lack of trained personnel.

The econometric results revealed higher returns to scale in the public psychiatric hospitals. But it was argued that this should not be the only argument for large asylums, because there are other economic as well as medical and social reasons which should also be taken into account. By further analyzing the operational parameters of occupancy rate and average length of stay it was found that the proposed policy of deinstitutionalization and the co-ordination of smaller psychiatric hospitals with general clinics and community mental health centers may provide significant economic benefits. The econometric results favour the announced reforms. It remains a challenge to the makers of social and health policy to demonstrate the required consistency in implementing the proposed plan.

References

Basaglia G (1969) "L'instituzioni della violenza" in "l'instituzione negata". A cura di Franco Basaglia Turin, Einaudi, pp 141–151

Culyer AJ (1976) Need and the national health service. Martin Robertson, London

Digby A (1983) Changes in the asylum. The case of York, 1977–1815. Econ History Rev 2nd series 36 (2): 218–239

European Economic Community (1984) Reform of public mental health care in Greece, study V/1147/84 EN

Fein R (1959) Economics of mental illness. Basic, New York

Foucault M (1971) Madness and civilization. A history of insanity in the age of reason. New America Library, New York

Haughton A (1979) Mentally disabled handicapped persons in Greece. Report, Fulbright Research Study

Johnston J (1960) Statistical cost analysis. McGraw-Hill, New York

Kennedy JF (1963) Message on mental illness and mental retardation. Feb 5, 1963, Congressional Record vol 88, no 1, CIX, part 2, 1744–1749

KEPE (1979) The regionalization of health services. Center for Planning and Economic Research Athens

Lave JR, Lave LB (1970) Hospital cost functions. Am Economic Rev 60 (6): 379–395

Law No. ψ. M. B. 1862 The Establishment of Psychiatric Hospitals, Issue 28, Athens

Law No. 104 (1973) Psychiatric Care, Issue 177, Athens

Law No. G_2B (3036) (1973) Psychiatric Care, Issue 1523, Athens

Law No. L_2B (5245) (1978) Psychiatric Care, Issue 983, Athens

Law No. (1397) (1983) National Health System, Issue 143, Athens

Madianos M (1983) Mental illness and mental health care in Greece. Public Health Rev 11 (1): 73

Mann N, Yett D (1968) The analysis of hospital costs. A review article. J Business, April: 191–202

McKechnie AA (1985) The development of an integrated psychiatric service in a Scottish community. Acta Psychiatr Scand 72: 97–103

Mangen S (1985) Mental health care in the European Community. Croom Helm, London

Stefanis C, Madianos M (1981) Mental health care delivery system in Greece. A critical overview: aspects of preventive psychiatry. Biblotheca Psychiatrica. Karger, Basel

Talbot JA (1978) The death of the asylum: A critical study of state hospital management services and care. Grune and Stratton, New York

Yfantopoulos J (1979) The economics of health and health care planning. A theoretical and empirical analysis with reference to Greece. PhD thesis, University of York, England

Yfantopoulos J (1985a) Health planning in Greece. Some economic and social aspects. National Centre of Social Research, Athens

Yfantopoulos J (1985b) Trends in health legislation in Greece. In: Health legislation in Europe. Country profiles. World Health Organization, Regional Office for Europe, Copenhagen, pp 93–109

Yfantopoulos J (1986) The political economy of the Greek psychiatric sector. Review of social research. National Centre of Social Research, Athens

World Health Organization (1953) Third report of the expert committee on mental health. Technical Report Series, No. 3. Regional Office for Europe, Copenhagen

World Health Organization (1976) Cost-benefit analysis in mental health services. Report on a working group. The Hague, June 21–25, Regional Office for Europe, Copenhagen

World Health Organization (1978) The future of mental hospitals. Report on a working group. Mannheim, (1976). Regional Office for Europe, Copenhagen

Wright K, Hay-Cox A (1985) Costs of alternative forms of NHS care for mentally handicapped persons. Working paper, University of York

Financing of Care for the Chronically Mentally Ill in the USA: A Patchwork of Policies

R. G. Frank, J. R. Lave, and H. H. Goldman

Introduction

Chronic mental illness poses a continuing public-policy challenge in the United States. A substantial number of Americans suffer from chronic illness, and the costs of providing services to them is very high. However, many people with chronic mental illness are poor and unemployable and thus do not have private health insurance – the primary method of financing health care in the United States. Thus, the responsibility of meeting the needs of these individuals falls mainly on the various levels of government in the United States, but the governments have not met this responsibility in any systematic way. In this paper we review some of the issues related to the financing of mental health services for the chronically mentally ill. We begin with an overview of the estimated number of people with chronic mental illness, their characteristics, and the costs of their medical care. Next, we briefly describe some of the financing programs that cover the medical care costs of the chronically mentally ill. We go on to examine the role that different types of institutions play in providing services to these individuals, with particular emphasis on the role of the general hospital. Finally, we examine some of the likely consequences of the current cost-containment movement in the United States for people with chronic mental illness.

Overview of the Chronically Mentally Ill

There are no central registries that provide an accurate count of the chronically mentally ill (CMI). However, using data from a number of sources, Goldman et al. (1981) estimated that based on the broadest definition of mental illness, (a definition which relies on a diagnosis of organic brain syndrome, schizophrenia, major affective disorder, and other psychoses) roughly 3 million people, or approximately 1.3% of the U.S. population were chronically mentally ill in 1977. Using the narrowest definition, one based on the diagnosis and on the extent and duration of the illness, they estimated that approximately 1.7 million people were chronically mentally ill.

Some of the economic, demographic, and social characteristics of the chronically mentally ill differentiate them from the rest of the population. First, since the

CMI are often unable to hold jobs, they tend to be quite poor. Second, they are disproportionately non-white, poorly educated, and unmarried.

The direct medical care costs of chronic mental illness, using the broadest definition, were estimated to be U.S. $ 7.4 billion (or approximately 39% of total mental health care costs) in 1981 (Goldman and Frank 1985). There have been no systematic estimates of the indirect costs associated with chronic mental illness. Indirect costs are defined as the loss of earnings to people who cease work in order to care for these individuals, the general costs of pain and suffering, and the costs imposed on society as a result of factors such as disruptive behaviors. However, these costs, in particular the loss of earnings, are likely to be substantial because of the debilitating nature of chronic mental illness. Benham and Benham (1982) have shown that there are substantial differences in both labor-force participation and earnings between those with a history of chronic mental illness and otherwise similar individuals. In addition, Frank and Kamlet (1985) estimate that roughly 14.5% of "disabled workers" in the United States are disabled due to a mental disorder.

Methods of Financing Care for the Chronically Mentally Ill

Prior to the 1950s much of the care rendered to the CMI was provided in state mental hospitals. However, since the beginning of the deinstitutionalization movement in the late 1950s and early 1960s public policy makers have searched for methods of financing care for these people. The system of financing that has emerged is rather diverse. All levels of government, federal, state, and local, finance some aspect of the care for this population.

Financing policy can perhaps be loosely divided into supply- and demand-side policies. Supply-side policies may be defined as those policies which are concerned with the direct provision of services. These are policies which directly fund the construction and operating costs of providers of services, which then have a mandate to provide care to the chronically mentally ill. Demand-side policies may be defined as policies which are targeted toward increasing the general access of the target population to the health care system. In this case, the providers of services are paid for rendering specific services to the target population.

The demand-side policies may contain important incentives for providers of care. For example, a per-case prospective hospital payment system creates strong incentives for hospitals to lower admission costs. Nevertheless, it is a demand-side policy, because the payment to a given provider is linked to a patient's decision to seek care from that provider. Thus, our characterization of policies reflects the extent to which payments are linked to individual patient actions. An overview is presented in Table 1.

Below we discuss the specific types of policies that have been developed to finance these services. It should be stressed that much care rendered to people is not provided through specialized programs or financed by the funding programs. Many of the CMI just appear at public general hospitals, or in emergency rooms or the outpatient departments of general hospitals. They receive various types of services in those settings, and much of their care is rendered in this fashion.

Table 1. Classification of mental health financing policies

Supply-side policies	Demand-side policies
State mental hospitals	Medicare
Community mental health centers	Medicaid
Other publicly owned providers	Mandated private insurance for mental
(a) General hospitals	health care
(b) Outpatient mental health clinics	
(c) Halfway houses	
Veterans Administration	
(a) Psychiatric services	
(b) General hospitals	

Supply-Side Policies

Financing policy in the mental health sector has historically emphasized the supply side (Dorris and McGuire 1981). This means that resources have been devoted primarily to the development of public providers of mental health care. The most important public providers are described briefly below.

State and County Mental Hospitals

In 1982 there were 277 state and county mental hospitals. These hospitals contained 140 140 beds. They are supported primarily from the budgets of the state governments. In 1980 expenditures for care given in these hospitals amounted to roughly $ 3.5 billion (Frank and Kamlet 1985), which is approximately 18%–20% of all expenditures on mental health care. According to the diagnostic definitions of chronic mental illness (schizophrenia, organic brain disease, major affective disorder), roughly 50% of the admissions to state and county mental hospitals are chronic mental patients (Manderscheid et al. 1985), while 70% of the inpatient days are for treatment of the CMI. At any one time there are about 88 000 CMI patients in state and county mental hospitals.

Community Mental Health Centers (CMHC)

The Community Mental Health Centers program was established in 1963 through federal legislation proposed by President Kennedy. This program provided assistance to communities for the development of treatment settings that were alternatives to the state and county mental hospitals for the prevention and treatment of mental disorders. Underlying establishment of CMHC was the notion of providing comprehensive mental health care in the community that would guarantee access and continuity of care. Federal participation was intitially visualized as providing "seed money" that would continuously decrease over an 8-year period (Taube 1983). The program grew from 197 centers in 1969 to 691 in 1980. Historically, about 12% of admissions to CMHC have had diagnoses that indicate chronic mental illness (NIMH 1981). In 1981 all federal dollars for CMHC were moved to state-administered block grants. These grants give states control over lump sums of federal money to fund mental health services, including CMHC. Recent analyses of block grants for mental health indicate that CMHC continue to receive substantial support (but less) under the new financial arrangements (GAO 1985; Logan et al. 1985). One notable change that has been reported in CMHC is that states have encouraged a shift in emphasis toward the care of the CMI under block grants.

Other State Programs

State governments also provide direct mental health care via ownership of: (a) general hospitals, (b) public outpatient mental health clinics, and (c) halfway houses. Halfway houses are sheltered living arrangements for the seriously mentally ill. The role of the public general hospital in treating the CMI is large and has continued to grow in the 1970s and 1980s. For example, the number of psychiatric beds in general hospitals increased by 39% between 1970 and 1982. Also, the portion of all discharges from general hospitals of patients who had a psychiatric diagnosis increased from 7.4% in 1975 to 8.3% in 1980. The portion of general hospital psychiatric discharges that are chronically mentally ill (by diagnostic group) is about 30%. This includes both public and private general hospitals. That implies that about 352000 discharges from general hospitals involve a CMI individual (Allen et al. 1983). This clarifies the scope of the role of the public general hospitals. Halfway houses and freestanding outpatient clinics play a considerably smaller role in treating the CMI.

The Veterans Administration (VA)

The Veterans Administration bears a large portion of the burden of caring for the CMI in the United States. Goldman and Frank (1985) estimate that the 1980 direct costs of treating the CMI population in the VA was U.S. $ 735 million. Eighty-two percent of the cost, or $ 606 million, was incurred in VA psychiatric services. The VA costs amounted to nearly 10% of the total direct costs of treating the CMI.

It should be noted that nursing homes treat a large variety of patients who might be classified as mentally ill. The issue of nursing homes is discussed in the context of Medicaid, below.

Demand-Side Policies

Since the 1970s, increased emphasis has been placed on demand-side policies. As noted above, the federal government has phased out its involvement with the CMHC via block grants. States have attempted to shift the responsibility for financing mental health from their budgets to private insurers and to the Medicaid program, which receives federal matching funds (McGuire and Montgomery 1982; Frank 1985). This shifting has focused attention on demand-side policies. We will now describe some of the demand-side policies, beginning with a discussion of two major health-financing programs which help cover the cost of treating the CMI. We discuss these programs in detail because they are the basic public medical care financing programs in the United States.

Medicare

The Medicare program was enacted in 1965 as Title XVIII of the Social Security Act. Initially, the program covered only people who were over 65 years of age and who were eligible for Social Security. In 1972, the program was amended to extend coverage to people under 65 who had been receiving disability payments for at least 2 years. (Social Security disability payments are given to workers who were employed long enough to be eligible for social security.) Approximately 14.5% of the people who have left the labor force because of disability are disabled as a result of a mental illness.

Medicare has two separate but complementary parts: Hospital insurance, known as Part A, and supplementary Medical Insurance known as Part B. Part A covers 90 days of hospital care per "spell of illness". There is no limit on the number of "spells of illness" an individual may incur. Moreover, there is a one-time 60-day lifetime reserve if the 90 days per spell limit are exceeded. Part A also pays for up to 100 days of care in a participating skilled nursing facility (SNF) following a hospital stay, as well as for an unlimited number of home health visits.

There are, however, some clear limitations on the use of psychiatric services under Part A. There is a lifetime limit of 190 days of care in participating psychiatric hospitals. Thus, there is a clear incentive to treat psychiatric patients in general hospitals and not in specialty psychiatric hospitals. This is particularly true for the CMI patients who may be heavy users of inpatient services over the course of their Medicare lifetime (which often begins prior to age 65). The nursing home benefits are also limited. Nursing homes which care primarily for persons with mental disorders are unlikely to qualify for Medicare reimbursement. In addition, the qualifying conditions for coverage for both home health and SNF care are very strict, and very few people with chronic mental conditions would satisfy them.

Part B is offered to all individuals eligible for Part A benefits. Part B is a voluntary program which entails the payment of a monthly "insurance premium". (These premiums cover only about 25% of the cost of the program; the remaining costs are met through claims on federal general revenues.) State Medicaid agencies may choose to "buy in" to Medicare Part B on behalf of the Medicare-eligible individual who also qualifies for Medicaid. Part B pays for 80% of the charges allowed for physician services and supplies after a deductible (British: an "excess") has been met. Outpatient psychiatric benefits under Part B are limited to $ 500 per year, of which the Medicare beneficiary must pay 50%. (Given an average fee of $ 50 for an hour of psychotherapy, this amounts to about ten visits per year.) Finally, only psychiatrists are eligible for Part B reimbursement. The services of other providers, such as psychologists and social workers, are not covered under the program.

Thus, Medicare will pay for a limited amount of the mental health services that are used by Medicare beneficiaries. It will, however, cover the cost of other acute care services used by these individuals. Currently, approximately 2% of total Medicare expenditures are for psychiatric services.

Medicaid
The Medicaid program was enacted in 1965 as Title XIX of the Social Security Program. Medicaid is a federally supported and state-administered program that pays for medical care services provided to eligible low-income individuals and families. One eligibility group is the permanently and totally disabled; thus, some of the CMI may be sufficiently disabled by their illness to qualify for Medicaid.

Subject to broad federal guidelines, the states can establish their own rules governing individual eligibility, provider reimbursement mode, and the amount, duration, and scope of covered services. State flexibility has increased considerably since 1980.

Medicaid is a very complicated program. For the purposes of this paper it is sufficient to say that Medicaid is a vendor-payment program. That is, the program pays qualifying providers fees for providing covered services to program eligibles. All states are required to cover hospital, physician, and skilled nursing care facilities. At their discretion they may cover (and most states do cover), intermediate care facilities – the type of nursing home that would provide services to the *CMI* population. Depending on the per capita income of a state, the federal government pays from 50%–79% of the cost of the program.

Medicaid financing of nursing home care for the CMI is a growing portion of expenditures for chronic mental illness. However, the role of the nursing home as a care provider for the CMI is seriously constrained. Medicaid will not pay for nursing home care if a facility has been defined as an institution for mental disease by the Health Care Financing Administration (HCFA) of the U.S. Government. The HCFA uses three criteria for determining whether a facility is an institution for mental disease. They are: (a) the facility is licensed as a mental institution; (b) 50% of the patients have a primary diagnosis of a mental disorder; (c) the facility provides specialized psychiatric services (Dickey and Goldman 1986). Criteria *b* has become the most important constraint because of the strong incentive it creates to either (a) not recognize and treat mental illness in nursing homes or (b) not admit mentally ill patients.

The states have taken advantage of the flexibility allowed under Medicaid to implement quite different types of reimbursement schemes and to impose different types of limitations on the use of services – both of which have implications for the chronically mentally ill. In 1985, for example, the majority of the states paid for hospital care on the basis of prospectively set per diem rates; six states have instituted per case reimbursement systems (which are likely to have particularly strong effects on the CMI, as discussed below), and 17 states continue to pay incurred costs. In addition, 15 states have imposed limits on reimbursable days under Medicaid. The limits range from 10 days per year to 40 days per illness spell. Clearly, the strict limits on annual days are likely to have more intense impacts on the CMI. The average length of stay in a general hospital for a schizophrenic patient was 14 days in 1981. Thus, in a number of states, a single average stay exhausts the annual inpatient benefit of a CMI patient.

A number of states have imposed specific limitations on psychiatric care with regard to both hospital outpatient and physician services. In general, the Medicaid program appears to encourage psychiatric outpatient care delivered in organized care settings (outpatient departments and clinics). A number of state programs have imposed restrictions on the use of office-based care, through setting a limit on the number of reimbursable visits, requiring a co-payment of the Medicaid recipient, or setting the fee level so low that physicians will not see Medicaid patients.

They are no very good estimates on the number of CMI who are covered by Medicaid. Birch and Davis (1980) estimated that Medicaid expenditures on the CMI in 1978 amounted to U.S. $ 2.04 billion.

Other Demand-Side Policies

In the United States, health insurance is an important and prevalent fringe benefit. That is, insurance coverage is often offered by employers in the United States as a non-taxed in-kind benefit. Although some insurance programs provide extensive mental health benefits, many do not. Consequently, much of the employed population may end up using public resources if extensive psychiatric care is required. A number of states have mandated that insurance policies cover some mental health benefits. This move is a result of activism by the mental health community as well as a desire on the part of states to shift some of the costs of paying for mental health services to employers. Frisman et al. (1985) show that when states pass legislation mandating minimum levels of private insurance coverage it serves to shift costs from the state budget to private insurors. This results in higher private insurance premiums often paid by employers.

As the above discussion indicates, there is no single approach to providing health care and other services to the CMI. The responsibility is divided among different agencies. There are programs that are specifically developed to provide services to this population whereas other programs, such as Medicare and Medicaid, facilitate the access of some of the CMI to the more general health care system where they may receive both mental health services and general medical services. This eclecticism is indicated by the source of funds for the care of the CMI. For example, as noted above, it is estimated that approximately U.S. $ 7.4 billion were spent on mental health services for the CMI. Of this, $ 2.3 billion were provided through the public mental hospitals, $ 2.08 billion by Medicaid, and $ 0.74 billion by the VA.

The Decline of the State Mental Hospital

Perhaps the most dramatic change that has taken place in the mental health delivery system has been the decline of the state mental hospital as the focal point of care for the CMI. This decline was facilitated by a number of factors, including (a) the development of psychotropic drugs, (b) the patient's rights movement, and (c) the deinstitutionalization movement. This decline was further stimulated by the enactment of the Medicare and Medicaid programs, which were a source of financing for care provided by general hospitals and private psychiatric hospitals and, in the case of Medicaid, in intermediate care facilities (nursing homes). In this section we document this shift by focusing on the changing locus of inpatient care.

The decrease in the importance of the state mental hospital was accompanied by an increase in the importance of the private psychiatric hospital and the general hospital. This shift in relative importance is dramatically revealed by the numbers. Between 1970 and 1982 there was a 38% increase in the number of beds in specialty psychiatric units in general hospitals, while at the same time there was a 52% decrease in the number of beds in public psychiatric hospitals. In addition to the increase in the number of beds in psychiatric units in general hospitals, there was an increase in the number of psychiatric cases seen in medical-surgical beds in those hospitals. This change in the distribution of beds is reflected in the shifting of the locus of treatment for inpatient psychiatric episodes. In 1969, 44.9% of all such inpatient episodes were seen in state and county mental hospitals while 42.2% were seen in private psychiatric and general hospitals; by 1981, only 29% of all inpatient episodes were seen in the former group of hospitals while 51.3% were seen in the latter group. (The remaining episodes were seen in the VA facilities as well as in an assortment of other facilities.)

One must be careful not to overstate the real role played by different institutions in caring for the CMI. For example, many of the people who have been seriously ill for a long time are likely to have no insurance coverage or to be covered by Medicaid as opposed to having private health insurance. Only 3.6% of the patients in the general hospitals and 0.96% of the patients in the private psychiatric hospitals were "no pay", as opposed to 45% of those in the state and county hospitals. In contrast, 23% of the patients seen in the private hospitals and 8% of those seen in the state mental hospitals were covered by Medicaid.

In order to more clearly understand the role of the general hospital in treating the CMI it is helpful to differentiate the publicly and privately owned general hospital. The privately owned general hospital exemplifies services provided in response to demand-side financing policies. In contrast, the public hospital represents a mix of supply- and demand-side financing effects. That is, direct subsidy of public hospitals from government budgets makes these facilities more willing to accept medically indigent patients. For example, 7% of psychiatric admissions to public general hospitals have no insurance while only 1.9% of psychiatric admissions to private general hospitals have no insurance coverage.

In the United States there is a continuing debate about the role of the specialty mental hospital (private and public) as well as the role of the public general hospital in caring for the CMI. Is the state mental hospital expected to decline further? Should the role of the public general hospital continue to increase? What should be the role of the private specialty hospital? These are questions whose answers may be resolved by the financing systems adopted for paying for inpatient psychiatric care. This is a clear departure from the past, when explicit goals were set for treatment of the mentally ill and financing policy was molded in an attempt to further treatment objectives. Thus, today the CMI are more likely to be treated in public facilities if there is no financing program for which they qualify.

The Role of Cost Containment

In response to the rapidly rising costs of health care in the United States during the 1970s the various levels of government and the business community are aggressively seeking ways to decrease the cost to them of providing health care services. New changes, unlike past policy initiatives, are not motivated primarily by a desire to improve the quality and access to mental health services. The CMI may be particularly vulnerable to the adverse consequences of cost-containment policies.

As noted above, the CMI are likely to be older (cases of dementia), not married, non-white, and poor. Because they tend to be poor, they rely to a lage extent on public hospitals and clinics and hospital emergency rooms for treatment. This means that the chronic mental patient does not enter the health care system through an office-based physician's practice. The office-based physician often serves as a patient advocate in dealing with organized care providers such as hospitals or specialty clinics. The reliance on providers other than office-based physicians (see Shapiro et al. 1985) for access to care often means that these *patients do not have advocates.*

Thus, it may be particularly dangerous for the CMI to rely on financing programs where incentives create an adversary relationship between providers and patients. These programs may work well for middle-class patients, who rely in part on their physician to inform them and advocate on their behalf. But careful thought should be given to the degree to which these mechanisms are sensible for the CMI.

There are a number of ways in which the current cost-containment efforts are likely to effect the CMI. These are discussed briefly below.

First, under pressure not to raise taxes and still to balance budgets, the funding of publicly owned specialty mental health organizations which provide services to the CMI population are threatened. Thus, supply-side programs are being put under pressure to shrink.

Second, as we noted above, a number of people with chronic mental illness receive their care through the emergency rooms and outpatient departments of public general hospitals. Many of these patients have no source of insurance, and the organizations have covered the cost of providing services to them by charging relatively high prices to the insured populations and subsidizing the care of those who cannot pay. As the health care system becomes more competitive, and as the private programs become more restricted, it becomes increasingly difficult for this cross-subsidization to continue. In response to new constraints these organizations may cut back on care to the CMI. This need to finance care for the medically indigent is one of the major public policy issues facing the United States today.

Existing demand-side financing programs have begun to change the way in which they pay providers for rendering services to covered populations. In October 1983, Medicare began implementation of a per case prospective payment system. A number of state Medicaid programs have either adopted a per case prospective payment approach or restricted the number of inpatient days of care they will reimburse. Under the per case system a hospital receives a fixed sum for treating a given patient. In economic terms, this means that as hospitals provide additional services to patients they incur incremental costs but receive no additional revenues. This situation not only provides incentives for hospitals to produce care efficiently but also creates incentives for hospitals to undertreat *all* patients. There are two dimensions to undertreatment: an inappropriate underutilization of nursing and ancillary services and an inappropriate number of days, leading to a patient's premature discharge. The incentive to reduce the length of stay will be strongest for the most costly patients – those patients on whom the hospital expects to lose money. The CMI may be overrepresented among that group. Moreover, as mentioned above, they are less likely to have advocates that could counter-balance the payment system incentives to the hospital. An important question is: Will hospitals respond inappropriately to the incentives built into the system, and will this response be particularly pronounced for the CMI? In order to address this question, we need to determine whether hospitals respond to the incentives and, if they do, whether those responses are inappropriate.

In a recent study, Frank and Lave (1985) found that providers of inpatient psychiatric care respond strongly to financial incentives. They studied the effect on the length of stay of Medicaid psychiatric patients to the imposition of limits on the number of days a state would pay for under per diem reimbursement systems. They found that the estimated effect of a limit of 25 days per admission was to reduce the average length of stay by about 28% relative to Medicaid cases in states that had no limits on the number of days covered. This result is particularly important, because the financial incentives to decrease lengths of stay under per diem reimbursement systems with covered day limits are significantly weaker than under a per case reimbursement system. Moreover, it was found that the response to the reimbursement limits was significantly more pronounced for two categories of schizophrenics (Frank and Lave 1986).

Payment mechanisms have been changed in order to evoke such changes. The question is: Is the nature of the supply response appropriate? What kind of quality/financial gain trade-offs have been made? The evidence on this issue suggests that there is reason for concern. For example, Rupp et al. (1984) found that the savings realized from a single hospital episode for Medicare psychiatric patients due to per case reimbursement in Maryland was accompanied by an offsetting increase in costs associated with readmission – a finding that implies that early discharges arising from per case payment may have been inappropriate. Frank and Lave (1985) found that limits on reimbursable days not only decreased the length of stay but also were associated with an increase in the probability of patient transfer to a state mental hospital (from .08 to .14). This type of behavior is undesirable, since the state hospital is viewed as a provider of last resort. The evidence suggests that provider response to new payment systems may be socially undesirable. Some more limited evidence implies that schizophrenics may be particularly vulnerable to such undesirable responses.

Alternative Approaches to Payment Reform

Concerns that traditional forms of health insurance (including Medicare and Medicaid) may overemphasize inpatient treatment of the CMI (Kiesler 1982) have led to a number of innovative financing proposals. The two financing alternatives receiving the most attention in the United States are capitation programs. Capitation financing involves payment of a lump sum of money to an organization responsible for meeting a broad range of service needs for a defined population. The lump sum payment places the responsible organization at financial risk and creates strong incentives to provide the needed services at least cost. There is also an incentive not to provide enough services. The capitation approach has become popular in the U.S. via the Health Maintenance Organization (HMO) model of care delivery. However, in the case of HMOs the populations served are primarily "healthy" and incentives to underserve members are mitigated because individuals are free to leave the program and find another health plan (such as traditional health insurance) if they are not satisfied. The situation is markedly different for application of such notions to the CMI population. If, for instance, a CMHC were to be the responsible organization, the CMI population would (a) have no alternate choice of provider, (b) have no advocate, and (c) be served by a provider with strong incentives to undertreat. A supply-side capitation experiment is currently underway in Rochester, New York.

An alternate to a supply-side capitation program is one which links dollars to patients and allows them a choice. The cornerstone of such approaches is a voucher system coupled with a so-called case manager. A voucher program provides each CMI patient with targeted purchasing power (Wallack 1981). Under a voucher system funding is tied to choices of the individual, thus decreasing the incentive to underserve patients if appropriate choice is exercised. The role of the case manager is to assist the CMI individual in making sensible choices. The case manager, in theory, is paid by a mechanism that is separate from the funding of patient care. This ensures that the patient's advocate neither gains nor loses financially as a result of treatment decisions made on the patient's behalf. The voucher-case manager approach allows for clinical judgement in the combination of services used, limits financial liability of the payor, and provides patients with enhanced decision-making power.

Voucher programs are thereby a demand-side policy that allows for considerable flexibility to meet the complex needs of the CMI. Typically, vouchers service as "cash" equivalents for the purchase of designated services. Thus, there is less flexibility than under a cash-transfer program. In the case of the chronic mental patients several types of vouchers might be issued, one set to be used for the purchase of housing, a second set for obtaining health, mental health, and social services, and finally vouchers for the purchase of food. Prior screening of providers and the use of case managers to guarantee minimum quality levels and assist in consumer choice serve to create the potential for a service system that may be more responsive to the CMI population than many traditional supply-side solutions are.

As yet, little experience exists upon which to judge the potential and practical difficulties associated with such approaches. In early 1987 a series of experimental programs for providing services to the urban CMI were begun in a number of cities in the U.S. These programs include a mix of voucher systems, capitation programs, traditional supply-side policies, and enhanced insurance coverage for the broad array of services needed by the CMI population. This experience will allow for the first systematic view of the problems and prospects of each type of approach.

Conclusions

Financing programs for the chronically mentally ill have evolved from predominantly paternalistic supply-side programs, where patient treatment is chosen by the provider, to demand-side programs, which rely almost entirely on the patient to "fend for him- or herself". The evidence of the "new incentives" contained in demand-side programs suggests that chronic patients may be particularly vulnerable to adverse provider responses. For this reason, mixed supply-demand approaches to financing may be the most desirable. Theoretically, the voucher-case manager approach has many desirable features for funding care for the CMI. However, a lack of experience with this approach makes it premature to tout it as a solution.

Acknowledgements. We are grateful to Herbert Zöllner for helpful comments on an earlier draft.

References

Allen G, Burns BJ, Cook W (1983) The provision of mental health services in the health sector. In: Taube C, Barret S (eds) Mental health U.S. 1983. USGPO, Washington, D.C., pp 41–49

Benham L, Benham A (1982) Employment, earnings and psychiatric diagnosis. In: Fuchs V (ed) Economic aspects of health. University of Chicago Press, Chicago

Dickey B, Goldman HH (1986) Public care for the chronically mentally ill: financing operation costs. NIMH working paper

Dorris W, McGuire TG (1981) Federal involvement in mental health services: an evaluation of the community mental health center program. In: Altmann S, Sapolsky H (eds) Federal health programs. Heath, Lexington, pp 83–102

Frank RG (1985) A model of state expenditures on mental health services. Public Finance Q 13 (3): 319–338

Frank RG, Kamlet MS (1985) Direct costs and expenditures for mental health care in the U.S. 1980. Hosp Community Psychiatry 36 (2): 165–168

Frank RG, Lave JR (1985) The impact of benefit design on length of stay and transfers to residential settings for Medicaid psychiatric patients. Hosp Community Psychiatry 36 (7): 749–753

Frank RG, Lave JR (1986) The effect of benefit design on the length of stay of Medicaid psychiatric patients. J Human Resources 21 (3): 321–337

Frisman L, McGuire TG, Rosenbach M (1985) Cost of mandates for outpatient mental health care in private health insurance. Arch Gen Psychiatry 10: 1074–1081

Goldman HH, Gattozzi D, Taube A (1981) Defining and counting the chronically mentally ill. Hosp Community Psychiatry 32 (1): 21–26

Goldman HH, Frank RG (1985) Evaluating the costs of chronic mental illness. Conference on the economics of disability, Washington, D.C.

Government Accounting Office (1985) Block grants brought funding changes to program priorities. Report to Congress, GAU-HRD 85-3

Kiesler CA (1982) Public and professional myths about mental hospitalization. Am Psychol 37 (12): 2216–2237

Logan BM, Rochefort DA, Cook EW (1985) Block grant for mental health elements of the state response. J Public Health Policy 6 (4): 476–492

McGuire TG, Montgomery JT (1982) Mandated mental health benefits in private health insurance policies. J Health Polit Policy Law 7 (2): 380–406

Manderscheid R, Witkin M (1983) Specialty mental health services: system and patient characteristics: U.S. In: Taube C, Barrett S (eds) Mental health U.S. 1983. USGPO, Washington, D.C.

NIMH (1981) Characteristics of admission to selected mental health facilities. USGPO, Washington D.C.

Rupp A, Steinwachs D, Salkever D (1984) The effect of hospital payment method on the pattern and cost of mental health care. Hosp Community Psychiatry 35 (3): 552–555

Shapiro S, Skinner EA, Kramer M, Steinwachs DM, Regier DA (1985) Need and demand for mental health services in an urban community. An explanation based on household interviews. Johns Hopkins University, Baltimore

Taube CT (1983) Professional versus public health goals: psychiatry and community mental health centers. Unpublished dissertation, American University, Washington D.C.

Wallack S (1981) Financing option for the chronically mentally ill. In: McGuire T, Weisbrod B (eds) Proc. of conference on the economics of mental health. USGPO, Washington, D.C.

Managing Chronic Psychotic Patients:
A Clinical and a Political Point of View

M. Kastrup and M. Bille

A massive growth in mental health services has taken place over the past 20 years as psychiatry has widened its boundaries (Richman and Barry 1985). But what has happened to the needs of the long-term psychotic patients in this era of deinstitutionalization? Have they been neglected despite the advances?

In a criterial review, Kirshner (1982) discusses the hospital stay of psychiatric patients from the point of view that the shortest stay possible in hospital is the best for the patient and the most cost-effective. One aim of cost-effectiveness analysis is to characterize that optimal treatment and disease prevention as well as the optimal allocation of resources. In the case of chronic psychotic patients, however, the question is complex.

The number of chronically mentally ill is increasing; it has become a serious problem in most Western countries and will become an equally serious problem in the less developed countries (Kramer 1980). Indeed, the problems have considerable implications for the allocation of resources. To solve the problems improved communication between psychiatrists and politicians is needed.

But what is the size of the problem? And what are the future perspectives for the mentally ill, particularly the chronic psychotic patients needing extensive care and treatment?

One way to throw light upon these problems is through the study of large-scale cohorts of psychiatric patients. Such studies are needed, but have hitherto been few due to the difficulties in following up a psychiatric population. In Denmark, the existence of a nationwide cumulative psychiatric register (Dupont 1983) provides an excellent opportunity to trace selected groups of patients. Since April 1, 1970, this register has received information on all inpatient admissions to Danish psychiatric institutions and since 1974 from all day-patient admissions. At present the register receives input from 86 institutions with about 10000 beds and with about 35000 inpatient and 5000 day-patient admissions annually. The information contained in the psychiatric case register is restricted to crude data concerning the admission in question and a diagnostic evaluation.

Based on information from the register, a cohort was analyzed consisting of all patients 15 years or older who were admitted for the first time to a psychiatric institution in Denmark during the period April 1, 1970, to March 31, 1971. The cohort comprised a total of 12737 patients, of which 46% (5881) were males and 54% (6856) females. This cohort was followed up in the psychiatric register until January 1, 1980, and all information available in the register was collected concerning admissions as in patients and day patients. The cohort had a total of 35 497 admissions. In the analysis no discharge of less than 10 days' duration was considered a discharge. This arbitrary limit, previously used in another study (Weeke et al. 1979), was chosen because we did not want short absences from hospital, for instance in connection with visits home, to influence the status of the patients.

In the cohort study 7.4% (947) became long-stay patients over the 10-year observation period, representing a 10-year incidence rate of long-stay patients of 22 men and 27 women per 100 000 total population. Long-stay patients were here divided into two groups; one group comprised 4.1%, the "new" long-stay patients – i.e., patients with a first admission lasting for more than 1 year, and the other group comprised 3.4% – the "late" long-stay patients with a later admission lasting for more than 1 year. Besides the long-stay population, another group of chronic patients needing consideration are the "revolving-door" patients. Many delineations have been put forward to define this group. In the present study 11.0% (1397) became "revolving-door" patients, representing a total of 42 men and 32 women per 100 000 total population. The "revolving-door" patients consisted of two partly overlapping groups. The groups were defined as those having at least four admissions, one group comprising 7.2% of the patients who were in and out of hospital with no hospitalization and no discharge period lasting for more than one quarter of the observation period, the other group comprising 9.1% of the patients who had at least four admissions concentrated over the first quarter of the observation period.

Diagnostically we found that long-stay patients were predominantly psychotics. Among the "new" long-stay patients 76.7% of the men and 79.7% of the women suffered from senile or cerebrovascular psychoses. In total, the psychotic group comprised 90.0% of the men and 94.1% of the women in the "new" long-stay group. This means that a total of 10.09 per 100 000 men and 14.91 per 100 000 women belong to the group of psychotic "new" long-stay patients.

Among the "late" long-stay patients, 32.9% of the men and 16.3% of the women suffered from schizophrenia and 21.9% of the men and 38.9% of the women from senile or cerebrovascular psychoses. In total, the psychotic patients comprised 77.1% of the men and 78.3% of the women in the "late" long-stay group. In other words, the chronic psychotic group becoming "late" long-stay patients amounted to 8.65 men and 8.95 women per 100 000 total population.

Among the revolving-door group the schizophrenics constituted the largest psychotic group, 17.1% of men and 8.9% of women. Non-psychotic patients comprised a relatively larger proportion among the revolving-door patients, and in total the psychotics comprised 34.5% of men and 46.7% of women, representing an incidence rate of psychotics of 14.2 men and 14.86 women per 100 000 total population.

Another question is: What proportion of psychotic patients become chronic in the sense delineated here? Using the ultimate diagnostic evaluation, we found that schizophrenic patients had the greatest likelihood of becoming chronic, as about 70% of the male and about 55% of the female schizophrenics belonged to one of the chronic groups. All in all, about 20%–25% of all first-time admitted psychotics ended up belonging to the chronic population.

On the whole, the concepts "long-stay patient" and "revolving-door patient" have been connected with in-hospital care. But as outpatient care has increased in importance, it seems natural also to comprise the psychiatric service outside institutions, taking into account how complex the system of care is, and that a chronic patient may not necessarily be lying in a "psychiatric" bed.

This view is further supported by our investigations (Kastrup and Bille 1980, Kastrup et al. 1984) of the comprehensive psychiatric service in a WHO pilot study area, showing that only 20% of a patient population at a given time are admitted as day and inpatients whereas the majority are treated as outpatients.

Using in this study the term "chronic" for any patient in continuous treatment for more than 1 year – whether as in-, day-, or out-patient or shifting from one kind of treatment to another – we found that 212 men and 118 women per 100 000 belonged to the chronic population. Of the schizophrenics, 89% belonged to the chronic group, and taking all psychotic patients together, 52.7% of the men and 36.8% of the women became chronic patients.

It is evident that the chronic psychotic population seeking treatment is large, and that new psychotic patients needing chronic care are constantly accumulating. Of all first-time admitted, 7% became long-stay patients and 11% became revolving-door patients. Not all of these were psychotics but of all the psychotics, 20%–25% ended up belonging to the chronic population, with the schizophrenics having the greatest likelihood of ending up as chronics.

In the study we have defined the chronic psychotics by their use of the existing services. No information was available on the number of chronic psychotic patients living in the community but with no contact to psychiatric services.

How do psychiatrists and politicians optimally attend to the needs of the psychiatric patients in general and of the chronic psychotic patients in particular? Both authors are psychiatrists, but one (Bille) is also a politician, and since 1970 member of the County Council of Aarhus, serving on the finance committee. Both authors believe that political abstinence is not a virtue, and from that angle the relation between psychiatrists and politicians is discussed.

Both physicians and politicians work to improve the general state of health. The physician seeks to help the individual patient, the politician aims to help groups of patients.

The distance between politicians and physicians is undoubtedly at its greatest where psychiatry is considered. Politicians find it easier to identify with a surgeon than with a psychiatrist. And perhaps psychiatrists do not always make it easy for themselves. It is not a good negotiation technique for psychiatrists to practice their professional skills with politicians, sitting back silently, listening, and waiting, so that politicians feel like patients under observation.

This relationship between politicians and psychiatrists has another facet. If a politician has undergone surgery, it is often a good topic of conversation with the surgeon. If, however, the politician has been a psychiatric patient, experience shows that it is wisest not to mention it.

Generally, psychiatrists and politicians do not show much understanding of each other's working conditions, and this may influence their assessment of one another. In 1972, for instance, at an international symposium in Mannheim on the Epidemiological Basis for the Planning of Psychiatric Services, Erik Strömgren (1973) said: "For some politicians the main goal of their activities within the field of mental health planning is not the reduction of the prevalence of psychiatric disorder in the population. Their main interest may be to reduce the cost of mental illness."

The lack of understanding between politicians and psychiatrists is due, among other things, to their relative ignorance of each other's working conditions. We believe that psychiatrists underestimate the difficulties of making social forecasts. Yet these difficulties are common knowledge.

Psychiatry plans are worked out on the assumption, among others, of a certain amount of economic progress. If this is not forthcoming, the basis of the psychiatric plans collapses. Projecting builds on present assumptions, but these never continue unaltered. Yesterday is not today. Plans are changed by external circumstances on which politicians have no influence: war and peace, exchange rates, oil crises, technological developments, and so on. Altered circumstances are often crucial for what actually happens in the planning phase. The conditions for planning tend to be forgotten, leading to the accusation that only the most spineless of people become politicians. But we must also plan for the adjustment of our standards of value, for some values fade faster than others.

Traditionally, we plan according to need, but in the given situation it is necessary to plan according to possibility, not least within psychiatry, where the offer to a great extent defines the demand. Psychiatrists tend to forget that other areas of the health services need financing, and that society also needs roads and schools and so on. In this respect psychiatrists are no different from other groups such as teachers and social workers, each of whom say that they are here to run the services, not to save money. In the case of psychiatry, matters are not improved by the belief, cherished by some, that in the long run society will accept offers of treatment whose efficiency remains undocumented.

An even more fundamental question than that of the cost-effectiveness of managing chronic patients is fixing an order of priority between chronic patients and other psychiatric groups, and setting *such* priorities could give rise to considerable discord.

Taking psychiatric patients out of institutions has been a positive step, but in many places it has been difficult to find the alternatives to take responsibility for psychiatric patients. The reason for this may be that the new places of treatment were to be set up just as the economic crisis began. The public, the politicians, and the psychiatrists may also have been more interested in *psychiatria minor* than in chronic patients.

The establishment of emergency psychiatric clinics can be seen as the expression of a progressive attitude. With only limited finance available, such initiatives can in fact be paid from funds previously set aside for chronic psychiatric patients. Psychiatria minor patients have many champions, chronic psychiatric patients only a few. Politicians have to adapt their views to the electors. Similarly, psychiatrists can feel the need to be on good terms with various pressure groups.

But if chronic patients are neglected, the following situation can arise: In 1955 there were over 93 000 inpatients in state hospitals in New York. In 1982 there were about 24 000. But in 1982 there were also some 30 000 chronic psychiatic patients living on the streets of New York City. A 1981 report by the state of New York (Marcos 1982) shows that of 885 homeless individuals, 20% were found to be in need of immediate psychiatric hospitalization. The Norwegian psychiatrist Leo Eitinger (1983) assessed the situation as follows: "Economic and ideological arguments have favored an uncritical discharge of patients. The therapeutic possibilities for chronic patients are few, but this does not exempt us from our medical and human obligations to this patient group."

When psychiatrists evaluate politicians, we believe that they often forget that the economic possibilities *are* limited, that these possibilities *are* influenced by circumstances over which politicians have no control, and that the justified demands from other sectors of society are *numerous*. The prevalence of treated psychiatric illness is influenced by activities outside hospital budgets, such as the efforts to reduce youth unemployment, the campaign to reduce road accidents, and so on.

Focusing on the management of chronic psychotics, three groups have the most obvious interest here in: the patients themselves, the psychiatrists, and the politicians. The chronic psychotic patients are rarely in a position to articulate their own needs. Most commonly, it is through their relatives that their interests are attended to. We do not know enough about the human, social, and economic costs for these patients and their relatives if deinstitutionalization is carried out uncritically, but that the strain on the families is great if they are not provided adequate social support has been recognized (Sainsbury 1975).

Psychiatrists need no epidemiological schooling to recognize the presence of chronic psychotic patients. Just the size of their files shows that patients in this group - despite treatment - tend to relapse. This fact may become a burden on the psychiatrist and the nursing staff of the institutions, who may prefer to spend their time on patients with diseases of a more favorable prognosis. It is our opinion that in Denmark work with chronic patients, particularly gerontopsychiatric patients, carries little prestige, e.g., compared with work with patients in psychotherapy. A reflection hereof can be seen in the requirements for becoming a specialist, as psychotherapeutic knowledge and training is compulsory, and gerontopsychiatric knowledge a facultatory topic.

Human contact is time consuming, and the number of patients of whom a psychiatrist has a personal knowledge is therefore limited. It will be the exception rather than the rule that the psychotherapist is in charge of the gerontopsychiatric patients and vice versa. Generally, the psychiatrist talks on behalf of a particular group of patients.

The role of the politician is quite different from the individual-oriented role of the psychiatrist. The expectations of the politician may be like those of Nils in Selma Lagerlöf's *Wonderful Adventures of Nils,* who could fly and see everything from above but at the same time be aware of all details. What politicians need is an overview, not details of specification. The politician receives information from the administrative system, partly from different pressure groups outside the political system. Chronic psychotic patients have a weak lobby to support them, and if psychiatrists pay more attention to other patient groups, the chronic psychotic patients may end up in difficulties. This is particularly the case in times of limited resources and is apparently what has taken place in the U.S.

In conclusion, it may be that the chronic psychotic patients comprise a large group, as 20%-25% of first-time admitted end up chronic, as defined here. Despite the fact that the therapeutic possibilities for this group are still unsatisfactory, the

health services should not be entitled to give less priority to them. Deinstitutionalization is appropriate, but not when carried out dogmatically and with no acceptable alternatives. Resources should be allocated to patients whose disorders, so to
speak, form the core of the psychiatric disease complex.

One of the tasks of the psychiatrist is to help patients toward a recognition of
the realities of life. A pious hope of a politician would be that psychiatrists will do
the same for themselves and recognize the multiplicity of demands and the limits
of available finance.

References

Dupont A (1983) A national psychiatric case register as a tool for mental health planning, re-
    search and administration. In: Laska EM et al. (eds) Information support to mental health pro-
    grams. Human Sciences Press, New York, p 257
Eitinger L (1983) Opening speech at the XX Nordic Congress of Psychiatry, Bergen 1982 (in Nor-
    wegian). Nord Psyk Tids 37: 79–82
Kastrup M, Bille M (1980) A census study with special regard to long-stay psychiatric patients.
    Acta Psychiatr Scand [Suppl] 285: 269
Kastrup M, Bille M, Weeke A, Dupont A (1984) The psychiatric service in a geographically deli-
    mited population. I: Utilization of institutionalized psychiatric care in the light of the use by a
    census population (in Danish). Ugeskr Laeger 146: 213–218
Kirshner LA (1982) Length of stay of psychiatric patients. J Nerv Ment Dis 170: 27–33
Kramer M (1980) The rising pandemic of mental disorders and associated chronic diseases and
    disabilities. Acta Psychiatr Scand [Suppl] 285: 382
Marcos LR (1982) Deinstitutionalization. Psychiatry News 17: 2
Richman A, Barry A (1985) More and more is less and less. The myth of massive psychiatric need.
    Br J Psychiatry 146: 164–168
Sainsbury P (1975) Evaluation of community mental health programs. In: Guttentag M, Struening
    EL (eds) Handbook of evaluation research. Sage, London
Strömgren E (1973) Epidemiological basis for planning. In: Wing JK, Häfner H (eds) Roots of
    evaluation. The epidemiological basis for planning psychiatric services. Oxford University
    Press, London
Weeke A, Kastrup M, Dupont A (1979) Long-stay patients in Danish psychiatric hospitals. Psy-
    chol Med 9: 551–566

Regional Approaches

Economic Analysis of Different Patterns of Psychiatric Treatment and Management of Chronic Psychotic Patients in the Basque Country

J. A. Ozámiz and J. M. Cabasés

Introduction

A systematic follow-up of the psychiatric population in the Basque Country has been developed in the last few years. This has been done as a part of the Basque Psychiatric Care and Mental Health Plan established by the Department of Health. One of the key aspects of this follow-up is the compilation of a Psychiatric Case Register that has been in operation since October 1983, providing data on an increasing number of psychiatric cases, the characteristics of the patients, and their care processes, through the systematic recording of every single care contact. This has made possible the estimation of the costs of mental health care.

The purpose of this paper is to describe the direct costs of treatment of chronic psychotics in the Basque Country. Cost calculations have been made by different diagnostic categories of chronic psychosis – organic, affective, schizophrenia, and alcoholic – and different patterns of care – outpatient, hospital, and a mix of both. If direct costs only are considered, outpatient care is the cheapest pattern of treatment, as expected. But health care direct costs are just a first step in cost calculation. The inclusion of other costs borne by families and social service departments, as well as indirect and intangible costs, might lead to different results.

The paper is divided into three sections. In the first we give an outline of our health care system and psychiatric care, as well as a description of the Psychiatric Case Register, its contents and main features. Section two focuses on the cost study, after describing the different types of chronic psychotics and patterns of treatment. We discuss the results in section three, where some proposals for further research are given.

Psychiatric Care in the Autonomous Basque Community

The Health Care System in the Basque Country

Euskadi (the autonomous community of the Basque Country) is situated in the north of Spain and has an area of 7261 km^2 and a population of 2135060 (according to the 1986 census). Fifty percent of the total population are immigrants from other autonomous communities in the Spanish state. The pyramidal age range has a wide base, as 20% of the population is under the age of 15. The present level of unemployment is 21% of the active population. Euskadi has had its own parliament and government since 1979.

The health care system in the Basque Country is based on social security, with 93% of the population covered. The financing is 77% public and 23% private, with a total spending of 5.76% of the gross domestic product (GDP) in 1982. A power-devolution process was started in 1979, that will result in an autonomous Basque health care system by 1988. Provisional figures give 5.5 beds per 1000 population (4 acute; 1.5 chronic) in hospital care, receiving 50% of the total health-care spending. Ninety percent of hospital care is financed publicly. One specific feature of publicly financed hospital care is that it is provided partly in publicly owned hospitals (65% of acute beds) and partly in private hospitals (35%).

Outpatient services are provided in public health centres and private clinics, with a strong presence of private practice.

Psychiatric Care in the Basque Country

Psychiatric care in Euskadi, as in the rest of Spain, was mainly custodial in nature until 1980. Over the past few years there has been an effort to change this in the autonomous Basque Community. At present there are six psychiatric hospitals, ranging in capacity from 175 to 400 beds. There are three psychiatric units in general hospitals with 20, 30, and 60 beds respectively. This gives us a ratio of 1.2 psychiatric beds per 1000 inhabitants. Although there is an adequate ratio of psychiatrists to population (eight per 100000 inhabitants), we have few psychologists and psychiatric nurses; 80% of our personnel are auxiliaries who mainly carry out tasks of a custodial nature.

Although we have promoted Mental Health Centres in the community, we are still far from establishing the full implementation of primary care. In this respect there is still no coordination between the staff in these centres and family doctors and general practitioners; there is practically no domiciliary service. The transformation of psychiatric care in the Basque Country has been continuous since 1979, and at present it allows the mid-term planning of a realistic community psychiatric-services network, which guarantees the setting of effective objectives. This is possible thanks to programs which were developed and materialized in 1982 in the *Psychiatric Care and Mental Health Plan,* which was published, presented in the Basque Parliament and accepted by all the political groups.

Nevertheless, the contents of this plan, although important and decisive for the transformation of a traditionally custodial psychiatric care service, are only a basic description of the resources, infrastructure, and typical work of a modern psychiatric care service.

Committees which have been formed under this plan have studied and proposed specific programs which are used to guide the development of child psychiatric care and psychogeriatrics, as well as establishing criteria and alternatives for the reform of legislation affecting psychiatric care.

The Psychiatric Case Register

As a basic aim in all our work we proposed to establish a system of continuous assessment of our achievements. We reached the conclusion that the Psychiatric Patient Register and the follow-up of its contacts with the health care services was an instrument fundamental to obtaining adequate knowledge and a technical assessment of the psychiatric services. In the Psychiatric Care and Mental Health Plan drawn up by the Department of Health, the Register, its use, functions, and the data it must contain are mentioned. It is distinguished from the conventional clinical history, which also has to be employed in the treatment of the psychiatric patient. Based on these criteria, the Advising Commission for Mental Health designed a register which is compiled by all different psychiatric services in the autonomous community. For the design of the register we had the advantage of the experience gained from similar registers (Camberwell and Groningen).

Dr. Giel, responsible for the Groningen Register, recommended that we take special care to register each and every contact made by the psychiatric patient with the different services, because only in this way would we adquire knowledge of the type of work involved with each type of patient.

The introduction of the register has required a great effort, above all a good deal of communication with each and every one of the psychiatric services and their qualified staff. The work has been carried out by three professsionals (two psychologists and one sociologist) and several administrative auxiliaries. These professionals have had to familiarize themselves with the terminology used by the personnel who work in the various services. Only in this way have they obtained collaboration in the collection of reliable data and useful information. One of the fundamental problems has been the collection of the data referring to the patients' characteristics. This has been solved by assigning a single anonymous code for each patient.

A preliminary interview was held with all the personnel of each of the centers to explain what the case register involves and the objectives which are sought. The register has two differentiating characteristics. First, each and every contact the patient establishes with the center is recorded, which professional has attended him, which type of contact is established, and whether any significant change is produced in the patient's personal life, work, or economic situation, as well as any change in diagnosis or treatment. Second, the idea is to fill in a card for each patient, on which the data of identification, family environment, psychiatric history, economic situation, occupation, diagnosis, and treatment all appear. This card is filled in on one sole occasion by the patient and the changes which occur appear in a box reserved for this on the daily contact sheets.

The attitude of the centres varies from one to another. Nevertheless, they are all ready to collaborate, although the attitude of some is skeptical regarding the use of this method. In this sense the effort which we are making to return the systemized information to each of the centres is fundamental. Generally, rapid feedback is required, but it is necessary to explain that adequate knowledge of the process of the services and the different types of patients requires a certain length of time.

The register was not introduced in a generalized form, but gradually, beginning with selected areas and services in October 1983.

To illustrate the operation of the register let us consider the collective data ac-cummulated by the end of 1985. On the December 31, 1985, there were 10 078 cases registered (an estimated 4.7 per 1000 inhabitants), with chronic psy-chotics constituting 30% of the population registered. The total number of first vis-its paid during 1985 was 4264 patients, 12.5% of which were diagnosed as psychot-ics.

The Cost of Treatment

Chronic Psychotic Patients in the Basque Country

The study concerned the population of chronic psychotics in the Basque Country who had entered the psychiatric case register before 1985 and were still receiving care at the beginning of 1986. This amounted to a total of 3243 patients, divided into four diagnostic categories: organic psychosis (ICD9-290/293/294) account-ing for 7.5% of all registered chronic psychotics; affective psychosis (ICD9-296) (20%); schizophrenic and other psychosis (ICD9-295/297/298) (69.5%); and alco-holic psychosis (ICD9-291) (3%). These figures show the relative importance of the third group, schizophrenics and others, constituting almost 70% of all regis-tered chronic patients.

Patterns of Treatment

In order to identify patterns of care, all the patients were followed up for the year 1985. This was possible using the information provided by the case register, which records every single professional-patient contact. Table 1 summarizes the number of patients receiving each of the three main types of care: hospital, outpatient, and mixed (a combination of hospital and outpatient), and shows the importance of hospital care, which accounts for 58.5% of the patients treated, followed by out-patient care (30.56%), and a slight trend to mixed care (11%) that might reflect a

Table 1. Chronic psychotics registered and patterns of care in the Basque Country, 1985

Type of psychosis	Treatment Pattern			Total	
	Hospital	Mixed	Outpatient	n	%
Organic	167	6	72	245	7.55
Affective	339	83	229	651	20.07
Schizophrenia and other	1315	264	676	2255	69.53
Alcoholic	76	2	14	92	2.84
Total	1897	355	991	3243	100.00
%	58.50	10.94	30.56		

mental health care system of a traditional hospital-focused structure. Hospital care is used more intensively by organic and alcoholic psychotics, while affective psychotics receive more outpatient care on the average.

Concerning outpatient care there are three main types of contacts: first visit, follow-up, and therapy, with a whole range of different therapies being recorded in the register. The patients normally receive different combinations of the three types of care. However, in order to facilitate cost calculations, and taking into account that nobody had his first contact in the period considered, we assigned all the outpatients to four groups, following Giel and ten Horn (1982), as shown in Table 2: those with only follow-up contacts, those with mostly follow-up contacts (up to 70%), those with only therapies, and those with mostly (up to 70% of the contacts) therapies. The most frequent or modal outpatient treatment is the first, i.e., only follow-up (74.5%) with an average of five contacts. This is true for all diagnostic categories. In only 12% of cases are therapies the dominating contact.

The distribution of patients who receive mixed care is shown in Table 3. Most patients (74.37%) belong to the group of schizophrenics, although only 12% of

Table 2. Outpatient care by diagnostic category for chronic psychotics, Basque Country, 1985

Type of contacts	Diagnostic category										
	Organic		Affective		Schizophrenic		Alcoholic		Total		
	n	$\bar{x}$ [a]	n	$\bar{x}$	n	$\bar{x}$	n	$\bar{x}$	n	%	$\bar{x}$
1 Follow-up only	68	3	185	5	476	5	9	3	738	74.47	4.79
2 Mostly follow-up	2	10	26	12	105	13	3	6	136	13.72	12.60
3 Therapies only	0	–	7	18	29	12	0	–	36	3.63	13.17
4 Mostly therapies	2	112	11	12	66	48	2	29	81	8.17	44.22
Total	72	–	229	–	676	–	14	–	991		

[a] $\bar{x}$, Average number of contacts

Table 3. Mixed care of chronic psychotics by diagnostic category, Basque Country, 1985

Type of contacts	Diagnostic category									
	Organic		Affective		Schizophrenic		Alcoholic		Total	
	n	$\bar{x}$ [a]	n	$\bar{x}$	n	$\bar{x}$	n	$\bar{x}$	n	$\bar{x}$
Outpatient										
First contact	0	–	1	1	2	1	0	–	3	1
Follow-up only	5	3	75	2	201	3	2	3	283	2.73
Mostly follow-up	1	11	6	9	32	25	0	–	39	22.18
Therapies only	0	–	1	1	5	40	0	–	6	7.66
Mostly therapies	0	–	0	–	24	47	0	–	24	47.00
Total	6		83		264		2		355	
Hospital										
<90 days	4	35.75	71	39.1	219	38	1	27	295	38.20
>90 days	2	114	12	156	45	146	1	122	60	146.50

[a] $\bar{x}$, Average number of contacts or hospital days

these patients receive mixed treatment. The mixed-treatment modal is the combination of "only follow-up" outpatient contacts (average three contacts) with a short hospital stay (average 38 days).

The Cost of Care

We estimated the direct costs of the treatment of chronic psychotics as measured by the resources health services use, e. g., manpower, equipment, buildings, consumable supplies. Other direct costs such as patients' and their families' resources, e. g., transport, home adaptation, personal time, were not included. Neither indirect (e. g., production losses because of mental illness) nor intangible costs were considered.

In searching for data for our cost calculations we ran into difficulties. They arose mainly because of the lack of developed cost-accounting procedures in the institutions providing care. We chose one hospital with reliable cost accounting[1] that supplied the hospital costs for long, medium, and short stays. Some outpatient centres which are affiliated with that hospital provided information for the calculation of the outpatient costs.

Outpatient Costs
We defined a "work unit" (w. u.) as the unit of outpatient care activity, so that any professional-patient contact could be converted into units of a single measure. The measuring rod was the professional's time devoted to care. Thus, because the shortest contact was a follow-up visit, this was taken as the work unit. One average first visit lasts four times a follow-up contact, i. e., equals 4 w. u. As for therapies, we had to summarize the wide range of them into a single concept of therapy, considering the professional time devoted to them, giving an amount of 4.25 w. u. for a therapy session. The cost of a work unit was calculated from the outpatient centers mentioned above, taking into account all running and capital costs and amounting to 652 Pts (U. S. $ 3.84 or 5.04 ECU) in 1985. The unit cost of the rest of the contacts is shown in Table 4.

Hospital Costs
The cost accounting of the hospital mentioned above allowed for the calculation of three different per diem costs, depending on the length of stay. Different lengths of stay are associated with different treatment patterns, yielding different costs. The cost per day of short-stay patients is double that of long-stay patients.

Tables 5 and 6 show the average treatment by diagnostic category and the corresponding costs of outpatient, mixed, and hospital care in each diagnostic group. Thus, the average chronic psychotic patient treated in outpatient institutions in the Basque Country in 1985 received 19.46 w. u., incurring a cost of 12688 Pts (U. S. $ 75). By diagnostic categories, this figure ranges from 7100 Pts

---

[1] We thank Sr. Mikel Aguirre, from the Hospital Psiquiátrico Las Nieves, in Vitoria, and Sr. José A. Aguirre, from the Mental Health Services, Osakidetza, Basque Government, for their most valuable help in our task

Table 4. Unit costs of treatment for chronic psychotics in the Basque Country, 1985

Outpatient care: cost per contact	Work units	Pts	U.S. $	ECU
First physician contact	4	2608	15.34	20.16
Follow-up visits only	1	652	3.84	5.04
Mostly follow-up visits	1.975	1288	7.57	9.95
Therapies only	4.25	2771	16.30	21.42
Mostly therapies	3.275	2135	12.56	16.5

Hospital care: costs per diem	Pts	U.S. $	ECU
Short stay (<90 days)	8129	47.81	62.87
Medium stay ($90<X<180$ days)	4573	26.89	35.37
Long stay (all year)	3793	22.31	29.33

Table 5. Average treatment of chronic psychotics by diagnostic category, Basque Country, 1985

	Outpatient	Mixed		Hospital
	Work units	Work units	Hospital days	Hospital days
Organic psychosis	13.66	5.97	62	365
Affective psychosis	10.89	3.13	56	365
Schizophrenia and other psychoses	23.01	27.72	56	365
Alcoholic psychosis	18.03	3	74.5	365
All chronic psychotics	19.46	21.15	56.5	365

Table 6. Average cost of care of chronic psychotics by diagnostic category, Basque Country, 1985

Diagnostic category	Treatment pattern					
	Outpatient		Mixed		Hospital	
	Pts	U.S. $	Pts	U.S. $	Pts	U.S. $
Organic psychosis	8906	52	371040	2182	1384445	8142
Affective psychosis	7100	42	377239	2219	1384445	8142
Schizophrenia and other psychoses	15002	88	387964	2282	1384445	8142
Alcoholic psychosis	11756	69	390650	2297	1384445	8142
All chronic psychotics	12688	75	385181	2265	1384445	8142

(U.S. $ 42) for affective psychotics to 15002 Pts (U.S. $ 88) for schizophrenics and other psychotics. The average patient under mixed treatment received 21.15 w.u. of outpatient care, being inpatient care for 56.5 days with a total cost for 1985 of 385181 Pts (U.S. $ 2265). Schizophrenics in this group with mixed treatment received more work units of outpatient care than schizophrenics in outpatient care only. Lastly, the cost of the average patient who was an inpatient during 1985 was 1384445 Pts (U.S. $ 8142).

Discussion

We have tried to explore the potential of the Psychiatric Case Register to calculate the costs of mental health care for chronic psychotics. Although the register is still in its infancy, it has been possible to follow up a cohort of more than 3000 patients for 1 year and to determine the patterns of care received by different diagnostic categories. Cost data were obtained from one hospital that had a satisfactory cost accounting and from the outpatient centres affiliated with it.

Before we comment on the results, there are some methological points that deserve attention. First, not all the potential of the case register has been used. Taking into account personal characteristics of the patients (age, sex, marital state, profession, etc.) some indirect costs could have been determined, e.g., production losses because of illness. Second, the potential of the case register is limited for a full economic evaluation. Only health care contacts are registered; this means that other types of care, such as informal care, are not considered. Moreover, the register lacks non-diagnostic measures of effectiveness such as functional status (e.g., scales of activities of daily living, quality-adjusted life years) and user's satisfaction. Although some effectiveness studies are being carried out currently in the Basque Country they are at too early a stage to be conclusive.

The costing exercise that has been done cross-sectionally, using 1 year of the treatment of each patient, has its pitfalls. One would like to follow up a cohort of patients for a longer time and compare the costs and effectiveness of different patterns of care, but this is not yet possible. The case register needs to be in operation for several years before we can study the cost of full processes of care.

Another methodological point is that the costs calculated are average costs. We took the average patient in each diagnostic category and pattern of treatment and obtained a unit cost of treatment. Decision-making is concerned more with marginal than average cost. In fact, looking at the cost of different patterns of treatment, and assuming for a moment that these could be considered as alternatives one has to strongly encourage outpatient care. However, if we think of marginal costs, i.e., the costs of providing care to a new patient, these may be very low in a hospital but perhaps very high in outpatient care in areas where this type of care is not yet well developed, areas that would need to incur new capital and running costs.

Finally, there is a lack of cost information in the institutions providing care, and they must be encouraged to fill this vacuum by developing cost-accounting procedures. Otherwise, our data on costs will not be reliable.

Looking at the results it is worth noting the large differences between the costs of the three patterns of treatment. Thinking of mixed treatment as a potential alternative to hospital treatment, the former seems to be a cheaper type of care, although one should not forget the transfer of the burden of disease from the hospital to the families or institutions receiving the patients. Deinstitutionalization processes have to be analyzed carefully, taking into account all the costs, especially those borne by the families.

The mixed pattern of treatment uses outpatient care more intensively than the outpatient pattern itself. This is especially true for schizophrenics. Although this may reflect a worse mental health status of the group receiving mixed treatment, it could indicate some degree of induced demand. This requires further research.

The outpatient care pattern is not well developed, though there has been an increase in the number of outpatient or community mental health centres in the Basque Country. One may expect an increase in the utilization of these facilities in the near future, including new patterns such as domiciliary care. Schizophrenics use these facilities much more intensively than other chronic psychotics, with annual cost per person that is twice the cost of treatment of affective psychosis.

Acknowledgements. We are grateful to Luis M. Puente, economist, Rakel Aguirre, psychologist, Ana Ugarte, psychologist, and the rest of the staff of the Psychiatric Case Register for their help in our task.

References

Giel R, ten Horn GHMM (1982) Patterns of mental health care in a Dutch register area. Soc Psychiatry 17: 117–123

Goldberg DM, Jones R (1980) The cost and benefits of psychiatric care. In: Robins L, Clayton P, Long J (eds) The social consequences of psychiatric illness. Brunner/Mazel, New York, pp 55–70

ten Horn GHMM, Giel R (1984) The feasibility of cost-benefit studies of the mental health care. Acta Psychiatr Scand 69: 80–87

Weisbrod BA, Test MA, Stein LI (1980) Alternative to mental hospital treatment. II. Economic benefit-cost analysis. Arch Gen Psychiatry 37: 400–405

Cost-Effectiveness of Health-Care Delivery to Chronic Psychotic Patients in Southern Alberta, Canada

R. Williams and J. T. Dalby

Demographic Features of Alberta

Alberta, one of ten provinces in Canada, is a frontier region of 255000 square miles (660411 km^2) inhabited by 2.3 million people. The province has a total area larger than that of Great Britain, Denmark, and West Germany combined, nations on a similar latitude in Europe (Figs. 1 and 2).

The 1981 National Census indicated that 77% of Alberta's population resides in urban areas, with over half of the total in the cities of Calgary and Edmonton. In 1983 Calgary registered 620692 residents, while Edmonton registered 560085.

Fig. 1. Geographic location of the province of Alberta, Canada

Fig. 2. Population and area comparison of
Alberta and the United Kingdom

Total population of Alberta - 2 348 800

Total area of Alberta - 255 000 sq. miles
                    - 660 411 sq. kilometers

Total population of the United Kingdom - 55 970 000

Total area of the United Kingdom - 94 216 sq. miles
                    - 244 019 sq. kilometers

Between 1971 and 1981 the province's population increased by 37%, but with the onset of economic recession in the early 1980s, caused by the fluctuating world price of oil, Alberta began to experience a significant emigration.

Albertans have an unusual age distribution, in that one third of the population is under the age of 21, another third is between the ages of 21 and 35 years, and the over-65 population is significantly lower than in most European countries. Two of every three Alberta residents have been born in the province, but one resident in five comes from outside Canada.

The region of Southern Alberta accounts for approximately 20% of the area of the whole province and contains half the population of the province.

Employment/Unemployment Statistics for the Province

It is important when looking at the services provided to a community to examine the level of employment and unemployment within the designated area. Table 1 gives the unemployment rates, which have risen in Alberta from well below the national average in 1974, when the unemployment level in Alberta was at 3.5%, crossing the critical threshold at which unemployment influences the probability of obtaining work for schizophrenics (Morgan and Cheadle 1979), to the level of 5% in 1982. At the beginning of 1984 the unemployment rate in Southern Alberta was 11.2% and this rose in 1985 to 11.9% as a consequence of the recession in the oil industry. We intend to examine the admission rates and unemployment rates among our population to assess the effects of rising unemployment on the employment rate of schizophrenics in Southern Alberta.

Health Services

The health services in each of the Canadian provinces are funded jointly by the federal and provincial governments. Due to the extensive oil revenues reverting to the provincial government of Alberta, there is adequate funding for such services. For patients suffering mental disorders there are inpatient and outpatient psychiatric facilities within general hospitals in Calgary, Lethbridge, and Medicine Hat and there is a regional hospital at Ponoka which serves the whole of the province, and which is a designated psychiatric facility taking those patients transferred under a mental health certificate.

There are 434 psychiatric inpatient beds within general hospitals for the entire province and 227 desginated psychiatric beds in general hospitals in Southern Alberta. There are additionally 485 beds at psychiatric hospitals, producing a total of 1004 designated hospital beds for psychiatric patients for a general population of 1200000 in Southern Alberta (i.e., 0.8 per 1000). Statistics are routinely compiled by the provincial authorities responsible for hospitals and are shown for Southern Alberta in Table 2.

Table 1. Unemployment rates of Canada, Ontario and Alberta (percent)[a]

	Canada	Ontario	Alberta
1974	5.3	4.4	3.5
1980	7.5	6.8	3.7
1984, Jan.	11.3	9.1	11.2
1985, Jan.	12.2	9.9	11.9

[a] Source: Statistics Canada

Table 2. Distribution of psychiatric patient-days and average percentage occupancy by unit in Southern Alberta

Hospital	Patient-days during a year: adults and children (psychiatric)	Average percentage occupancy: adults and children (psychiatric)
Lethbridge Municipal	6727	87.9
Medicine Hat and District	4018	61.2
Calgary, Holy Cross	12423	79.2
Calgary, Foothills provincial	15108	59.1
Calgary, General	22596	82.5
Total	60872	74.0

Pathways of Psychiatric Care

Routes to psychiatric are summarized in Fig. 3. Patients enter the psychiatric system in Southern Alberta through self-referral to psychiatric emergency departments located in general hospitals or through referral from their family physician.

If schizophrenia of moderate severity is diagnosed, patients are most likely to be treated as outpatients. It is likely in Southern Alberta that all schizophrenic patients will be hospitalized at some point in time. They will typically be admitted to a general hospital inpatient psychiatric ward if they are willing to accept treatment. If, however, patients do not perceive their need for treatment and they fulfill the criteria for admission under a provincial mental health warrant, they will then be transferred to a designated hospital inpatient facility (Alberta Hospital Ponoka) where they will receive mandatory assessment and treatment. Once psychotic symptoms abate in an inpatient facility, either a general hospital or a designated hospital, the patient will generally be transferred to a general hospital outpatient (day hospital) facility for medication follow-up and rehabilitation. Some of these patients will then be transferred to the Alberta Mental Health Clinics which operate in both urban and rural regions.

In Southern Alberta there are 67 licensed specialists in psychiatry who work largely in either a hospital facility or an Alberta Mental Health Clinic or occasionally in a combination of these. Alberta Mental Health Services (AMHS) is an agency funded through the Social Services Department of the provincial government to provide care to patients with mental disorders discharged into the community or requiring treatment other than on an inpatient basis. AMHS funds a number of clinics which have nurses, social workers, and psychologists, in addition to psychiatrists, who operate on a team basis to provide acute aftercare in both rural and urban regions of Southern Alberta (see Table 3).

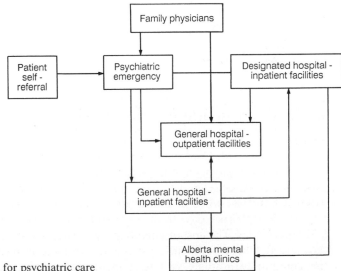

Fig. 3. Pathways of referral for psychiatric care

Table 3. Alberta mental health clinics and staff allotment, fourth quarter 1984–1985, in the Calgary and southern regions

	Calgary region	Southern region
Main clinics	4	2
Sub-clinics	5	4
Travelling clinics	12	9
Psychiatrists	8.62	2.99
Psychologists	17.32	8.00
Nurses	19.33	8.00
Social workers	20.33	15.00
Total staff	65.60	33.99

Community Services

The Department of Social Services and Community Health, through which community mental health clinics operate, has the responsibility of ensuring the availability of mental health treatment services to all areas of the province, both urban and rural. Community mental health services are delivered through nine mental health clinics and 30 sub-offices, as well as through regular visits by professional mental health teams to smaller rural centres. Services are provided free of charge and consist of assessment and diagnostic services. Two categories of rehabilitation and treatment support service programs are funded: community residences and non-residential programs. Of the community residences, 91 are approved homes providing a total of 270 beds. These residences are generally not approved for more than four residents at a time. The residents of these facilities are typically discharged psychiatric patients, usually with a chronic psychotic disorder who are ready for a family-like environment. There are 16 other community residences supporting between 5 and 25 residents each. The division of mental health funds 16 non-residential programs throughout the province. All but three of these are day-activity and socialization programs that emphasize skill development. All clients in a supported residence are required to be enrolled in either a day-activity program or an employment or pre-employment program.

Costs of Care to Schizophrenic Patients

The Alberta Health Care Insurance Commission requires diagnostic formulations (ICD-9) prior to payment to physcians. The total number of individuals diagnosed as having schizophrenia and receiving medical care in Southern Alberta in 1984 was 1318. In 1984 a bed in a designated facility (i.e. specialized psychiatric hospital) cost $ 191.00 per day. In the inpatient units in general hospitals the cost was $ 357.00 per day. The cost of attending a psychiatric day Hospital was $ 203.65 per day, and for those psychiatric patients maintained on medication and residing in the community a single visit to a medication clinic at a hospital facility cost

Table 4. Exchange rates for the Canadian dollar at January 1986

U.S. dollar	0.7200
Deutsche mark	1.8157
French franc	5.5335
Swiss franc	1.5104
Italian lira	1233
Pound sterling	0.4838

$ 18.33. To assist with international comparisons, Table 4 provides exchange ranges as of January 1986.

The costs of health care include the costs of direct services (nursing, occupational therapy, social work, medical) and of capital expenditure costs and depreciation, and are those costs calculated by the government in determining health care expenditure in relationship to specific illnesses.

Current Research on Health Care Evaluation and Cost-Effectiveness of Services to Chronic Psychotics in Southern Alberta

The Alberta Heritage Trust Fund, which derives its income from the province's rich oil resources, funds a great deal of medical research in Alberta. At the end of September 1983 the fund's assets stood at 13.3 billion dollars. There are four universities in the province, the University of Alberta in Edmonton, the University of Calgary, the University of Lethbridge, and Athabasca University; the first two offer courses in medical education.

A team of clinical researchers from the University of Calgary and AMHS are in the process of examining various aspects of services to chronic psychotic patients in the community. The provincial authorities have provided access to data bases on the characteristics and locations of patients treated for mental disorders. Dr. Williams and his colleagues at the Calgary General Hospital have identified a subject pool using a structured interview based on DSM-III diagnostic criteria to confirm the diagnosis of schizophrenia in 200 patients drawn from the community. The research team has been examining the quality of life of individuals with psychotic disorders living in the community and comparing this measure with those of chronically physically disabled and non-disabled subjects. As an additional independent variable, employment status was examined within each of these groups. In this study the questionnaire developed by A. F. Lehman and colleagues (Lehman 1983) was used, which examines both subjective and objective estimates of quality of life and includes specific measures of living arrangements, family background, finances, contact with others, leisure activities, employment, religion, and involvement with legal agencies either as an offender or as a victim. Data collection has been completed and analysis is underway.

In the initial analysis the questionnaire responses of 199 subjects were examined. Two global indices of quality of life were extracted from the extended questionnaires as dependent variables. The first was a 7-point Likert-type rating of general feeling about one's life, from terrible (1) to delighted (7). The second measure was a sum of seven 7-point Likert-type ratings which asked subjects to evaluate their life in general on several dimensions (e.g., boring-interesting; discouraging-encouraging).

A three-way analysis of variance was conducted: group (psychiatric; physically disabled; non-disabled) X employment status (employed; unemployed) X type of dependent measure. A significant main effect emerged for employment status, and no significant interactions were seen. This showed that employed individuals reported a higher quality of life attitude than unemployed individuals and their relationship held across all groups and with all dependent measures.

The magnitude of difference in the groups between employed and unemployed individuals was inspected. In the unemployed sample the non-disabled controls scored lower than the two disabled groups while in the employed groups the non-disabled controls scored higher than the disabled samples. This would suggest that a disability may buffer the perception of quality of life by diminishing the positive consequences of employment and perhaps the negative aspects of unemployment. More in-depth analyses of our data are in process.

A second area of study for our group is the development of a questionnaire which is completed by relatives of schizophrenic patients. With this questionnaire we are seeking to examine the impact on the family of having a relative with a schizophrenic disorder. Included in this measure are items tapping the attitudes of the family to the services their relative has received and items that indicate the impact on the family in economic terms and in emotional terms, particularly focusing on the strain on marital relationships.

A third study, from which we present preliminary data here, concerns the efficacy of a medication group established in one of the outpatient departments of a general hospital in Calgary. This medication clinic accepts referrals from all psychiatrists who have utilized the Day Hospital Program as part of the rehabilitation program for schizophrenics under their care. The Day Hospital is predominantly a social skills program where issues such as the need for medication and family problems are discussed in group settings. This is an educational program that prepares patients for the medication clinic and for life outside of a hospital environment.

The medication clinic was started in 1981 by Dr. Michael Lee to meet the needs of the schizophrenic patients who had indicated that, rather than just come for injectable medications, they would like to opportunity to socialize with patients living like themselves outside the hospital and to gain support from one another. To be accepted into the medication clinic patients have to agree to attend the patient-support meeting from 4:30 to 5:30 p.m. before receiving their injection. The patients may come weekly or only on the days when they are due to receive medication (i.e. every 2nd, 3rd, or 4th Tuesday); many attend regularly, even when not receiving injections and indicate that they come to socialize with people who are in a situation similar to their own. In any given week 20–40 patients attend and sit around one of two tables where coffee and snacks are available. Three nurses attend these meetings and socialize with the patients. The unemployed patients say they gain much from hearing of other patients who are working and

Table 5. Characteristics of 35 patients admitted to a medication clinic

Means of financial support	Sex	Cumulative hospitalization in previous 2 yrs (wks)	Post-clinic admissions (days)	Income $/month
Family	M=2 F =4	12.67 ± 10.7 (range 0–32)	0 ± 0	0.00
Earned wages	M=4 F =3	34.00 (range 3–104)	0	671.43 (range 350–1200)
Welfare payments	M=12 F =10	30.00 (range 7–104)	2.2	557.00 (range 380–1000)

leading "normal" lives in spite of the disabilities and impairments they suffer as a consequence of their illness. Patients are supportive of those individuals who relapse, and many say that to see people remaining well for 2 years after periods of illness is uplifting for them. One group tends to be quiet while the other patients participate in lively discussion. Patients say they value the situation of not being in organized therapy and enjoy meeting friends and gaining mutual support.

Thirty-five patients with a diagnosis of schizophrenia were admitted to the medication clinic (Table 5) for this study. All patients had been diagnosed as having a schizophrenic illness which had originally been diagnosed more than 2 years prior to admission to a medication clinic, and they had been followed up by private psychiatrists for outpatient aftercare until admitted to this study. We compared the 2 years prior to admission to the medication clinic with the 2 years after with regard to rates of utilization of hospital services. Since their admission to the clinic the rate of re-admission to hospital for these patients has dropped substantially. From Table 5 it can be seen that six of the thirty-five are financially supported by members of their family, usually a spouse, seven are earning wages, and 22 are receiving welfare payments.

Vaughn and Leff (1976) have indicated that after the first episode of a schizophrenic disorder, even among those who return to a family with a low level of expressed emotion and who take medication, the minimum relapse rate in the first 9 months after discharge from hospital is on the order of 12%. Other studies (Johnson 1974; Parkes et al. 1962) have indicated that without social support networks or with failure of patient compliance the relapse rate is nearer 60%.

Of 35 patients attending the medication clinic from 1983 to 1985, in the post clinic period six were supported financially by their families, no patient was re-admitted to the hospital as an inpatient, and the day-patient attendance totalled 195 days, i.e. a mean of 32 days per patient, at a cost of $ 203.65 per day. None of the seven patients earning wages were re-admitted to hospital, to Day Hospital, or to outpatient facilities after admission to the medication clinic. Among the group receiving payments (22) there were a total of 48 days re-admission to hospital, a mean of 2.2 days per person, and a total of 575 days of further psychiatric day-hospital attendance, a mean of 26.1 days per individual. This is substantially lower than has been found in most studies. Participation in an educational program prior to discharge which prepares them for living once more in the community is important to patients. When this is combined with a support group after discharge, which stresses the importance of medication as well as social factors, the relapse rate can be substantially lowered. Recent independent research also suggests the powerful role of social-skills training in reducing relapse (Liberman et al. 1986).

In Alberta, as in other parts of the world in general, there is increasing emphasis on providing cost-effective psychiatric care both in traditional hospital settings and in other treatment models (Sharfstein 1985; Friedman 1985). We must ensure that the drive for economic health is balanced with humane care.

References

Friedman RS (1985) Resistance to alternatives to hospitalization. Psychiatr Clin North Am 8: 471–482

Johnson DAW (1974) A study of the use of antidepressant medication in general practice. Br J Psychiatry 125: 186

Lehman AF (1983) The well-being of chronic mental patients: Assessing their quality of life. Arch Gen Psychiatry 40: 369–373

Liberman RP, Mueser KT, Wallace CJ (1986) Social skills training for schizophrenic individuals at risk for relapse. Am J Psychiatry 143: 523–526

Morgan R, Cheadle AJ (1979) Unemployment impedes resettlement. Soc Psychiatry 10: 63–67

Parkes CM, Brown GW, Monck EM (1962) The general practitioner and the schizophrenic patient. Br Med J 1: 972

Sharfstein SS (1985) Financial incentives for alternatives to hospital care. Psychiatr Clin North Am 8: 449–461

Vaughn CE, Leff JP (1976) Influence of family and social factors on the course of psychiatric illness. Br J Psychiatry 129: 125–137

Schizophrenia: Results of a Cohort Study with Respect to Cost-Accounting Problems of Patterns of Mental Health Care in Relation to Course of Illness

D. Wiersma, R. Giel, A. de Jong, and C. J. Slooff

Introduction

No drastic changes in inpatient psychiatric care like those that have taken place in the USA, Canada, the United Kingdom, and Italy have occurred in the Netherlands. The number of days spent in mental hospitals per year decreased by 11% during the early 1970s, but it has been stable since 1978. The admission rate is also constant: 3.8–3.9 per thousand of the total population (Haveman 1984). The policy of the Dutch government is nevertheless oriented towards a reduction of mental hospital beds in favour of an extension of outpatient and day care. In the next 5 years 2000 long-stay patients will be transferred to sheltered living arrangements. Further bed reduction is aimed at by preventing admission.

In this report we will present some results of our research on a cohort of new schizophrenic patients (see also Wiersma et al. 1983; de Jong et al. 1984, 1985; Giel et al. 1985). We will focus on the relationship between course of illness (psychosis) and the pattern of care during a period of 3 years from the onset of psychosis. Direct costs of mental health care according to different types of course and pattern are calculated. We will use an incidence approach to costing disease, similar to the one Andrews and his colleagues (Andrews et al. 1985) applied in their study of the economic cost of schizophrenia in New South Wales, Australia. This approach, stemming from Hartunian et al. (1980), is based on the principle that the stream of costs associated with an illness should be assigned to the year in which the stream begins. The central question is: What will new cases of disease occurring in year Y cost directly and indirectly in the long term when valued in year-Y dollars? The incidence approach is more appropriate than the prevalence approach when the aim of the exercise is to make decisions about the implementation of a treatment or research strategy. Prevalence-based costing is more relevant in case of cost control.

Finally, some problems encountered in the cost accounting of experimental alternatives of day and community care versus traditional inpatient care will be discussed.

The WHO Collaborative Study

The data come from the WHO Collaborative Study on the Assessment and Reduction of Psychiatric Disability, which was initiated in 1976 to explore the applicability, reliability and validity of a set of instruments and procedures designed to evaluate impairments and disabilities in a population of patients with potentially severe mental disorders (Jablensky et al. 1980). The aim of the study was to accumulate a cohort of consecutive new patients coming from a geographically circumscribed area and suffering from functional psychosis of a non-affective type. Screening criteria were:

- Age 15–44 years
- Residence in one of two neighbouring provinces, Groningen and Drenthe, in the north of the Netherlands, with a population of 420 136 between the ages of 15 and 44 years
- No evidence of organic brain disease (including epilepsy), severe mental retardation, severe sensory defects, or alcohol or drug dependency
- The presence of at least one of the following symptoms: hallucinations, delusions of a non-affective type, bizarre or grossly inappropriate behaviour, thought and speech disorder other than retardation or acceleration
- A recent onset of psychotic illness: i.e. not more than 24 months prior to our screening of the files of the institutions providing the cohort

The selection of cases depended on the type of institution collaborating in the study. There are four mental hospitals, six psychiatric units in general hospitals, including the university department of psychiatry, and two social psychiatric services with outpatient clinics in various locations in the two provinces. We asked the services to extract from their files all first admissions with a clinical diagnosis of schizophrenia (ICD-295), paranoid state (ICD-297) or other non-organic psychosis (ICD-298.3–9), while applying the criteria for residence and age. One of the psychiatrists of the research team went to each of the institutions to screen the case notes of the patients selected by the services. This second screening served to ascertain that the cases selected concerned first episodes of non-affective psychosis without evidence of an organic basis. Several patients selected by a social psychiatric service were also reported to us by a mental hospital following their referral; only one patient avoided admission altogether. The cases were selected from April 1978 to December 1979, during which period about 230 patients were reported to the research team. The secondary screening eventually yielded a total of 100 cases, all involving a recent onset of psychotic symptoms. The majority of excluded patients were chronic cases whose illness dated back many years. Here we report on the 82 patients who participated in the study. Men and women were almost equally represented (52% and 48%) without any evidence of an earlier onset in either six. Sixty-one percent were aged less than 25 years and 63% were still single. At the onset of their first episode of psychosis 37% held ordinary jobs, 28% were at school or university, 16% were housewives, and 19% were unemployed or had never held a job.

Indicators and Patterns of Mental Health Care

In general, actual treatment of schizophrenia by Dutch psychiatrists can be described as follows. First admission for most patients is relatively brief (less than 3 months), during which time diagnostic procedures, neuroleptic treatment and supportive therapy are prominent. Discharge is mostly followed by less frequent contacts with the social psychiatric service or with the outpatient department of the mental hospital. During this period of aftercare, medication will gradually be stopped.

A relatively small group of patients (e.g. students) is referred to a therapeutic community for long-term treatment. On such wards medication is deliberately avoided as much as possible. In case of chronic or recurrent psychosis three possibilities will emerge:

1. Admission to a long-stay department of a mental hospital or to a sheltered living accommodation
2. Intensive outpatient treatment and guidance of the patient and his family with continuation of medicatin and, if possible, finding a sheltered workplace
3. No contact with mental health care or social services at all

The reality of care given to our patients is of course much more complex. We have characterized the care and treatment actually given by means of several indicators: number of admissions, number of weeks in mental hospital, number of outpatient contacts, and percentage of time of follow-up in inpatient care and in total mental health care.

Actual care received by the patients during the course of their illness is given in Table 1. The number of admissions includes transfer from one treatment setting to another (e.g. therapeutic community), either within the same or to another hospital, because the patient has to go through a new intake procedure with rather strict criteria for admission. The mean number of 2.8 admissions per patient includes one patient (1%) who was never admitted, 26% who had one admission, 23% who had two admissions, and 50% who were admitted between three and eight times. The standard deviation from the mean reflects the large number of patients who were not readmitted repeatedly.

On average, each patient had spent 41 weeks in hospital and received 16 face-to-face outpatient contacts. Nevertheless, in the first, second and third year respec-

Table 1. Indicators of in- and outpatient care during first year and during 3 years after onset of psychoses ($n = 82$)

	During first year		Total follow-up of 3 years	
	Average no.	(SD)	Average no.	(SD)
Number of admissions	1.7	(1.0)	2.8	(1.0)
Number of weeks in hospital	16.0	(13.9)	41.2	(40.9)
Number of outpatient contacts	6.8	(13.2)	16.4	(23.7)

Table 2. Percentage of patients receiving in- or outpatient care from onset of psychosis

	(n)	%	Time in hospital				Time in outpatient care		
			None	3 months or less	3–10 months	more than 10 months	None	less than once monthly	at least once monthly
First year	(82)	100	6	48	37	9	29	58	13
Second year	(79)	100	47	16	24	13	51	25	24
Third year	(71)	100	49	17	16	18	52	32	16

tively, 6%, 47%, and 49% of the patients stayed outside the hospital. Figures from Table 2 show the tendency that after the first year a growing percentage of patients was hospitalized for longer periods.

Outpatient contacts before, during or after hospital stay vary greatly among patients, with large groups having no such contacts at all during follow-up: 22% of the patients did not receive a single face-to-face contact during the 3 years. Nine percent had an average of one contact a month (although not precisely at such an interval) during this period.

Generally, the average percentage of time in in- and/or outpatient care during 3 years was 58%. The figure for inpatient care only was 29%. This means that a large part of the cohort was not under any kind of care for considerable periods of time, which can also be illustrated in another way by the finding that every 6 months about 40% of the patients had not received any treatment for at least the preceding 4 weeks. In spite of the often chronic course of the illness, 'chronic' care will not automatically be delivered.

Besides counting days in hospital and outpatient contacts we constructed a typology of consecutive treatment periods which includes different patterns of care. Each pattern characterizes a continuous spell of care without an interruption of more than 3 months of no contact at all. Six categories or patterns of care were possible, two of which refer to more than one continuous spell of care during the 3 years. Table 3 contains the details of this typology.

Two categories are important because of the numbers of patients involved: a single spell of care characterized by several admissions and outpatient contacts (pattern IV) and two or more spells of care with a combination of in- and outpatient care (pattern VI). The main difference between the two categories lies in the continuity of care. Patients with one spell of care got twice as much inpatient care as those with two or more spells of care but the same number of outpatient contacts. Pattern V and, to a lesser extent, pattern IV point to the phenomenon of the 'revolving-door' patients with high numbers of admissions. Patients with no outpatient contacts emerge in pattern II and again in V. Each pattern of care is quite different from the others with respect to the number of admissions, weeks in hospital, outpatient contacts, and proportion of time in care.

Table 3. Patterns of mental health care and their costs per patient over a period of 3 years from onset of psychosis ($n=82$), in Dutch guilders and at 1978/1979 prices

Type of pattern	n	%	Average number of			Percentage of time in		Average costs per patient (×1000 guilders)		
			Admissions	Weeks in hospital	Outpatient contacts	Hospital	Any kind of m. h. care	Hospital care	Outpatient care	Total care
I One spell of care: outpatient only	1	1	0	0	8.0	0	14.0	0	1.3	1.3
II One spell of care: hospital only	9	11	2.3	60.8	0	41.3	42.9	72.3	0	72.3
III One spell of care: admission and outpatient care	12	15	1.0	19.9	27.2	13.0	63.4	23.7	4.4	28.1
IV One spell of care: several admissions and outpatient care	21	26	3.2	56.0	20.2	36.2	76.5	66.6	3.3	69.9
V Two or more spells of care: hospital care only	7	9	4.1	75.9	0	51.0	52.6	90.3	0	90.3
VI Two or more spells of care: hospital and outpatient care	24	29	2.9	28.0	23.2	18.1	48.9	33.3	3.8	37.1
Insufficient data	8	10	2.6	26.1	3.6	35.8	46.1	31.1	0.6	31.7

Direct Costs of Mental Health Care

Our cohort study enabled us to estimate the direct costs of mental health care. In calculating the actual costs for each individual patient we ran into problems. As patients were admitted to several psychiatric hospitals during the period of follow-up we should take into acount all the different hospital costs per diem. For example, the hospital fee for the psychiatric department of the university clinic is more than twice that of most mental hospitals. The same applies to outpatient contacts: a face-to-face contact with the social psychiatric service is much more expensive than a visit to the outpatient department. The difference has to do with the way of financing mental health care: for the latter a system of fees for each contact and for the social psychiatric service a budgetary system for all kinds of activities: face-to-face contacts, prevention, consultation, etc. (see ten Horn and Giel 1984).

By taking the average costs per day in a mental hospital in the Netherlands over the years 1978 and 1979 we came to the amount of 169.95 in Dutch guilders (about U.S. $ 57 at the rate of 3 to 1). As to the cost per face-to-face contact, we followed the calculation of ten Horn and R. Giel (1984), resulting in 162.28 guilders per contact at the outpatient department of a mental hospital (at 1978 prices; about U.S. $ 54). In our calculation of the direct health costs we did not take into account costs of medication, general health costs, visits to the general practitioner, or rate increases and inflation.

The right part of Table 3 shows that there are large differences between the various pattern. The most costly pattern was characterized by at least two spells of hospital care (pattern V). The most important patterns, IV and VI, as far as number of patients are concerned differ greatly with respect to these costs.

The average cost per patient over 3 years totals 51 556 guilders (about U.S. $ 17 000), 95% of which is chargeable to the mental hospital. We also calculated the direct costs for mental health care during the first year of the illness, which appeared to be 20 138 guilders (about U.S.$ 6700). This is much more than ten Horn and Giel (1984) found for patients with a personality disorder or a neurotic depression who were followed-up 1 year after their first contact with the mental health service by means of a psychiatric case register: 5477 and 3390 guilders respectively. This is because outpatient contacts dominate the pattern of care (42% and 65% respectively). The importance of inpatient care in case of schizophrenia can also be demonstrated in another way. The proportion of costs for outpatient contact in the national expenditures of mental health care (van der Grinten 1985) is 14%, which is nearly three times the figure in our cohort. We agree with Andrews et al. (1985) that schizophrenia is a costly disease. According to their calculations, the direct costs for new patients aged 15–44 years at onset totals (in 1975) U.S. $ 8320.- per patient in NSW, Australia, which is about $ 1600.- higher than we estimated for our patients. One reason for this difference could be the estimated standard number of days in hospital and of outpatient contacts for each category of good, medium and poor outcome. Andrew and his collaborators assume a direct relationship between course and outcome of illness and pattern of care. We will investigate our data with respect to this assumption and its consequences for costing analysis. The question is whether it matters which pattern of care a patient received.

Course and Outcome of Illness

Many follow-up studies of schizophrenia are hampered by a lack of precise dating of the onset of psychosis, including the criteria specifying the first presence of psychotic symptoms. Therefore, the comparison of patients with respect to course of illness and pattern of care was frequently dependent on the time they were seen at admission or at a follow-up contact with the psychiatrist. In the WHO Collaborative Study we took great pains to establish the date of the very first appearance of the schizophrenic psychosis on the basis of the symptomatology of sections 13–15 of the PSE (Wing et al. 1974). We followed up the patients for a period of 3 years after the outbreak of psychosis: mean number of weeks was 144 (standard deviation of 25 weeks is heavily influenced by five patients who died earlier). We classified the illness course according to the number of psychotic episodes – defined by the presence of positive signs and symptoms of delusions and/or hallucinations – and according to the situation after 3 years: complete remission, a neurotic syndrome, or a personality change. The chronic or lengthy episodes of psychoses and the suicide cases have been considered in separate categories (Table 4).

The proportions of patients with a complete (type I) or an incomplete (types II and III) remission, or a chronic course including suicide (four certain and one uncertain case of suicide; types IV and V) were about equal: 35%, 36%, and 30% respectively. Mortality of 6% during these years is a high figure. Furthermore, Table 4 gives data on total amount of time in a psychotic episode. The greater part of the cohort (71%) suffered a mean time of 16% from psychosis (i.e. 5 months) whereas the smaller part (24%) were psychotic nearly all of the time: 87%, or 2.5 years. The deceased patients (6%) hold the middle of these two groups.

Stated otherwise, the general course of schizophrenia from the beginning to the end of the third year is a chronic and sometimes fatal one: 6% died, 14% were psychotic all the time, and 47% had at least one relapse. Andrews and his col-

Table 4. Course and outcome of illness during the 3 years after onset

Type of course	No. of patients (total 82)	Percentage (total 101)	Percentage of time in psychosis ($\bar{x} = 52\%$)
I Complete remission	29	35	16
(a) After one episode	16	20	13
(b) After two or more episodes	13	15	19
II Neurotic syndrome	16	20	15
(a) After one episode	8	10	15
(b) After two or more episodes	8	10	15
III Personality change	13	16	21
(a) After one episode	3	4	16
(b) After two or more episodes	10	12	22
IV Chronic psychosis	19	24	87
(a) All the time	11	14	100
(b) Two or more lengthy episodes	8	10	69
V Deceased (suicide)	5	6	36

leagues estimated the outcome in the long run for 25% as good (only a single episode), for 40% as medium, and for 35% as poor. This is not very different from our 3-year follow-up findings, although the criteria for outcome differ greatly. Andrews et al. (1985) defined outcome categories by a standard period of time in hospital and a number of outpatient visits for the sake of simplicity of cost analysis. A good-outcome patient was defined as having only a single episode requiring, 60 days in the hospital, six subsequent visits to the physician, medication for 6 months, 6 months out of work because of illness, and no further disability. A medium-outcome patient was defined as requiring close to the overall average admissions per year (i.e. 135 days), six physician visits per year, continuous medication for the rest of the patient's life, and being in the work force for only 4 months each subsequent year. A poor-outcome patient was defined as needing about twice the overall average admissions to the hospital per year, never being able to work, and requiring monthly physician visits and continuous medication when out of hospital.

We will now turn to the question of whether patients with a good outcome received different patterns of care than those with a poor outcome. In Table 5 patterns of care are ordered from average low to high costs in connection with the main types of course of illness.

The relationship between patterns of care and type of course appears to be rather weak and not statistically significant. Patients with each type of course show up in any category or pattern of care. It is therefore difficult to establish the

Table 5. Patterns of care in relation to types of course of illness, in absolute numbers of patients, and average cost per patient ($\times 1000$) in Dutch guilders and at 1978/1979 prices

Patterns of care	Type of course of illness					Average Cost per patient ($\times 1000$)
	I Complete remission	II Neurotic syndrome	III Person-ality change	IV Chronic psychosis	V Deceased (suicide)	
I One spell of care: outpatient care only	–	1	–	–	–	1.3
III One spell of care: one admission and outpatient care	3	3	1	4	1	28.1
Insufficient data	4	1	1	1	1	31.7
VI Two or more spells of care: in- and outpatient care	10	4	4	5	1	37.1
IV One spell of care: several admission and outpatient care	6	2	7	5	1	69.9
II One spell of care: inpatient care only	4	3	–	2	–	72.3
V Two or more spells of care: inpatient care only	2	2	–	2	1	90.3
Average cost per patient ($\times 1000$)	32.9	55.1	65.6	72.2	38.8	51.6

effectiveness of the most costly pattern (V), characterized by at least two spells of inpatient care, because two of the seven patients with such patterns of care had a complete remission, another two patients had a neurotic syndrome, and the remaining three were chronic patients. The same difficulty applies to one of the cheapest patterns of two or more spells of care with a combination of in- and outpatient care (VI): of the 24 patients with such a pattern, ten had a complete remission, four a neurotic syndrome, four a personality change, and six a chronic or fatal course.

With respect to the various types of courses of schizophrenic illness, it is evident that a chronic psychosis (type IV) is the most expensive one, costs being more than twice the costs of type I, complete remission: 72202.- guilders vs. 32845.- guilders over 3 years. However, a remarkable finding is the wide range of average number of admissions, weeks in hospital, and outpatient contacts between patients with or without a relapse in the same main type of course, which is reflected in costs of mental health care. For example, a patient with a neurotic syndrome after at least one relapse (type IIb) ranked highest with a total of 81398.- guilders and a patient with a neurotic syndrome withouth a relapse (type IIa) ranked lowest at 25886.- guildes.

Finally, our incidence-based approach to costing showed to complex relationship between course of illness and pattern of care. It is very difficult to discern the better alternatives. It is in any case premature to draw conclusions about outcome of illness from particular patterns of mental health care. One might wonder about the central role of the mental hospital. The basic question facing new research in the Netherlands will be whether day treatment and strengthening of outpatient care could be a cheaper and/or more effective alternative to inpatient treatment.

Discussion

A study of a cohort of patients with a first episode of schizophrenia or other non-affective functional psychosis enabled us to compare patterns of mental health care and types of course of illness. The results showed that our characterization of patterns of care was not related to the outcome of the illness 3 years after onset. Nevertheless, it appeared that patients with a personality change or chronic psychosis on average spent more days in hospital and had more face-to-face contacts, resulting in higher direct costs than those for patients with a complete remission or a neurotic syndrome. But results differed greatly within subgroups of patients. Therefore, the validity of patterns of care based on quantitative criteria of consecutive spells of inpatient and/or outpatient care without periods of 3 months or more of no contact at all is rather questionable. It seems necessary to somehow include qualitative aspects of care. Our findings suggest that a quantitative approach to costing analysis like that of Andrews and his colleagues might not be realistic. An assessment of relative effectiveness of patterns of care is currently not feasible. Whether day treatment and community care lead to better psychosocial functioning of patients and less costs to the community will have to be decided by new research in the Netherlands. The essential features of a so-called substitution project are:

- The development of appropriate treatment strategies for patients who would otherwise have been admitted full time for several weeks (excluding patients with senile dementia for whom day-care facilities already exist)
- A close cooperation between hospital staff, the outpatient department of the hospital, and the social psychiatric service in order to garantee continuity of care at night and on the weekends at home
- An evaluation of this process of organizational change from beds to chairs and of the cost-effectiveness of such an approach

Part of this project is a clinical trial consisting of a random assignment of patients to the experimental condition of day treatment with continuous outpatient care in the community and to the usual inpatient care (cf. Herz et al. 1971; Hoult et al. 1983; Stein and Test 1980). The study is aimed at an investigation of patients in both the experimental group and the control group for a period of at least 2 years after admission in order to establish the course of the patient's psychiatric illness, state of remission, the change in psychosocial functioning, and constraints on the family. All patients will be monitored by a psychiatric case register following their career through mental health care facilities. With respect to the economic aspects, much attention will be paid to direct and indirect costs of both treatment procedures. Cash flows caused by the patient's illness will be analyzed from the viewpoint of the patient and his family, as well as from the viewpoint of the rest of the community (Goldberg 1985). The assessment of level and quality of care in both conditions includes a close surveillance of actual treatment and guidance procedures with respect to time spent by the professional staff on help with basic activities of washing, going to the toilet, etc.; on supervision and guidance; on therapeutic activities; on contact with the family; on staff meetings, consultation with outside helpers, and so on. In addition to a quantitative assessment of the supply of services, attention will be drawn to some qualitative aspects of care: to what extent is day care considered a less than optimal alternative? does lack of compliance on the part of the patient and/or his family occur more frequently than usual? Are patients satisfied with the kind and availability of care? Can the emotional burden on the family be minimized or avoided altogether? Is more help from other resources required, e.g. the general practitioner, the social work services, the police?

It is difficult to predict in advance which component in the new program could be held responsible for differences in outcome with respect to chronicity and disablement. Various possibilities could be mentioned: staying in the social network; better cooperation of clinical staff and social psychiatric service; less drop-out from treatment; longer continuation of day treatment than hospital treatment; more compliance to drug treatment; attitudinal change of professionals in being more motivated to treatment of patients.

It may be that no difference will be found. The reason for this might be that high expectations generated by the new project also affect other professional workers in and outside the mental hospital and lead to a general change in attitude to ward patients: e.g. getting them discharged earlier than usual and/or being more attentive to their needs before actual admission.

Apart from outcome, the basic issue is whether a reorganization of mental

health care which links in- and outpatient services, day and community care closely to each other is feasible at the same or a preferably higher level of quality of
care and at the same or a preferably lower level of costs.

References

Andrews G, Hal W, Goldstein G, Lapsley H, Bartels R, Silove D (1985) The economic costs of
    schizophrenia. Arch Gen Psychiatry 42: 537–543
Giel R, Sauer HC, Slooff CJ, Wiersma D (1980) Over de epidemiologie van functionele psychos-
    en en invaliditeit. Tijdschr Psychiatrie 11/12: 710–722
Giel R, de Jong A, Slooff CJ, Wiersma D (1985) Social disability and chronic mental disorder. In:
    Helgason T (ed) The long-term treatment of functional psychoses. Cambridge University Press,
    Cambridge
Glass NJ, Goldberg D (1977) Cost-benefit analysis and the evaluation of psychiatric services. Psy-
    chol Med 7: 701–707
Goldberg D (1985) Cost-effective analysis. In: Helgason T (ed) The long-term treatment of func-
    tional psychoses. Cambridge University Press, Cambridge
Grinten TED van der (1985) Mental health care in the Netherlands. In: Mangen SP (ed) Mental
    health care in the European Community. Croom Helm, London, pp 208–227
Hartunian NS, Smart CN, Thompson MS (1980) The incidence and economic costs of major
    health impairments: a comparative analysis of cancer, motor-vehicle injuries, heart disease and
    stroke. Lexington Books, Lexington
Haveman MJ (1984) De-institutionalisering van de intramurale psychiatrische zorg. Tijdschr Soc
    Gezondheidszorg 18: 698–706
Herz MI, Endicott J, Spitzer RL (1971) Day versus inpatient hospitalization: a controlled study.
    Am J Psychiatry 127: 1371–1382
Horn GHMM ten, Giel R (1984) The feasibility of cost-benefit studies of mental health care. Acta
    Psychiatr Scand 69: 80–87
Hoult J, Reynolds I, Charbonneau-Powis M, Weekes P, Briggs J (1983) Psychiatric hospital versus
    community treatment. The results of a randomised trial. Aust NZ J Psychiatry 17: 160–167
Jablensky A, Schwarz R, Tomov T (1980) WHO collaborative study on impairments and disabili-
    ties associated with schizophrenic disorders. A preliminary communication: objectives and
    methods. Acta Psychiatr Scand [Suppl] 285
Jong A de, Giel R, Slooff CJ, Wiersma D (1984) Foulds' hierarchical model of psychiatric illness
    in a Dutch cohort. Psychol Med 14: 647–654
Jong A de, Giel R, Slooff CJ, Wiersma D (1985) Social disability and outcome in schizophrenic
    patients. Br J Psychiatry 147: 631–636
Platt S, Weyman A, Hirsch S et al. (1980) The social behaviour assessment schedule (SBAS): ra-
    tionale, contents, scoring and reliability of a new interview schedule. Soc Psychiatry 15: 43–55
Stein LI, Test MA (1980) Alternative to mental hospital treatment. Arch Gen Psychiatry 37:
    392–397
Wiersma D, Giel R, de Jong A, Slooff CJ (1983) Social class and schizophrenia in a Dutch cohort.
    Psychol Med 13: 141–150
Wiersma D, Giel R, de Jong A, Slooff CJ (1984) Chroniciteit bij functionele psychosen. Tijdschr
    Psychiatrie 26: 402–419
Wiersma D (1986) Psychological impairments and social disabilities: on the applicability of the
    International Classification of Impairments, Disabilities and Handicaps to psychiatry. Int Re-
    habil Med 8: 3–7
Wing JK, Cooper JE, Sartorius N (1974) Measurement and classification of psychiatric symp-
    toms. Cambridge University Press, Cambridge
World Health Organization (1976) Cost-benefit analysis in mental health services. Report on a
    working group, The Hague, 21–25 June. WHO Regional Offices for Europe, Copenhagen
World Health Organization (1980) International classification on impairments, disabilities and
    handicaps. WHO, Geneva

Cost-Effectiveness
of Managing Chronic Psychotic Patients:
Italian Experience Under the New Psychiatric Law

A. Marinoni, M. Grassi, D. Ebbli, A. Brenna, S. Silva, and E. Torre

Introduction

Since the 1970s a profound renovation has taken place in the modalities of psychiatric care in Italy; however, not much is known about the practical consequences these changes will have on the patients, on the health care services, and on the families of those being treated. Very few evaluative studies have been carried out in our country, and practically none of them have taken the economic aspects into consideration. For this reason we felt it would be useful to do a study that would evaluate the treatment costs for certain psychiatric patient groups, from both an economic and a social point of view. In particular, we wanted to ascertain the "burden" that these psychiatric patients represent for the public services and for their families in relation to the severity of their illness, their degree of physical and psychological autotonomy, and the way in which they utilize the health care services.

Since this kind of a cost-effective evaluation is only possible in a relative sense, we identified two groups of psychiatric service utilizers, both of which consisted of patients diagnosed as psychotic. In fact, from our previous research we found that psychotic patients, with respect to their history of contacts with the public services, fall into (a) a high-user group, characterized by frequent contacts over a with the psychiatric services long period of time, and (b) a "dropped-out-of-sight" group, composed of patients who disappear after having been in contact with the services for a variable period of time. On the basis of these observations we felt it was important to investigate both groups for the possible implications this difference might have on both monetary and nonmonetary costs.

Since we had at our disposal several care services that had organized a psychiatric case register, we decided to use one where the personnel declared they were willing to cooperate with the study and where the administrators supplied part of the funds necessary for the research. The service center chosen was Local Health Care Unit (USL) No. 4 Albenganese in Liguria.

Catchment Area and Services

The area studied was that served by USL No. 4 in the northwestern Italian region of Liguria, known as Albenganese. This area consists of 20 communities, five of which are on the coast and contain more than four fifths of the inhabitants; the remaining 15 are situated inland, mostly on the hillsides. Table 1 summarizes the principal sociodemographic characteristics of the population.

We wish to emphasize that the net increase in population registered in the 1981 census is the result of a positive migration balance, while the natural population balance (births vs deaths) has been negative since 1976.

With respect to national statistics, the population of Albenganese is relatively young and has a larger number of active members. More than 60% of the active population is involved in business, vegetable farming, and tourism.

The psychiatric care services in this area are limited to the territorial service, located in the central part of the city of Albenga. This center began its activity in May 1980 in the context of a radical transformation in the Mental Health Center of the province of Savona, which (in compliance with Law 180 regarding psychiatric care reform) was completely decentralized into four independent Territorial Services, corresponding to the province's four Local Health Units. The center is open every week day and is staffed by a team composed of four psychiatrists, two psychologists, two social workers, six nurses, and a secretary.

Psychiatric hospital care is supplied by the General Hospital of Savona, where a 15-bed Psychiatric Service for Diagnosis and Treatment has been operating since July 1978; patients from all parts of the province of Savona come to this hospital, which serves almost 300000 people. The hospital of Savona is about 45 km from Albenga.

The psychiatric hospital to which patients from this area are referred is in Cogoleto, 70 km from Albenga. At the present time it has been turned into a health care headquarters. This headquarters accepts all service utilizers from the province of Savona. Assistance is provided by a team of doctors and nurses and consists ecxlusively of inpatient care. Readmission of patients is still possible, but only if they are ex-patients from this hospital, and only under particular circumstances.

Table 1. Sociodemographic characteristics of the USL no. 4 Albenganese (census 1981)

Total population	56022
Inhabitants per km^2	185
Male/female ratio	0.92
% aged 0–14 years	16.38
% over 65 years	18.27
% economically active (aged over 15 years)	50.4
Occupation:	
% in agriculture	17.7
% in manufacturing	20.7
% in trade and services	61.5

General Organization of the Service

The service has a single office in Albenga. Work begins every morning with a meeting of all the personnel. The first order of business is the calls and requests for appointments that the secretary received the day before. The actions to be taken in cases that require attention during the course of the day are decided, and the appointment schedule is checked. Then the day's activities are organized, the staff agreeing on the use of the rooms for patient interviews, on the use of the cars for home visits, and on the assignement of new cases. Finally, each member of the team informs the group about his/her appointments and other activities the previous day. This part of the meeting has expanded with the increase in the number of cases handled. An attempt has been made to have each person be as concise as possible in his/her presentation without leaving out anything important. Despite this problem, everyone considers the morning meeting the primary working tool and one of the most important characteristics of the service. No appointments are made before 10 a.m., except in unusual cases.

As far as clinical activities are concerned, home visits and outside consultations are mostly taken care of during the morning, while the afternoon is reserved mainly for office patients.

The Psychiatric Case Register

Since July 1, 1980, a record of patients using the service and of the therapeutic measures taken by the staff has been kept at the Territorial Psychiatric Service; it is modeled after the "Psychiatric Case Register" used at Camberwell (Wing et al. 1968) and after those of Lomest (Pavia) and Genoa in Italy (Torre et al. 1977; Marinoni et al. 1981).

A comparison between the data from the Lomest and Albenganese Psychiatric Case Registers was first made in 1982 (Torre et al. 1982). This methodological tool has the following essential features:

- It is a collection of data from all the public psychiatric agencies utilized by the service patients in the area
- It is based on a well-defined population, which in our case is represented by the residents of the area
- It is cumulative, in the sense that it permits the patient contacts with the service to be updated over time

Most of all, these aspects enable us to avoid duplications of data since no patient is counted more than once, even if he/she has had contacts with more than one agency; furthermore, they make it possible to calculate the rates of contact for the entire population of service utilizers, and finally, they point out any changes over time in the relationship between service and utilizers.

Among the limits this form of registration possesses, it should be remembered that, on the one hand, it does not take the mobility of the population into account, and, on the other, it is restricted by the lack of data from other health care agencies that furnish psychiatric help (private specialists, hospital and territorial general medicine facilities, etc.).

It is believed (Wing et al. 1972; Marinoni et al. 1978) that the usefulness of the Psychiatric Case Register in evaluating the psychiatric services lies fundamentally in these features:

- It permits collection of systematic descriptive statistics.
- It constitutes a base for collecting other information that can be of use in specific research projects.
- It offers a proper sample for more complex and intense studies whose results can be generalized.
- It represents a starting point for comparative studies with different population groups.

The diagnoses for the Albenganese Psychiatric Case Register, like those of the others cited earlier, are formulated by a psychiatrist in accordance with the terminology used in "A Glossary of Mental Disorders" (Her Majesty's Stationary Office 1968), which is based on the eighth revision of the International Classification of Diseases, Accidents and Causes of Death.

On the basis of the data from the Psychiatric Case Register it was possible to calculate the prevalence rates of the service utilizers from 1981 to 1984 (Table 2).

Table 2. One-year prevalence (rate per 100000) of the patients in contact with the Mental Health Services of the USL no. 4 (Albenga, Italy) by sex, year, and type of contact

Type of contact	1981						1982					
	M		F		T		M		F		T	
	n	Rate	n	R	n	R	n	R	n	R	n	R
A	19	85.4	11	44.67	30	64.03	20	89.9	11	44.67	31	66.17
B	21	94.4	17	69.07	38	81.11	16	72.0	21	85.9	37	78.98
C	14	63.0	11	44.67	25	53.3	15	67.4	9	36.5	24	51.23
D	32	143.9	36	146.2	68	145.1	48	215.8	73	296.4	121	258.2
Total	86	386.7	75	304.6	161	343.6	99	445.2	114	463.0	213	454.6

Type of contact	1983						1984					
	M		F		T		M		F		T	
	n	Rate	n	R	n	R	n	R	n	R	n	R
A	8	80.9	6	24.3	24	51.23	18	80.9	7	28.4	25	53.3
B	26	116.9	20	81.2	46	98.19	16	72.0	17	69.0	33	70.4
C	21	94.4	25	101.5	46	98.19	30	134.9	27	109.6	57	121.6
D	44	197.8	62	251.8	106	226.2	40	179.9	72	292.4	112	239.0
Total	109	490.2	113	458.9	222	473.8	104	467.7	123	499.5	227	484.5

A, Inpatients on December 31 of previous year; B, not A, but admitted during the year; C, not A or B, outpatients on December 31 of previous year; D, not A, B, C, but outpatient contact during the year; F, female; M, male; T, total

The psychiatric service utilizers are subdivided into two groups of hospital patients (A and B) and two outpatients groups (C and D).

Aims of the Research

The aim of this study is to evaluate the costs and the benefits of health care for the chronic psychotic patients who utilize or have utilized the mental health service.

The specific objectives we proposed for ourselves can be summarized in the following questions:

1. Are the monetary costs borne by the public services different for the two patient groups being considered, i.e., chronic psychotics in contact with the mental health service and chronic psychotics no longer in contact?
2. Are the monetary and nonmonetary costs which the presence of these patients involves for their families different?
3. Is there a relationship between the two patient groups and the quality of physical, psychic, and social life of these patients?

Methodology of the Study

In order to accomplish the proposed objectives, it was necessary to carry out an ad hoc investigation. A cohort study was used for this purpose: a historical cohort based on information available in the psychiatric Case Register, and a follow-up of patients which terminates with an interview using a questionnaire at least 3 years after the patient's first contact with the service. In addition to the patient, a family member or a close acquaintance who is familiar with the patient's life style (informant) is also interviewed.

The Cohort

The cohort consisted of all patients who made contact with the service for the first time in 1981 or 1982 (Table 3), who ranged in age from 21 to 64 years old, and

Table 3. Patients on the register by sex, diagnosis, and age (1981–1982)

Diagnosis	Men – age-group				Women – age-group				Total			Total
	20–44	45–64	65+	Total	20–44	45–64	65+	Total	20–44	45–64	65+	
Schizophrenia	19	14	3	36	18	14	5	37	37	28	8	73
Affective psychosis	5	5	2	12	4	10	4	18	9	15	6	30
Neurosis	13	5	1	19	24	18	5	47	37	23	6	66
Other	21	5	7	33	8	9	4	21	29	14	11	54
Total	58	29	13	100	54	51	18	123	112	80	31	223

who had a diagnosis of schizophrenia (ICD VIII: 295) or paranoid syndrome (ICD VIII: 297); the psychiatric case register supplied the sampling frame.

Sixty-one patients satisfied the criteria for admission to the study; of these, 30 had a previous psychiatric history, in that they had been admitted to a mental hospital, while 31 had no history of institutionalization or of any contact with public psychiatric services. On the basis of information contained in the psychiatric case register it was possible to divide the 61 patients into two groups: those who could be considered "under care" by the service at the beginning of the study (January 1, 1985), in that they had had at least one contact with it during 1984 (38 patients), and those who could be considered "dropped out of sight" on January 1, 1985, in that they had had no contact with the service during 1984 (23 patients; see Fig. 1).

Modality of Data Collection

The questionnaires were filled out and the interviews conducted by a physician specializing in psychiatry and a social worker with psychiatric training; neither worked for the service, and both were hired and hoc for this research project. In order to locate and get in touch with the patients we used the collaboration of all the Territorial Psychiatric Service personnel in the area.

In choosing the informant we tried to identify the person 'closest' to the patient, the one most knowledgeable of the patient's problems, present and past. For some of the cases this was not possible, so we fell back on the most accessible person. For the most part, the choice of the informant was made on the basis of indications provided by the personnel at the service; in very few cases was it made on the indications of the patient.

When contacting the "dropped-out-of-sight" patients and their respective informants, the decision was made case by case whether to communicate directly by mail, making an appointment to see the person at home, or whether to seek the mediation of the attending physician or the Psychiatric Service operator who had followed up the patient at the time.

An effort was made, whenever possible, not to allow any time lapse between the interview with the patient and that with the informant. In only one case did we receive indirect information supplied by the family doctor or other sources. We encountered only one explicit refusal to cooperate on the part of the patient and one on the part of a patient's family. No great difficulties were encountered in administering the questionnaire to the patients, even in the most severe cases. There were some problems in many of the interviews with the informants concerning the questions relating to economic matters. These stemmed both from a general resistance to reveal one's own financial situation and from the objective difficulty in itemizing the family budget into the various entries requested by the questionnaire.

The average length of the interview was about 1 h for the patient and about the same for the informant, with variations ranging from 45 min to 2 h.

There were some difficulties in locating certain "dropped-out-of-sight" patients because they had moved; other problems were also encountered because of the psychopathological conditions of certain patients, as a result of which, although there was no explicit refusal, it was very difficult to carry out the interview.

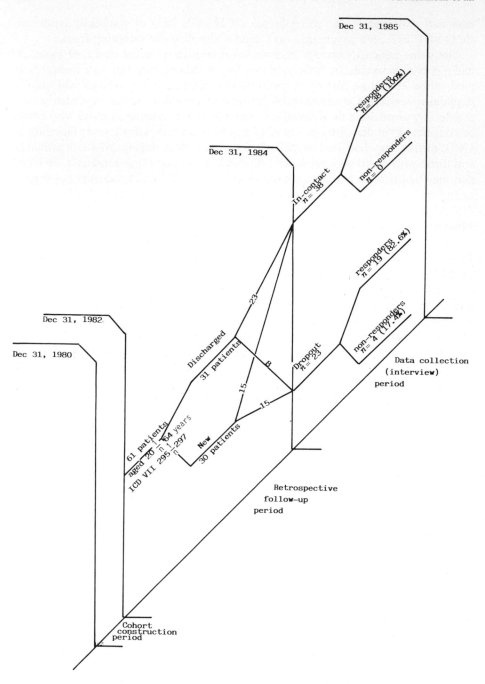

Fig. 1. Pathway of the research: three periods of patients' follow-up: entering period and retrospective and interview period

Variables Collected

The variables collected concern different aspects of the patient and of the context in which he/she lives:

1. Patient's general background – this includes information such as age, sex, marital status, place of birth, occupation, with whom he/she lives, etc.
2. Psychiatric care background – these variables are concerned with the health-care history of the patient: psychiatric records, diagnosis, how and why the first contact was made, type of treatment, number of hospital and office contacts, length of hospital stays during the last year of the follow-up, the Service operators' opinion about the prognosis of the patient at the first contact. The source for these variables is the case register, rounded out by an interview with the Service personnel who treated the patient at the time of the first contact.
3. Patient's quality of health and of life at the time of the interview – the areas investigated here cover behavior, mood, physical and mental health, social performance, stressful events occurring in the past 3 months, and the patient's opinion about the health care services (Questionnaire Group A).
4. Variables regarding the interviewer's opinion of the behavior, affectivity, and language of the patient during the interview; monetary costs, defined as goods consumed or earnings lost through failure to use alternative resources; non-monetary costs, i.e., inconveniences caused to the family by the presence of the patient (Questionnaire Group B).

From an operational point of view, the cost elements were identified according to the following outline:

- Institutional and macroeconomic costs: these are the costs documented by routine administrative data (USL budgets, etc.)
- Living costs: these are costs for the patient's family, calculated from the questionnaire the informant was given in order to investigate the expenses incurred by the family in maintaining the patient in their home
- Social costs: those expenses incurred by society in maintaining the patient (help for household tasks, social support, etc.)
- Benefits the family derives from the patient's presence, whether monetary or non-monetary.

Methodology for Cost Evaluation

Cost evaluation was formulated in such a way as to be as comprehensive as possible. For this reason costs were classified on the one hand as monetary or non-monetary, according to their ability to be expressed in terms of money, and on the other hand as private or social, according to the party that in effect bore the burden, namely the family for the former costs and all the other possible parties for the latter. This double classification is briefly summarized in Table 4. Obviously some nonmonetary burdens, those not having an immediate monetary worth, are

Table 4. Double classification of costs

	Private costs	Social costs	Total costs
Monetary	Expenses borne by the family	Expenses borne by third parties	Total expenses borne by anyone
Nonmonetary	Nonmonetary burdens borne by the family	nonmonetary burdens borne by third parties	Total nonmonetary burdens borne by anyone
Total	Total burden, monetary and nonmonetary, borne by the family	Total burden, monetary and nonmonetary, borne by third parties	General total

monetizable, i.e., they can be converted into monetary value. Nevertheless, we did not attempt, at least at first, to quantify burdens of this nature with a monetary yardstick because they were so disparate: instead we chose to list them in numerical order. For example, such burdens are represented by the daily number of work hours the family dedicates to the patient (non-monetary costs for the family) or by the services provided by third parties such as social and health-care operators (non-monetary burdens for society).

Only in the final paragraph did we attempt to give a monetary evaulation to these burdens – an evaluation which should, however, be taken with the necessary caution.

Table 4 does not require any particular comments since the meaning of the various cost categories listed there is sufficiently clear. However, once again we feel it necessary to point out that one of the biggest problems encountered on the empirical level is the possible duplication of costs, especially given the diverse sources from which the data are derived. For a more detailed analysis, see the Appendix.

Methods of Statistical Analysis

Preliminary data analysis consisted of examination of the univariate frequency distributions of the collected variables within the two groups of patients (dropout/in contact).

The aim of descriptive analysis is to show some evidence, if any, of different costs and benefits of management for the patients in contact with the mental health services and those no longer in contact, by summarizing the variables related to monetary costs borne by the public service and by the family and the variables related to physical, psychic, and social life of the two groups of patients. Given the fact that the number of cases in the data matrix is small while the variables are numerous and, moreover, many items in the questionnaire have possible substantive meaning only if considered in association with others, it is useful to reduce the number of variables to summary indices with social or psychiatric meanings of their own.

For this purpose, we performed as a scaling method, the multiple correspondence analysis (Greenacre 1984) on each set of items relative to different aspects of the patient's situation.

The aim is to arrange the categories of a set of nominal variables in the best possible order according to the individuals which they exhibit. This allows transformation of the pattern of the attributes of each variable to continuous scales, and often the continuum obtained represents a meaningful index that discriminates between subjects. The technique is often used (Lebart et al. 1984) to provide a descriptive, graphic representation in two or three principal axes of the joint two-way relationship between categorical data. It can also be shown (Greenacre 1984, Chap. 4) that the coordinates with respect to the first axis of the categories assign scale values (called optimal weights) in order to obtain for each individual a new measure (called optimal score); i. e., the optimal score for a subject can be calculated as the average of the optimal weights of these modalities of the subject's character.

The weights and the scores (or the coordinates with respect to the principal axis) maximize (minimize) various criterian: Guttman's correlation ratio, Cronbach's reliability index, weighted least-squares approximation.

The output follow-up variable is dichotomous, and the logistic regression model (McCullagh and Nelder 1983) is an appropriate method for determining the effect of a stimulus variable, adjusted for potential confounding effects attributed to other regressours. Though the logistic model allows the inclusion of both continuous and categorical explanatory variables, together with interactions of various orders, the method has potential drawbacks if the number of the regression parameters is large relative to the number of cases.

We therefore used logistic regression to estimate associations between dropout/in-contact output and a set of few variables and principal axes obtained from the data-reduction phase.

To select the final model we followed an interactive procedure. Preliminary-variable screening was carried out using 'all-subsets' discriminant analysis (see Brenn and Arnesen 1985 for discussion of alternative methods) and, in a following step, the interaction terms in the few subsets identified during the previous phase were examined.

Marginal and conditional likelihood tests (Benedetti and Brown 1978) were performed in order to select a concise interaction logit model that fits the chosen set of data satisfactorily. These statistics indicate the order of magnitude of the change in "deviance" when the effect term is either entered (marginal test) or deleted (conditional test) from "base models."

In addition, in the final model, the regressor (stimulus) effects are expressed in odds ratio terms. To help visualize and check the meaning of the continuous regressors, partial residual plots (Landwehar et al. 1984) are also reported.

Statistical computing was performed using the packages SPAD (Lebart et al. 1985) and GLIM (Baker and Nelder 1978).

Results

The results are subdivided into two parts: the first part concerns the descriptive analysis of the data, and the second part deals with the multivariate data analysis.

Descriptive Analysis

Tables of the preliminary descriptive analysis should be interpreted with great caution. Because of the large number of variables and the small sample size, one should not rush to definite conclusions; the results are useful as an aid in interpreting and discussing the output of the successive multivariate analysis.

Demographic and Personal Information and Psychiatric Assistance Variables

Table 5 presents the distribution of the personal and demographic characteristics of the patients studied; the data are divided according to the status of the patients at the end of the follow-up period i.e., either in contact or dropped out of sight. Both sexes are equally represented, with a slightly greater number of women found in the group still in contact and slightly more men in the dropped-out-of-sight group.

The mean age is 46 years and is slightly higher in the dropped-out-of-sight subjects. Immigrants, those persons born outside the Liguria region (for the most part in Southern Italy), make up 42.1% of the patient population, while in the general Italian population between the ages of 20 and 65 years immigrants represent only 33%. This confirms a possible association between immigration and psychosis.

Table 5. Distribution of sociodemographic characteristics within the two groups of patients at the first contact

Characteristics	In-contact ($n=38$)		Dropout ($n=19$)		Total ($n=57$)	
Sex						
Male	16	(42.1)	11	(57.9)	27	(47.4)
Female	22	(57.9)	8	(42.1)	30	(52.6)
M/F	0.72		1.36		0.90	
Birthplace						
Native in Liguria	23	(60.5)	10	(52.6)	33	(57.9)
Immigrant to Liguria	15	(39.5)	9	(47.4)	24	(42.1)
Marital Status						
Married	26	(68.4)	9	(47.4)	35	(61.4)
Not married	6	(15.8)	7	(36.8)	13	(22.8)
Widow or divorced	6	(15.8)	3	(15.8)	9	(15.8)
Age						
Average	45.42		48.47		46.08	
Standard deviation	10.80		12.46		10.11	
Living arrangement						
Alone	6	(15.8)	5	(26.3)	11	(19.3)
In family	26	(68.4)	8	(42.1)	34	(59.6)
With relatives	3	(7.9)	1	(5.3)	4	(7.0)
In institution	3	(7.9)	5	(26.3)	8	(14.0)
Occupational status						
Employed	7	(18.4)	5	(26.3)	12	(21.1)
Unemployed	6	(15.8)	8	(42.1)	14	(24.6)
Retired	25	(65.8)	6	(31.6)	31	(54.4)

Sixty-one percent of patients were married, with the still-in-contact group having a higher percentage of conjugal partners. Almost 60% (59.6%) of the patients lived with their families, either the original family or an acquired family: for the in-contact group this figure rises to 68.4%, while among the dropped-out-of-sight group there are more "anomalous" situations, i.e., persons living alone, in institutions, or with relatives.

The distribution of the occupational status is interesting. It is the only variable distributed in significantly different ways in the two groups ($\chi^2 = 6.672$; $P < 0.05$): there is a majority of retired people among the still in contact patients, while employed or unemployed subjects prevail in the dropped-out-of-sight group. It should be stressed that since these are patients under 65 years of age, the retirement referred to here is an early retirement. Table 6 summarizes the distribution of the psychiatric-assistance variables regarding the ways in which the subjects came to have their first contact with the psychiatric service.

About half (52.6%) of the patients had a history of mental hospital experience, the percentage being higher (60.5%) among those still in contact. Examination of

Table 6. Distribution of psychiatric assistance characteristics within the two groups of patients

Variables	In-contact ($n = 38$)		Dropout ($n = 19$)		Total ($n = 57$)	
Past psychiatric history						
Hospitalized	23	(60.5)	7	(36.8)	30	(52.6)
Not hospitalized	15	(39.5)	12	(63.2)	27	(47.4)
Channel of referral						
Patient	2	(5.3)	1	(5.3)	3	(5.3)
Relative	9	(23.7)	2	(10.5)	11	(19.3)
Family doctor	5	(13.2)	2	(10.5)	7	(12.3)
Social service	12	(31.6)	8	(42.1)	20	(35.1)
GHPU[a]	6	(15.8)	3	(15.8)	9	(15.8)
Police	1	(2.6)	2	(10.5)	3	(5.3)
Other	3	(7.9)	1	(5.3)	4	(7.0)
Motivation						
Request for admission to hospital	1	(2.6)	2	(10.5)	3	(5.3)
Request for treatment	15	(39.5)	6	(31.6)	21	(36.8)
Aggressive behavior	5	(13.2)	5	(26.3)	10	(17.5)
Consultation	1	(2.6)	1	(5.3)	2	(3.5)
Social assistance	16	(42.1)	5	(26.3)	21	(36.8)
Main treatment						
Pharmacological-psychotherapeutic	3	(7.9)	4	(21.1)	7	(12.3)
Pharmacological-rehabilitative	34	(89.5)	11	(57.9)	45	(78.7)
Social assistance	1	(2.6)	4	(21.1)	5	(8.8)
Prognostic opinion of psychiatric operators						
Favorable	15	(39.5)	5	(26.3)	20	(35.1)
Unfavorable	23	(60.5)	14	(73.7)	37	(64.9)

[a] General hospital psychiatric unit

the ways in which the patients arrived at the psychiatric service shows that the main channel was through the social services (35.1%); about one quarter either came spontaneously or were brought by relatives. Fifteen percent came to the service following a period in the psychiatric unit of a general hospital.

The only noticeable differences between the two groups, even though they are not statistically significant, are that more patients in the still-in-contact group were brought to the attention of the service through their relatives and more in the dropped-out-of-sight group through the social services.

The most frequent motivation for the first contact with the service was the request for treatment, followed by the request for social assistance (financial aid, work, etc.). Not to be overlooked was the number of requests for intervention motivated by aggressive behavior on the part of the patient (17%).

Two-thirds of the patients were given a pharmacological rehabilitative-type treatment by the service; 8.8% received social-supportive assistance.

The distribution of these types of help is significantly different between the two patient groups ($\chi^2 = 8.283$; $P < 0.01$), in the sense that the pharmacological-rehabilitative treatment was proportionately higher for the still-in-contact patients than for those who had dropped out of sight, while the latter group had a higher percentage of social-supportive interventions.

The psychiatric service operators expressed an unfavorable prognosis in 65% of the in-contact cases; this was higher in the dropped-out-of-sight group (73.7%).

Life Events During Last 3 Months Before the Interview

During the follow-up period, 26% of the patients suffered an organic illness (Table 7). Thirty-seven percent of the subjects declared they had experienced stressful events in the past 3 months; this percentage was not homogeneous throughout both groups but was significantly ($\chi^2 = 8.534$; $P < 0.01$) higher among those still in contact. An analysis of the type of life events described shows that the most frequent problems were related to the health of family members or were of an economic nature. There was a high percentage of unexpected events and setbacks (Table 8).

Behavioral, Mood, and Social Performance Disturbances

In both groups, varying percentages of the patients answered positive to the items concerned with behavioral and mood disturbances (Table 9), with lower percent-

Table 7. Distribution of life events within the two groups of patients in the last 3 months before the interview

Variables	In-contact ($n = 38$)		Dropout ($n = 19$)		Total ($n = 57$)	
Organic diseases						
Yes	11	(28.9)	4	(21.1)	15	(26.3)
No	27	(71.1)	15	(78.9)	42	(73.7)
Life events (number)						
None	19	(50.0)	17	(89.5)	36	(63.2)
One	12	(31.6)	1	(5.3)	13	(22.8)
Two or more	7	(18.4)	1	(5.3)	8	(14.0)

ages concerning the items regarding intrapersonal relationships and higher percentages for those exploring the perception of anxious and depressive symptomatology. A comparison of the two patient groups shows that those still in contact gave an overall higher number of positive responses. The percentage difference is higher especially in the questions that indicate a depressive state (fear, sadness, etc.); furthermore, the positive responses in the dropped-out-of-sight group were higher for those questions that explored harsh and violent behavior toward others.

We wish to emphasize the high percentage of positive replies (50%) this latter group gave to the "feeling of tiredness", perhaps an indication of a somatization of otherwise not recognized depressive disturbances. Weight loss (13.54% vs 6.3%) and insomnia (62.1% vs 43.1%) were more frequent among the in-contact patients. Examination of the distribution of the responses to the items concerning social

Table 8. Type of life events in last 3 months before the interview (percentage of positive answers)

Type of problems	In-contact ($n=38$)	Dropout ($n=19$)	Total ($n=57$)
Illness in family	24.3	6.25	18.9
Work or study	10.8	6.25	9.4
Economic difficulty	13.5	–	9.4
Legal	5.4	–	3.8
Divorce or marriage	2.7	–	1.9
Unexpected events	18.9	18.7	18.9
Mishaps	13.5	6.25	11.3

Table 9. Behavior and mood of patients during the last month (percentage of positive answers)

Behavior	In-contact ($n=38$)	Dropout ($n=19$)	Total ($n=57$)
Misery	45.9	12.5	35.8
Withdrawal	29.7	12.5	24.5
Slowness	35.1	50.0	39.6
Forgetfulness	16.2	6.25	13.2
Indecisiveness	27.0	12.5	22.6
Worrying	32.4	43.7	35.8
Fearfulness	18.9	12.5	17.0
Obsession	18.9	12.5	17.0
Odd ideas	35.1	43.7	37.7
Overactivity	32.4	37.5	34.0
Unpredictability	29.7		20.8
Irritability	40.5	1.2	37.7
Rudeness	5.4	25.0	11.3
Violence	8.1	18.7	11.6
Parasuicide	18.9	6.25	15.1
Offensive behavior	10.8	6.25	9.4
Heavy drinking	2.7	6.25	3.8
Self-neglect	21.6	12.5	18.9
Complaints of bodily pains	32.4	31.2	32.1
Odd behavior	29.7		20.8

Table 10. Social performance during the last month (percentage of positive answers)

Social performance	In-contact (n = 38)	Dropout (n = 19)	Total (n = 57)
Household tasks	64.8	43.7	60.4
Household management	45.9	31.2	41.5
Interest in children	13.5	12.5	13.2
Caring for children	13.5	12.5	13.2
Bringing up the children	8.1	12.5	9.4
Spare-time activity	37.8	31.2	35.8
Relationships with the family	67.5	31.2	56.6
Support	81.0	31.2	66.0
Affection, friendliness	70.2	56.2	66.0
Sexual problems	24.3	6.25	18.9
Work-study	27.0	18.7	24.3
Decision-making	70.2	25.0	56.6

performance (Table 10) shows that the answers were positive, with values exceeding 50% for half of the questions.

The in-contact patients gave a higher quota of positive answers, and large differences were especially evident in the items pertaining to decision-making ability, performance of household chores, and relationships with family members and others.

Mental Health

A study of the members of the two groups for possible signs of specific disturbances related to their psychopathological condition (Table 11) revealed that one-fifth of them presented hallucinatory symptoms at the time of the interview and one fourth symptoms of delirium.

Examination of the two groups separately showed that the dropped-out-of-sight group in general expressed a greater number of more severe symptoms. In particular, auditory hallucinations and a sense of persecution were present in larger measure in these subjects as compared with those still in contact. However, this latter group had a slightly higher percentage of certain thought disturbances.

Behavior During the Interview

Table 12 reports the data relative to behavioral disturbances noted by the interviewers during the interview.

About one-third of all patients appeared to be indifferent, with slow reflexes, or agitated; one-fifth were easily distracted. Indifference and distractibility were observed more often in the dropped-out-of-sight subjects.

Table 13 shows the distribution of the occurrence of symptoms of anxiety during the interview: anxiety, blunted affectiveness, and suspiciousness were found to be prevalent. Overall, there is a generally higher number of symptoms among the dropped-out-of-sight patients, who displayed anxiety, blunted affectiveness, and suspiciousness in more than 50% of the cases. The especially high values for anxi-

Table 11. Check list of symptoms present during examination of psychotic patients (percentage of occurrence)

During the last 3 months	In-contact ($n=38$)	Dropout ($n=19$)	Total ($n=57$)
Perceptual disorders (not hallucinations)			
Something odd is going on	18.9	18.7	18.9
Unusual smell or taste	10.8	12.5	11.3
Thought reading, insertion, echo, broadcasting	–	–	–
External influences	24.3	18.7	22.6
Thought insertion	2.7	6.25	3.8
Thought broadcasting	18.9	12.5	17.0
Thought stealing	5.4	6.25	5.7
Hallucinations			
Auditory	16.2	31.2	20.8
Visual	2.7	–	1.9
Gustative	8.1	12.5	9.4
Delusional elaboration	2.7	12.5	5.7
Delusions			
of control	2.7	18.7	7.5
of reference	18.9	18.7	18.9
of persecution	18.9	43.7	26.4
of assistance	2.7	6.25	3.8
of grandiose ability	16.2	6.25	13.2
of grandiose identity	2.7	6.25	3.8
religious	16.2	18.7	17.0
paranormal phenomena	13.5	43.7	22.6
of alien force penetration	8.1	12.5	9.4
of guilt	2.7	–	1.9
of jealousy	5.4	–	3.8
of appearance	2.7	–	1.9
of depersonalization	10.8	6.25	9.4
of catastrophe	10.8	6.25	9.4

Table 12. Behavior during interview (percentage of occurrence of symptoms)

Behaviour	In-contact ($n=38$)	Dropout ($n=19$)	Total ($n=57$)
Self-neglect	24.3	37.5	28.3
Bizarre appearance	–	6.25	1.9
Slowness	29.7	25	28.3
Agitation	21.6	18.7	20.8
Gross excitement	–	6.25	1.9
Irreverent behavior	5.4	–	3.8
Distractibility	10.8	25.0	18.9
Embrassing behavior	2.7	–	1.9
Mannerism	–	–	–
Stereotypical	5.4	–	3.8
Behaves as if hallucinating	2.7	–	1.9
Catatonic	2.7	–	1.9

Table 13. Affect during interview (percentage of occurrence of symptoms)

Affect	In-contact (n = 38)	Dropout (n = 19)	Total (n = 57)
Observed anxiety	40.5	50.0	43.4
Observed depression	18.9	6.25	15.1
Histrionic	5.4	–	3.8
Hypomanic affect	5.4	12.5	7.5
Hostile irritability	2.7	6.25	3.8
Suspicion	24.32	56.2	34.0
Perplexity	18.9	31.2	22.6
Lability of mood	–	12.5	3.8
Blunted affect	32.4	56.2	39.6
Incongruity of affect	13.5	37.5	20.8

Table 14. Speech during interview (percentage of occurrence of symptoms)

Speech	In-contact (n = 38)	Dropout (n = 19)	Total (n = 57)
Slow	29.7	25.0	28.3
Pressured	27.0	31.2	28.3
Non-social	2.7	6.25	3.8
Muteness	2.7	–	1.9
Restricted quantity	45.9	43.7	45.3
Neologisms	2.7	6.25	3.8
Incoheret	5.4	25.0	11.3
Flight of ideas	–	–	–
Poverty of content	8.1	6.25	7.5

ety and suspiciousness in this group might be the expression of a greater difficulty of the patient in interacting with the interviewer. Slightly more than one third of the patients presented speech disturbances (Table 14).

Interview with the Informant

Fifty-three informants replied to the interview, 37 for patients still in contact and 16 for those dropped out of sight.

The informants indicated the presence of behavioral disturbances in one third to one half of the patients (Table 15). Informants for the dropped-out-of-sight group gave a higher number of positive responses. Among the informants for the patients still in contact, there was a greater number of positive replies to the items referring to depressive signs or behavioral disturbances that reflect negatively on the patient.

In the other group positive responses were more numerous regarding behavioral disturbances with respect to others, both in the sense of violent or aggressive behavior and in the sense of embarrassing conduct. It is interesting to note the low agreement between the subjective perception of uncomfortable situations and the

Table 15. Informant's spinion of behavior and mood of the patient (percentage of occurrence of symptoms)

Behavior	In-contact ($n=37$)	Dropout ($n=16$)	Total ($n=53$)
Misery	40.5	18.7	33.9
Withdrawal	37.8	56.2	43.4
Slowness	37.8	18.7	32.0
Forgetfulness	13.5	31.2	18.8
Indecisiveness	56.7	43.7	52.8
Worrying	51.3	50.0	50.9
Fearfulness	35.1	25.0	32.0
Obsession	13.5	37.5	20.7
Odd ideas	37.8	56.2	43.3
Overactivity	37.8	50.0	41.5
Unpredictability	16.2	18.7	16.9
Irritability	27.0	43.7	32.0
Rudeness	18.9	37.5	24.5
Violence	18.9	31.2	22.6
Parasuicide	8.1	–	5.6
Offensive behavior	10.8	31.2	16.9
Heavy drinking	10.8	18.7	13.2
Self-neglect	37.8	37.5	37.5
Complaints of bodily pains	43.22	37.5	39.6
Odd behavior	21.6	18.7	20.7
Weight loss	10.8	31.2	16.9
Insomnia	32.4	43.7	35.8

Table 16. Informant's opinion of social performance of the patient (percentage of positive answers)

Performance	In-contact ($n=37$)	Dropout ($n=16$)	Total ($n=53$)
Household tasks	59.4	50.0	56.6
Household management	59.4	43.7	54.71
Helping children	40.5	31.2	37.7
Caring for children	56.7	18.7	45.28
Spare-time activity	37.8	62.5	45.28
Relationships with the family	62.2	50.0	58.49
Support	81.1	81.3	81.13
Affection, friendliness	54.0	50.0	52.8
Sexual problems	21.6	18.8	20.7
Workstudy	48.6	37.5	45.3
Decision-making	35.1	25.0	32.1

opinion of the informant; the agreement on each item had an overall value of 60%. This is a discrepancy that we feel requires further study.

The informants gave positive responses regarding patients, performance of social activities (Table 16) in an average of half of the cases. Looking at the two groups separately, it is evident that the higher values are always found among the still-in-contact patients, except for the question regarding free time.

Table 17. Informant's report of life events occurring to the patient during the last 3 months before the interview

Type of life event	In-contact (n = 37)	Dropout (n = 16)	Total (n = 53)
Illness of relative(s)	8.10	6.25	7.5
Problems with work	10.8	–	7.5
Economic difficulty	16.2	6.25	13.2
Legal problems	5.4	12.5	7.5
Marriage or divorce	2.7	12.5	5.6
Mishaps	8.1	31.2	15.1

The number of life events reported was rather low, without noticeable differences between the two groups (Table 17). The agreement leven between the informant's answers and those of the patient averaged about 70% for these items; the percentage was higher for those still in contact but not homogeneous in the various items.

Economic Variables

Table 18 displays the distribution of monetary and nonmonetary costs for the family and for society, according to the definition given earlier. Monetary costs for the family were significantly higher for patients not in contact, and the expenses for society were also considerably higher for this group.

About 53% of the in-contact patients represented high costs for society as compared with 10% for the dropped-out-of-sight group: it is reasonable to suppose that patients in contact with the psychiatric services are the ones who are most likely to make use of public services in general, and this results in a minimization of costs borne by the family.

The differences in benefits found between the two groups were not significant, although greater monetary income and more modest help provided to the family on the part of the dropped-out-of-sight patients seems consistent with their greater degree of independence (Table 19).

Table 20 presents a comparison of monetary costs among the different types of assistance for the psychotic patients. These expenses were gathered in part from the questionnaire and in part from the bookkeeping records of the mental health institutions and service centers.

The kinds of assistance considered are diverse; some refer to the patient sample we studied (groups 4 and 5), others to estimates made on the basis of the financial records of institutions (groups 1, 2, and 3). Analysis of the results shows a decreasing trend in the costs from residential-type assistance to outpatient care. Obviously, the lowest costs are found with respect to patients not in contact with the service; however, this cost should be considered an underestimate because it is difficult to document all the sources of costs.

As far as the costs for patient assistance on the part of the territorial services are concerned (type 4), these seem to be definitely lower than those for all institutionalized patients; however, calculating the average net monetary value of the costs and the nonmonetizable benefits, the figure of 615000 lire should be in-

Table 18. Monetary and nonmonetary costs for the family and society

Variables	In-contact		Dropout		Total	
Monthly monetary costs						
($\times$ 1000 lire)	($n=38$)		($n=19$)		($n=57$)	
Average	220.26		331.84		257.44	
Standard deviation	88.25		150.55		100.15	
Family burden	($n=34$)	(%)	($n=10$)	(%)	($n=44$)	(%)
None	8	(23.5)	1	(10.0)	9	(20.5)
Low	8	(23.5)	3	(30.0)	11	(25.0)
Medium	12	(35.3)	4	(40.0)	16	(36.4)
High	6	(17.7)	2	(20.0)	8	(18.1)
The presence of patient is	($n=33$)	(%)	($n=11$)	(%)	($n=44$)	(%)
Welcomed	27	(81.8)	9	(81.8)	36	(81.8)
Indifferent	4	(12.1)	1	(9.1)	5	(11.4)
Unpleasant	2	(6.1)	1	(9.1)	3	(6.8)
Society burden	($n=34$)	(%)	($n=10$)	(%)	($n=44$)	(%)
None	2	(5.9)	5	(50.0)	7	(15.9)
Low	14	(41.2)	4	(40.0)	18	(40.9)
Medium	14	(41.2)	–	–	14	(31.8)
High	4	(11.7)	1	(10.0)	5	(11.4)

Table 19. Monetary and nonmonetary benefits for the family

Variables	In-contact		Dropout		Total	
Monthly income	($n=38$)		($n=19$)		($n=57$)	
($\times$ 1000 lire)						
Average	383.04		404.37		390.28	
Standard deviation	187.15		200.17		182.00	
Nonmonetary benefit	($n=33$)	(%)	($n=11$)	(%)	($n=44$)	(%)
No	14	(42.4)	6	(54.5)	20	(45.5)
Low	12	(36.4)	4	(36.4)	16	(36.4)
Medium	7	(21.2)	1	(9.1)	8	(18.2)

Table 20. Monthly monetary costs of the different types of assitance

Assistance	Monetary costs ($\times$1000 lire)			
	To the family	To the outpatient psychiatric service	To the inpatient service	Total
1. Inpatient in general hospital psychiatric unit	–	–	4940.00	4940.00
2. Patient in rehabilitation center	–	–	3000.00	3000.00
3. Patient resident in nursing home	–	–	750.00	750.00
4. Outpatient in continuous contact	220.26	297.00	98.00	615.26
5. Outpatient dropout	331.84	–	–	331.84

creased on average by about 250000–300000 lire a month, which brings the overall average monthly expense to about 860000–910000 lire, slightly less than that required for care in a non-medical institution but much less than that of all the other medical health-care alternatives.

Multivariate Analysis

The analysis, conducted so far separately for every item, has shown some differences between the two groups. Given the large number of variables and the predictable interdependence among them, we thought it best to use a multivariate approach in order to answer the questions we had set out to resolve, questions which were reformulated as follows:

1. Did chronic psychotic patients who remained in contact with the service present characteristics, at the first contact, different from those of patients who dropped out of sight?
2. Did chronic psychotic patients who remained in contact with the service have monetary and non-monetary costs different from those of patients who dropped out of sight?
3. Did chronic psychotic patients who remained in contact with the service have, at the end of the follow-up period, a state of physical, psychic, and social health different from that of patients who dropped out of sight?

Because of the large number of variables being examined and the limited size of the sample, the statistical analysis was carried out in two phases, using multiple correspondence analysis to summarize large amounts of available information into synthetic indices, and using multiple logistic regression in the modelling process.

Multiple Correspondence Scaling

The results of multiple correspondence analysis on the questions concerning personal behavior, social performance, psychotic symptoms, and the interviewer's opinion, performed on the total of the patients, are shown in Figs. 2–5. The displays present graphically the original items on the optimal plane with respect to the first and second principal axes. On the maps, points near to each other correspond to similar modalities whereas distant points represent dissimilar modalities.

The personal behavior items on the first axis appear homogeneous (Cronbach index = 0.85) and the score is positive when deviant behavior symptomatology is present. In particular hyperactivity, misery, and worrying appear to be the most relevant symptoms.

For the items set relative to social performance the homogeneity among the items on the first axis is satisfactory (Cronbach index = 0.715). The axis has a positive score when activities are absent. The items with more contribution are decision-making, household management, household tasks, and informant-patient support.

The items concerning psychotic symptoms on the first axis are very homogeneous (Cronbach index = 0.83). The direction of the axis is positive when many symptoms are present, and consequently it is an index of the seriousness of psy-

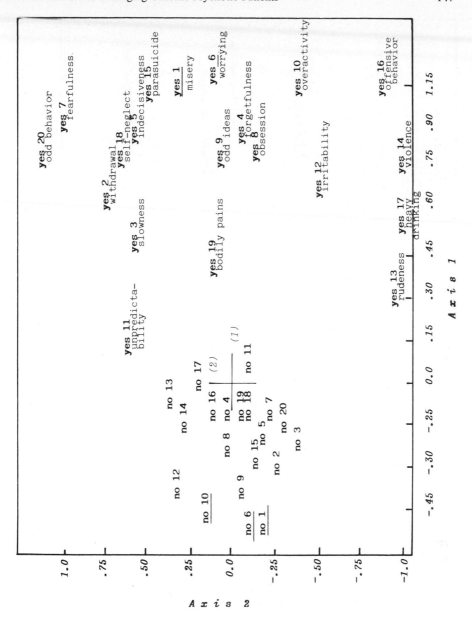

Fig. 2. Optimal two-dimensional display (goodness of fit 61.3%) by multiple correspondence analysis of the set of 20 (yes/no) items concerning patient's behavior. On the map near points correspond to modalities similar with respect to each other, distant points represent dissimilar modalities. The *underlined* options have a high (more than twice the average value) contribution to the variance of the first principal axis; the bipolar direction of the first axis tends to be an index of deviant behavior

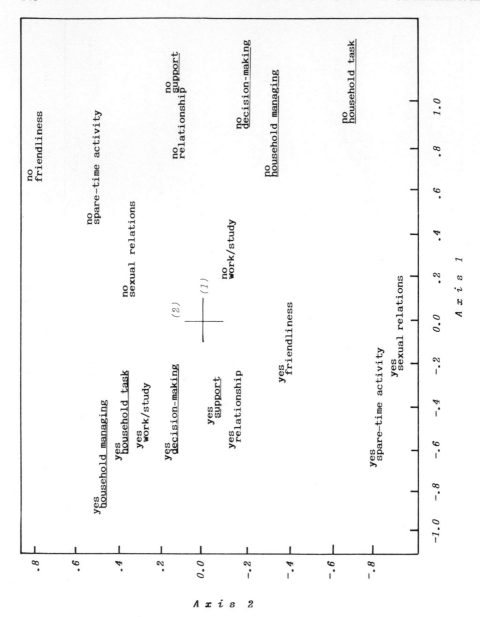

Fig. 3. Optimal two-dimensional display (goodness of fit 71.2%) by multiple correspondence analysis of the set of nine (yes/no) items concerning patient's performance. On the map near points correspond to modalities similar with respect to each other, distant points represent dissimilar modalities. The *underlined* options have a high (more than twice the average value) contribution to the variance of the first principal axis; the bipolar direction of the first axis tends to be an index of poor social performance

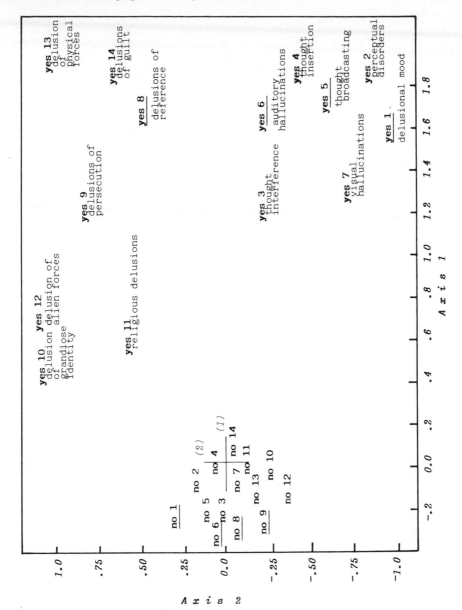

Fig. 4. Optimal two-dimensional display (goodness of fit 77.1%) by multiple correspondence analysis of the set of 14 (yes/no) items concerning the psychotic symptomatology. On the map near points correspond to modalities similar with respect to each other, distant points represent dissimilar modalities. The *underlined* options have a high (more than twice the average value) contribution to the variance of the first principal axis; the bipolar direction of the first axis tends to be an index of seriousness of psychotic symptoms

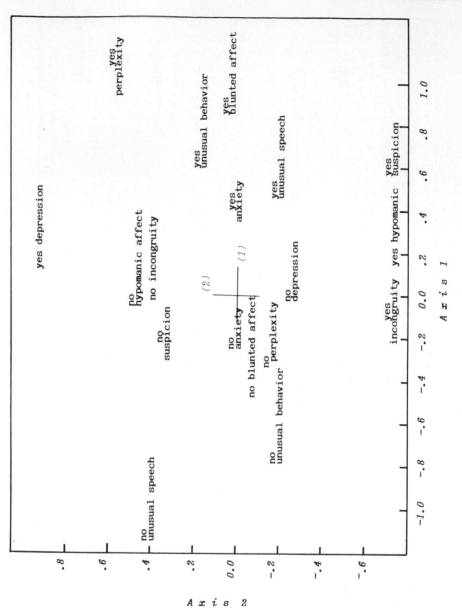

Fig. 5. Optimal two-dimensional display (goodness of fit 66.1%) by multiple correspondence analysis of the set of nine (yes/no) items concerning the interviewer's opinion. On the map near points correspond to modalities similar with respect to each other, distant points represent dissimilar modalities. The *underlined* options have a high (more than twice the average value) contribution to the variance of the first principal axis; the bipolar direction of the first axis tends to be an index of poor communication

chotic symptomatology. The most important symptoms are auditory hallucinations, delusional mood, delusions of reference, and thought broadcast.

As for the interviewer's opinion items, the fact that the Cronbach index has a value of only 0.633 raises the suspicion that at least two axes are necessary to summarize the items, i.e., they may not be unidimensional. Figure 5 shows that the direction of the first axis is associated with the poor communication characteristics of the patient during the interview. The second axis appears to be more associated with the items related to the mood of the patient (observed depression vs hypomanic affect and incongruity of affect).

Only two of the variables obtained from the psychiatric case register (11 questions) proved to be significantly associated with the evolution of care: occupational status and treatment received (see Tables 4-5). Therefore, we used multiple correspondence analysis on this set of variables in order to identify a composite index which takes into account the joint two-way relationships of all background variables (see Fig. 6).

The display represents about one half (49%) of the variance of the modalities of the background variables. Only sex and place of birth do not contribute to the principal directions of the first two axes. The first axis is determined basically by five variables: living arrangement, motivation channel, occupational status, prior psychiatric history and marital status.

In particular, the modalities of those subjects who live in institutions and those who ask to be followed up by the social or psychiatric services either in the outpatient clinic or at home are located at the negative end of the axis. These attributes are also associated with the group of persons no longer in the labor force, most of whom receive disability pension checks. The typology of these modalities is that of former psychiatric hospital patients, i.e., people with a psychiatric history that precedes Law 180 (1978).

At the positive end of the axis are found the modalities relative to subjects who have jobs or are looking for work, who are married, and who were brought to the services by relatives or by the family doctor because of aggressive behavior and frequent claims for economic subsidy. They do not have a past history of institutionalization and are therefore new for the services.

In brief, we could interpret this axis as a "historical" axis: at one end are those types who were once mental hospital patients and who have become excluded from the labor force (even though they are still below retirement age), and at the other end, the new psychotic patients, who are integrated in the family and in the work force, with disturbed behavior (violent and aggressive). The intermediate situations are found between these two extremes.

The second unipolar axis is dominated by pharmacological-psychotherapeutic treatment. Given the practical importance of this variable, we decided in the following analyses to keep the treatment categorical rather than as the score of the second axis.

At the end of the scaling analysis we were left with nine variables, five of which were principal axes:

1. Age (recorded in 1985)
2. Planned treatment (1 = rehabilitative, 0 = other)

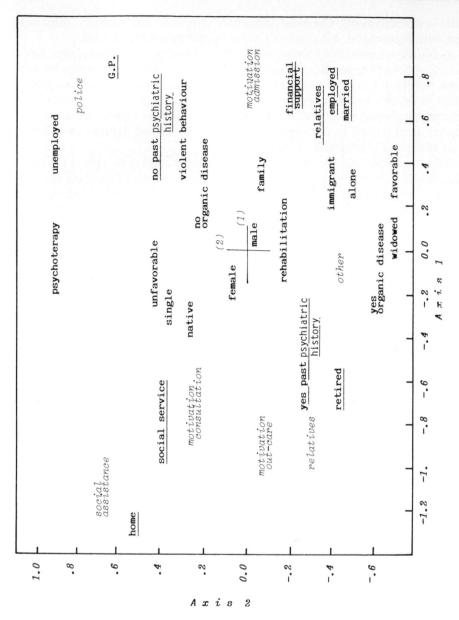

Fig. 6. Optimal two-dimensional display (goodness of fit 49%) by multiple correspondence analysis of the set of 11 variables concerning the background of the patients. On the map near points correspond to modalities similar with respect to each other, distant points represent dissimilar modalities. The modalities of the items not in boldface in the map have not determined the directions of the axes; the *underlined* points have a high (more than twice the average value) contribution to the variance of the first principal axis; see text for interpretation of axes

3. Background axis (at first contact)
4. Personal behavior axis
5. Social performance axis
6. Psychotic symptoms axis
7. Interviewer's opinion axis
8. Number of life events (max. 6)
9. Percentage of the patient's income spent on assistance

Multiple Logistic Regression Modeling

Table 21 reports the mean values of the variables and of the scores for the two groups of patients: in the subjects still in contact, pharmacological-rehabilitative treatments predominate, the social performance is better (negative score), especially for the items "ability to make decisions" and "ability to manage one's own domestic and economic affairs". This group also has a higher frequency of life events referred.

The correlation matrix of these variables and scores did not indicate highly collinear variables; therefore, we have to screen the whole set with respect to drop-out/in-contact output. After a preliminary selection of regressors we have chosen the three-variables set containing background axis *(bk)*, social performance axis *(sp)*, and rehabilitative treatment *(rt)* as the more appropriate regressors pattern between "minimal adequate" sets (see Fig. 7).

We tested whether all of them were truly useful for the identification of a minimal model; the marginal and conditional tests were performed on the main effects and on the interaction effects. The results are reported in Table 22. Among the main effects, the marginal test of the background axis was not significant; in contrast, the conditional test was significant. This is likely due to the confounding effect of the high inverse correlation between sp and bk ($r = -0.43$).

According to both tests, only the interaction between the social performance axis and the treatment planned is significant. As a result, the logit model selected is the following (in GLIM form):

$$1n\ odds(dropout) = 1 + bk + sp*rt$$

Table 21. Mean values and standard deviation of variables and principal axes within two groups of patients

	In-contact		Dropout		t-value	P-value
	Mean	SD	Mean	SD		
Age (in years)	45.4	10.8	48.5	12.5	0.94	0.355
Rehabilitative (1 = yes)	0.89	0.31	0.58	0.49	2.91	0.005
Background axis	−0.09	0.82	0.05	1.26	0.49	0.631
Behavioral axis	−0.07	1.02	0.14	0.94	0.72	0.480
Social performance axis	−0.26	0.90	0.51	1.01	2.86	0.006
Mental health axis	0.04	0.94	−0.07	1.11	0.36	0.723
Interview-opinion axis	−0.04	0.96	0.10	1.07	0.51	0.699
Life events (number)	0.68	0.77	0.16	0.49	2.69	0.009
% income/assistance expenses	68.1	35.1	76.8	24.8	0.95	0.348

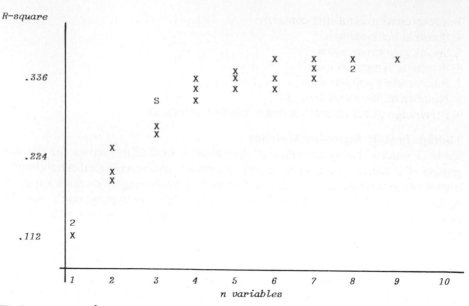

Fig. 7. Values of R^2 for 3-discriminant subsets of 1, 2, ... 9 variables. 'S' shows the selected sub-·set: background axis, social performance axis, and planned treatment

Table 22. Marginal and conditional likelihood-ratio tests for term in the logit models with the variables background axis *(bk),* social performance axis *(sp),* and rehabilitative treatment *(rt)*

Source	Marginal			Conditional		
	df	dev	P	df	dev	P
bk × sp × rt	1	0.004	ns	1	0.004	ns
bk × sp	1	1.75	ns	1	1.38	ns
bk × rt	1	3.88	0.05	1	3.63	ns
sp × rt	1	8.67	0.01	1	7.41	0.01
bk	1	0.25	ns	1	6.70	0.01
sp	1	7.57	0.01	1	9.86	0.005
rt	1	7.23	0.01	1	7.74	0.01

It expresses 38.1% of the linear association between the log odds and the stimulus variables and correctly predicts 84% of the output variable. The estimates of the regression parameters, the relative standard errors, the odds ratio, and the relative 95% CI are reported in Table 23. The figures quantify the increase (decrease) in the odds of becoming a dropout for a one-standard deviation increase in background and social performance regressors and for the presence of rehabilitative treatment with respect to others in treatment regressor.

For descriptive purposes, the partial residuals plot relative to the background axis is displayed in Fig. 8 as a function of the background itself, conditional to the two different treatment values. The plot does not appear to be linear when the

Table 23. Estimates of the parameters, of the odds, ratios, and of their approximate 95% confidence limits, for the Logit model: ln odds (dropout) $= 1 + bk + sp*rt$

Effect	Estimated coefficent	Standard error	Odds ratio	Confidence limits	
				Lower	Upper
Background axis	1.62	0.571	5.05	1.65	15.5
Social performance axis					
(rt = rehabilitative)	0.797	0.467	2.22	0.888	5.55
(rt = other)	4.96	2.43	143.00	1.22	
Rehabilitative/other					
(sp = mean)	−2.06	1.22	0.127	0.012	1.38
(sp = 1 SD)	−6.22	2.87	0.002	0.000	0.552

treatment is rehabilitative; this is possibly due to an interaction effect between the background and the treatment itself, which is also visible from the plots. Some possible transformations of the score variable did not seem to give more linear plots, and the polynomial terms did not appear significant with the conditional test, so we chose to retain the model selected.

The partial residuals plot was also displayed for the social performance axis (see Fig. 9), conditional to the two treatment values: interaction effect between social performance and treatment are clearly visible from the different slopes of the two plots. An outlier is evident, but its deletion did not influence the fitted regression coefficients.

In brief, there seems to be a positive relationship between the "historical" axis and the output: the attributes pattern of old psychotic patients is more associated with the in-contact response and the pattern of new psychotic patients with the drop-out response.

The social performance and treatment also seem related to output: when a rehabilitative option is not present, the drop-out response increases for the patients with poor performance. In others words, a rehabilitative treatment seems to be an important protecting factor with respect to drop-out patients if they have a poor social performance.

Discussion

The analysis performed allows us to respond to the questions we had formulated. First, the psychotic patients who remained in contact with the services at the end of the follow-up period (2–3 years) presented personal, social, and historical characteristics which were statistically predictive of their destiny.

In fact, multivariate results showed that the risk of becoming a dropout at the end of the follow-up period increased (descreased) fivefold if the background axis increased (descreased) by one standard deviation; i.e., one end of the background spectrum, constituted by the old institutionalized, who have an old clinical history and minimal occupational possibilities, receives a great deal of public care; the

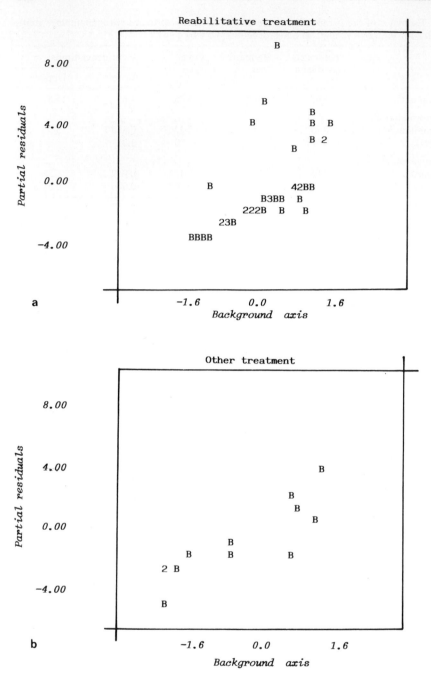

Fig. 8 a, b. Partial residual plots for the background axis, conditional on the reabilitative treatment (**a**) and the other treatments (**b**). B = one case; 2 = two cases; 3 = three cases; 4 = four cases

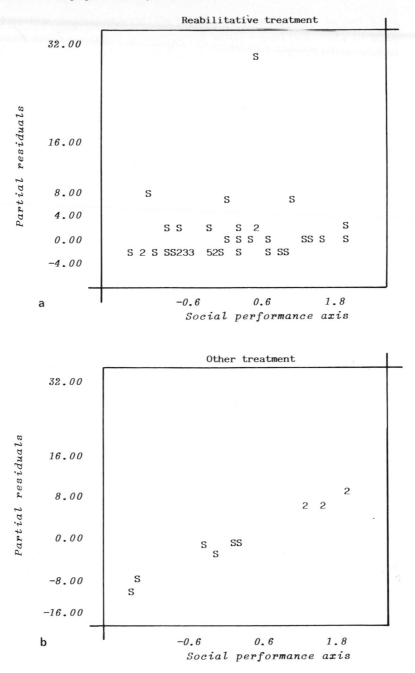

Fig. 9a, b. Partial residual plots for the social performance axis, conditional on the reabilitative treatment (**a**) and the other treatments (**b**). S=one case; 2=two cases; 3=three cases; 4=four cases

other end of the spectrum, constituted by the new patients who have jobs and some of whom had been referred for aggressive behavior, shows poor social performance and dropping out after a few clinical contacts. Other patient patterns are found between the two ends of the care spectrum.

As far the second question is concerned, it is obvious that chronic psychotic patients still in contact with the services involve greater expenditures on the part of the public structures for assistance than do those no longer in contact; furthermore, this latter group utilizes fewer medical and social services, even outside those offered by the psychiatric centers. In addition, contrary to our expectations, the monetary and non-monetary burdens borne by the family were not greater than those for the patients still in contact.

The last question requires a more detailed response. Analysis of the two groups of subjects at the end of the follow-up period does not reveal any substantial quantitative difference with regard to the scores for specific psychiatric symptomatology and for behavioral and mood disturbances (see Table 21). However, the difference between the two groups seems qualitative: a greater prevalence of depressive and anxious states, insomnia, and referral of life events is noted in the subjects still in contact, while in the dropped-out-of-sight group, aggressive and violent behavior prevails, with more evident psychiatric symptoms, i.e., hallucinatory and persecutional (see Tables 9 and 11).

Behaviour during the interview also confirms only qualitative differences between the two groups, in the sense that among the dropouts more disturbed attitudes prevailed.

The interview with the informant also corroborated the prevalence of depressive and anxious states among the patients in contact, and of more aggressive and violent states among the dropouts. The social performance is different in the two groups: it is significantly better in the subjects still in contact. Multivariate results also point up the direct association between good social performance and having remained in contact with the services; the treatment interacts with this association, in the sense that when it is not of the rehabilitative type, the risk of becoming a dropout increases for those with a poor social performance.

Of course, one has to be careful in interpreting the final logit model; indeed, the social performance of the subjects was assessed only after their evolution had already taken place. So social performance cannot be viewed as a risk factor but only as a concomitant variable; it could possibly be analyzed as an output variable in a future study. The treatment planned by the psychiatrists proved to be associated with the evolution of the service relationship. There are two possible reasons for this: either rehabilitation was prescribed for patients who were going to keep in touch with the service anyway, i.e., the psychiatrists somehow made a sort of implicit prognostic evaluation while prescribing the treatment, or the treatment itself actually modified the evolution of the service relationship. The fact that poor performance is associated with an interruption of service utilization when rehabilitative therapy is not used also generates interesting hypotheses for future research.

Appendix: Sources and Nature of the Economic Data

The sources supplying the data needed to complete the cost classification described in Table 4 are essentially represented by (a) the questionnaire given to the informant, and (b) the budget and general bookkeeping records of the centers and institutions that offer psychiatric care. In particular, the first source was used to obtain information relative to the monetary and non-monetary costs sustained by the families and the non-monetary costs borne by society. Furthermore, information was also obtained from this first source regarding monetary and non-monetary benefits which the families realized from the presence of the patient in the home; these latter were inserted as negative costs.

The second source, on the other hand, supplied only data regarding the monetary costs of psychiatric care provided by the mental health services and by other institutions.

The specific content of the part of the questionnaire dedicated to costs is summarized as follows:

1. The first group of questions concerns the amount of actual expenses incurred by the family for the support of the patient, expenses for housing, food, clothing, medical care (if this requires the presence of paid personnel), entertainment, and money given directly to the patient. The expenses considered here are entirely monetary and are due exclusively to the presence of the patient (in other words, they are expenses the family would not incur if the patient were not present).
A minimum of 100000 lire a month for food costs was calculated for patients living with their families, even in cases where the informant denied this cost.
2. The second group of questions was aimed at finding out information about the time burden the patient represented for the family (or for those who lived with him/her). "No burden" means a patient is completely self-sufficient; "low burden" means less than 50 h per month dedicated to the patient; "medium burden" corresponds to between 51 and 100 h per month; and "high burden" more than 100 h per month.
3. The third set of questions explored the possible burden the presence of the patient caused the family or co-inhabitants in terms of uneasiness, inconvenience, embarrassment, or mental anguish. That the patient's presence is welcomed is a sign that there is no additional psychological burden (usually this acceptance is justified by the satisfaction found in helping the person or by the conviction that in any event he/she is better off within the family), in the sense that the quality of family life does not suffer as a result of the patient's presence. If the family is indifferent to his/her presence, or if they find it unpleasant, this takes on the significance of a growing burden for the family or the patient's co-inhabitants.
4. The fourth set of questions was meant to evaluate the non-monetary burden the patient represented for society. In general, this involved care and services obtained free of charge by the patient's family outside the centers and institutions charged with providing specific assistance, in other words the services provided by the National Health Services, by old psychiatric hospitals (PH) that are dis-

appearing, by long-stay institutions (usually private), by general hospital units, by the community social services, by general practictioners – all these are services and institutions whose monetary costs have been inferred from their bookkeeping records.

The burdens considered here were classified as none, low, medium and high, according to the presumed cost of the free services offered, using a system designed to weight each service (e.g., maid service $= 1$, social worker and the like $= 2$, doctor $= 3$).

This is the entry that presents the greatest risk for duplication, as was mentioned earlier, basically for two reasons: first, because there is the chance that at least a part of the services in question were furnished by the mental health centers (in which case there is a diplication with the service costs gathered from the bookkeeping data); second, when dealing with services that must be paid in full or partially (ticket) there is a possibility that these expenses have already been declared among the monetary costs borne by the family (see point 1 above). So for these reasons as well, it is worth adding, we preferred not to assign a monetary value to these burdens.

The specific content of the part of the questionnaire dedicated to economic benefit is summarized as follows:

1. Patient's monetary income

   Such income, expressed as monthly average of the annual income, once again presents a certain risk for duplication in that it was not possible to separate the part which derives from retirement money or other type of subsidy from that coming from a job activity or personal estate the patient might have. If the income was the result of retirement payments (or public subsidy), from the point of view of the entire collectivity this does not represent creation of income but a simple transferral of funds.

2. Non-monetary benefits

   This regards the help offered by the patient to the family in terms of carrying out domestic tasks. This kind of benefit was considered low if it amounted to less than 50 work hours a month and high if it was greater than that number.

As far as the monetary costs sustained by society are concerned, as we said before, these were inferred from the bookkeeping records of the centers and institutions involved. These structures included hospitals for long-stay psychotics previous insane asylums), general – hospital psychiatric services, and institutions – usually private – offering mental health care and assistance. The costs recorded for these three structures are annual figures, while those for the mental health care centers refer to the expenses for every contact. Nevertheless, these are average cost figures, whose total amount depends, among other things, on the extent to which the various services are utilized, an extent that can vary greatly from one year to the next.

References

Baker RJ, Nelder JA (1978) The GLIM system, release 3. NAG, Oxford

Benedetti JK, Brown MB (1978) Strategies for the selection of log-linear models. Biometrics 34: 680–686

Brenn T, Arnesen E (1985) Selecting risk factors: a comparison of discriminant analysis, logistic regression and Cox's regression model using data from the Tromso heart study. Stat Med 4: 413–423

Greenacre MJ (1984) Theory and applications of correspondence analysis. Academic Press, London

Her Majesty's Stationery Office (1968) A glossary of mental disorders. HMSO London

Landwehar JM, Pregibon D, Shoemaker AC (1984) Graphical methods for assessing logistic regression models. J Am Stat Assoc 79: 61–71

Lebart L, Morineau A, Warwick KM (1984) Multivariate descriptive statistical analysis. Wiley, New York

Lebart L, Morineau A, et al. (1985) SPAD: Systeme portable pour l'analyse des donnees. CESIA, Paris

Marinoni A, Torre E, Allegri G (1978) Il registro dei casi come strumento metodologico di analisi in epidemiologia psichiatrica. Riv Psichiatria 13: 126–151

Marinoni A, Torre E, Allegri G, Comelli M (1983) Lomest psychiatric case register: the statistical contest required for planning. Acta Psychiatr Scand 67: 107–117

McCullagh P, Nelder JA (1983) Generalized linear models. Chapman and Hall, London

Torre E, Marinoni A (1977) Prime esperienze di utilizzazione del registro dei casi psichiatrici. Proc. XXXIII Congresso Nazionale della Società Italiana di Psichiatria, Naples

Torre E, Marinoni A, Allegri G, Bosso A, Ebbli D, Gorini M (1982) Trends in admissions before and after an act abolishing mental hospitals: a survey in three areas of Northern Italy. Compr Psychiatry 23: 240–246

Wing J, Branley L, Hailey A, Wing JK (1968) Camberwell cumulative psychiatric case register. Part I. Aim and methods. Soc Psychiatry 3: 116–123

Wing JK, Hailey A (1972) Evaluating community psychiatric services: the Camberwell register 1964–1971. Oxford University Press, London

Institutional Approaches

The Application of Modified Cost-Benefit Analysis in the Evaluation of a Hostel Ward for Chronic Psychotic Patients

K. Bridges, D. Goldberg, C. Hyde, K. Lowson, C. Sterling, and B. Faragher

Williams and Anderson (1975) have shown how methods of cost-benefit analysis may assist in making choices between various health service projects. In a conventional cost-benefit analysis all the effects of a service are, in principle, quantified and expressed in monetary terms – the 'hard' costs and benefits. A major problem with this form of analysis, however, is that many of the deleterious or beneficial effects of a service, such as the relief of symptoms and distress or the benefit of not needing to be in hospital, cannot be expressed in financial terms.

Glass and Goldberg (1977) have proposed a modification of the usual cost-benefit framework in which investigators, who wish to compare two services, carry out a conventional cost-benefit analysis but measure the 'soft' non-monetary effects as a separate exercise. These effects may be called 'soft' costs if they involve symptoms or impairment of psychosocial function and 'soft' benefits if they represent improvement in psychosocial adjustment. The results of the economic comparison can be condensed to a single figure called the 'net effect' of the comparison between two services, and this is then used to interpret the overall balance sheet of soft costs and benefits. If a service which produces more soft benefits is also cheaper, then it is said to 'dominate' the other service. If the service with more soft benefits is more expensive, health planners will at least have objective data to help them decide whether the extra quality is worth the extra price.

The utility of this approach has been demonstrated in research comparing the services of a psychiatric unit of a district general hospital (DGH) with those of a large mental hospital for patients with schizophrenia (Jones et al. 1980). The purpose of this paper is to provide a further example of this Glass-Goldberg model of cost-benefit analysis by reference to research at Manchester, which will be reported in greater detail elsewhere (Hyde et al. 1987), in which the care of chronic patients in a hostel ward in the community has been compared with care provided by a psychiatric unit of a DGH. The background to the study and the form of care provided by the hostel ward are described first, followed by a brief evaluation.

The Manchester Study

Some patients with chronic psychotic illnesses remain severely ill and require continuous nursing care in hospital for prolonged periods. The Department of Psychiatry at the University Hospital of South Manchester was opened in 1971. It is a

DGH unit in a teaching hospital which has a full catchment-area responsibility for over 200 000 people. Despite the constant pressure on beds it has accumulated several severely ill patients under the age of 65 years who have needed intensive nursing for periods longer than 6 months and who have presented formidable problems of rehabilitation.

It has not been possible to allocate beds within the unit in such a way that these 'new long-stay' patients are nursed in one particular ward in a milieu appropriate for their needs. They are distributed throughout the busy adult psychiatric wards, often to their disadvantage. From time to time the social milieu of these wards can become too emotionally arousing and cause them to relapse into florid symptomatology. At times they can be taken for granted by staff when their attention is distracted by the needs of the floridly disturbed short-stay patients.

Care on the general psychiatric wards can also have the disadvantage of progressively disabling the patient for life in the outside community: the management practices of the wards prevent patients from being responsible for domestic tasks as well as outside activities such as shopping and gardening.

Following the pioneering work of Dr. Douglas Bennett and Professor John Wing in developing a hostel ward at the Maudsley Hospital in London and subsequent reports on the benefits of caring for chronic psychotic patients in this residential setting (Wykes 1982; Wykes and Wing 1982), a suitable property was acquired in Manchester and has been used as an alternative location for the care of some of the 'new long-stay' patients of the DGH unit. This property – called Douglas House – is located in the community, about a mile from the hospital. It was opened in 1982, and the form of care that it provides is being evaluated to test the hypothesis that the care of the 'new long-stay' patients in a hostel ward is clinically and socially advantageous to the patient and financially advantageous to the community compared with care provided by the DGH unit.

Comparability of Services

The Psychiatric Unit of the DHG

The patients on the psychiatric wards of the DGH have access to a comprehensive service provided by the rehabilitation facilities within the DGH which are shared with day patients. These include an industrial workshop, woodwork and craft rooms, clerical and household facilities, and other activities organised by the nurses and occupational therapists. There is a daily social-skills group which most of the longer-stay patients attend from time to time, a literacy group and a rehabilitation flat. Other activities are provided by the social and recreational departments of the hospital, and patients are usually able to use community facilities as they wish.

Douglas House

Douglas House has been described by Goldberg et al. (1985). It is a large Victorian house situated in a pleasant neighbourhood near to shops and other social facilities. Within the limits of the resources available the living environment is domestic and fosters a social atmosphere that is much less arousing than a hospital ward. Downstairs there are two large lounges, a dining room, a kitchen and a small office for nursing staff. Upstairs there are five bedrooms, a bathroom and an office used for staff meetings. Outside there is a large mature garden, a garage, and a patio which the residents constructed behind the house.

Douglas House does not have any domestic staff; it is not dependent on the hospital for catering, laundry or social activities, and the residents are not expected to spend their time in workshops, day centres or occupational therapy departments. Emphasis on daily living skills at the hostel ward are regarded as more appropriate re-enabling activities for patients who have spent much time in hospital than those offered by these other services. So that the hostel ward can function independently of the hospital, it has a comprehensive range of equipment for cooking, cleaning, laundry and gardening. The patients are expected to contribute to the catering, household cleaning and maintenance, laundry, shopping, gardening, etc. as part of their rehabilitation.

The hostel ward should be staffed during the day and night by a nursing establishment of one charge nurse, one ward sister, one staff nurse, 3.75 State Enrolled Nurses and 2.25 nursing assistants, but in practice the actual numbers have been short of this. A clinical psychologist provides a service on a sessional basis, and other staff such as social workers and speech therapists provide assistance when this is necessary. The overall clinical responsibility for individual patients remains with the referring consultant, but while they are resident at Douglas House their care is managed by psychiatrists with clinical responsibility for this service.

During the period of the evaluation the number of patients living there has never been more than ten because of the disadvantages that greater numbers may have on the social and therapeutic milieu of the building and because of the intensive nursing care that these patients need.

The care of an individual patient is eclectic and may involve a number of different forms of interventions such as drugs, psychotherapy, speech therapy and educative procedures. Within the limits of a group-living situation, the management of each resident is individually formulated and structured by a personal rehabilitation programme which addresses itself to several areas of behaviour: self-care, domestic skills, social and community skills, and specific problem behaviours. The patients are encouraged to focus their attention not upon their illnesses but on the things that seem to prevent them from enjoying the kind of things that ordinary people do, and to be responsible for their own activities.

Nursing is organised on behavioural lines under the supervision of the clinical psychologist with a reward system of points which are exchanged for money on a weekly basis. This money is in addition to the patients' private incomes, which are usually state benefits. This system is flexible, so that more is expected of the less disabled patients; the very disabled patients are all given points for behaviours which less disabled people must exhibit without reward, so that the most disabled persons can earn the same total number of points as the least disabled. A system of fines for serious misconduct is used sparingly, and patients can be transferred back to the hospital if they hit a member of staff or develop intolerable behaviours that cannot be managed at the hostel ward.

In addition to the rehabilitation programmes, patients are encouraged to pursue their own leisure and social pursuits, and they invariably take part in group activities that they arrange for themselves with the staff such as going to the cinema, theatre, pubs and restaurants.

The Evaluation

The Patients

In order to be eligible patients had to have been in hospital for at least 6 months – the admission period currently used to operationally define the long stay in this study, aged between 16 and 65 years, in need of 24-h nursing care, and thought not to constitute a serious hazard to public safety. The first 18 patients eligible for the study were carefully arranged into two matched groups which were comparable in terms of duration of illness and hospitalisation, clinical diagnosis – including the presence of organic brain disease, the extent of psychological impairments and remedial problem behaviours as measured by standardised assessments. They also turned out to be matched for age, sex and research diagnosis determined by the ID-CATEGO system (Wing et al. 1974). The index group to be transferred to the hostel ward was chosen by the toss of a coin. The control group continued to receive their care in the hospital. As places subsequently became available at the hostel ward, we identified further eligible patients and introduced them into the study in pairs, whilst ensuring that the two groups remained broadly comparable with one another.

The data referred to in this paper are concerned only with patients who have been in the study for at least 2 years, i.e. 11 pairs. Overall, their average duration of illness since first admission was 12 years (range 0.5–29.5 years), the average cumulative time spent in hospital was 5 years (range 0.5–14.4 years), and the average period of their current admission prior to the start of the experiment was 3.5 years (range 0.5–8.5 years). The average age was 43 years (range 21–63 years) and each group had six men and five women. The most common diagnosis was schizophrenia ($n = 13$); other patients had affective disorders and some had evidence of organic brain disease in addition to a psychotic illness.

Measures of Non-monetary Effects

Each patient was interviewed using standardised instruments which assessed different aspects of their clinical morbidity, their psychosocial function and their satisfaction with different aspects of the care they were receiving. These instruments included the Present State Examination (Wing et al. 1974), the Krawiecka Scales –

KGV (Krawiecka et al. 1977), the Psychological Impairment Rating Scale – PIRS (Jablensky et al. 1980), the Mini-Mental State – MMS (Folstein et al. 1975), and various scales developed for use at the Maudsley Hostel Ward assessing patients' satisfaction with their care, use of social facilities and remedial problem behaviours (Wykes 1982). These assessments were carried out before the patients were allocated to their respective experimental group and repeated every 6 months. They were also carried out on patients even after they were discharged. In addition, standardised time budgets were made annually in order to assess how the patients were spending their time.

Assessment of Monetary Effects

Four categories of costs associated with each form of care were considered: capital costs, revenue costs, Local Authority and Home Office costs, and social costs. The capital costs were those of replacing and upgrading the hostel ward compared with the equivalent costs of replacing the total psychiatric unit. These were converted to an annual equivalent using a discount rate of 5%.

The revenue costs included the costs of care provided by nursing and nonnursing staff, investigations and treatment costs, and general service costs. Information was derived from medical and nursing records, prescription charts and other records of the services used by each patient throughout the 2 years of the evaluation.

For the assessment of care costs for the hostel ward the index patients were regarded as a homogeneous group for the purposes of calculating average costs per patient. The assessment of the care costs was more problematic for the psychiatric unit, as the control patients were distributed thoughout different wards. They were also regarded as a homogeneous group, but the care resources they used were individually calculated and then aggregated in order to derive an average cost per patient. For this purpose a professional-time cost exercise was carried out in the hospital. This involved all professional staff systematically recording on standardised forms the amount of time that they had spent indirectly and directly on each of the control patients over a designated period of 14 consecutive days and nights. In order not to influence their normal practices other patients were included and staff were not told the main reason for the exercise. The staff were of all ranks and training and there was 100% cooperation.

General service costs were provided by the Health Authority; their accounting system was such that those costs which were specific to Douglas House and to the individual wards of the psychiatric unit were recorded separately.

It was necessary to include Local Authority and Home Office costs, as two patients from the control group lived in hostels and night shelters after their discharge from the DGH and a third patient spent time in prison. With regards to social costs an attempt was made to examine the financial burden on families, but this proved to be negligible, and no patient in the study gained any employment. As these costs were similar in both groups they were ignored in this analysis, along with welfare payments such as social security benefits. Further, the total revenue costs did not include the costs specifically concerned with the evaluation.

Results

In the course of 2 years, three patients had to be transferred from the hostel ward back to the DGH unit permanently: one had a deteriorating organic condition and could no longer be managed in a domestic setting, owing to a severe ataxia; two others who had spent many years in institutions developed unremitting behavioural problems including fire-setting, exhibitionism and aggressive outbursts, which quickly remitted once they were back in hospital again. It was therefore important to analyse the outcome data (a) irrespective of whether patients were able to benefit from the new service and (b) in terms of the effects that the new service had on patients who did not have to return to hospital together with their matched controls. Only data referring to the reduced group are presented here as an illustration of non-monetary effects; the full details of these effects for all the patients are reported in Hyde et al. (1987).

The Non-monetary Effects

The results of the analysis between the two groups over time for some of the measures of 'soft' costs and benefits, are shown in Table 1. There was no significant

Table 1. Comparison of some non-monetary and monetary effects of two services

	Superior service
Soft costs	
Psychotic symptoms (KGV, PSE)	Neither
Psychological impairments (PIRS)	
'Psychomotor inhibition'[a]	Hostel ward
'Non-assertiveness'[a]	Hostel ward
'Indifference'	Hostel ward
Overall impression score	Hostel ward
Total item score	Neither
Reduction in neuroleptics prescribed	Neither
Remedial problem behaviours	Neither
Soft benefits	
Domestic skills	Hostel ward
Use of community facilities	Hostel ward
Constructive behaviours (time budgets)	Hostel ward
Hard costs	
Costs to the NHS	
Capital costs	Hostel ward
Revenue costs	
Nursing care	DGH Unit
Non-nursing care	Hostel ward
Drugs investigations	Hostel ward
General services	Hostel ward
Total	Hostel ward

[a] Factor scores derived from the PIRS (A. Jablensky, personal communication)

difference between the two groups in terms of their experience of affective and psychotic symptoms such as delusions and hallucinations as measured by the KGV. In some respects, however, the patients who we were able to care for in the hostel ward experienced significantly fewer psychotic impairments than their controls over the 2 years of the evaluation. This appeared to be because the controls seem to continue to acquire such defects, while the index group remained relatively unchanged or improved (Figs. 1–3). The members of the index group also developed superior domestic skills, used more facilities in the community and were more likely to be engaged in constructive activities. In addition to this, the patients at the hostel ward – apart from the two who were transfered back to the DGH unit – were consistently satisfied with life there, and the majority preferred it to being in hospital.

The Monetary Effects

Table 1 also shows which service proved to be cheaper. The 'hard' costs to the NHS for providing each service were calculated as the average costs per patient per day. Different levels of patient occupancy and nursing establishment at the hostel ward gave rise to a wide range of nursing costs, but in spite of this, the cost of providing care in the hostel ward remained less than that of the DGH unit. The total costs based on actual occupancy and staffing levels were £ 29.38 and £ 42.89 respectively. The nursing costs represented 31% of the hospital costs but 60% of the costs at the hostel ward. This was not unexpected because of the small number of patients being nursed there but was, however, offset by the much lower costs for general services for the hostel ward, which represented only 22% of the total costs compared with 44% for the DGH unit. This was due in part to the fact that the hostel ward does not have domestic and catering staff, and that the patients themselves are involved in these kinds of tasks as part of their daily lives.

Some patients from the hostel ward had to return to the hospital, and for these occasions the costs of the hospital care were charged to the hostel ward. Apart from the permanent transfer of the three patients mentioned above, these admis-

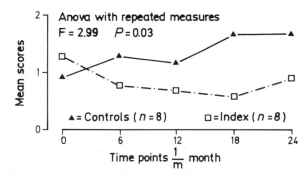

Fig. 1. PIRS Factor 3 – non-assertiveness. Comparison of mean scores of both groups with time. *Anova,* analysis of variance

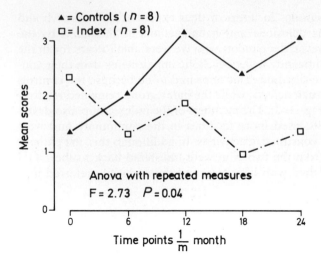

Fig. 2. PIRS Factor 10 – indifference. Comparison of mean scores of both groups with time

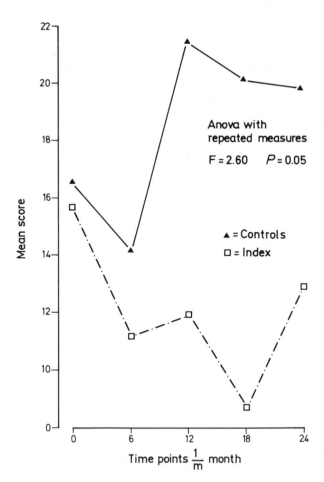

Fig. 3. PIRS Overall impression score. Comparison of mean scores of both groups (8 pairs) with time

sions were usually for brief periods. They were necessary during episodes of florid psychosis associated with disturbed behaviour that could not be managed at Douglas House and when patients required more specialised medical and surgical care which could be provided only at the hospital. Patients from the control group also needed medical attention in other departments of the hospital and some spent time, after discharge from hospital, in Local Authority hostels, night shelters or prison. In order to calculate the costs to the community of providing each service these additional costs had to be taken into account, and it was also found that the care of the index group was cheaper: the average annual cost per patient was £ 10284 for the index group compared with £ 11504 for the control group.

Discussion

Although modified cost-benefit analysis cannot say whether it is worth having a service at all, it can show which of two services is preferable. By the same token, there may be some third way of running the service which is better than either of the services that have been compared (Goldberg and Jones 1980).

This study shows that in several respects the hostel ward provides a better service than the DGH unit for severely ill 'long-stay' patients who need intensive nursing care. That is, according to Glass and Goldberg (1977), it 'dominates' the DGH unit. The assessment of the non-monetary effects suggests that it has an important function in preventing or at least slowing down the development of psychotic impairment and that it provides a more suitable environment for rehabilitation than the psychiatric wards of the hospital. The assessments of the 'hard' costs show that these 'soft' advantages do not have to be purchased at a price, since they are achieved at a lower cost to the NHS and to the community. These results support the advantages reported for 'long-stay' patients being cared for in the hostel ward at the Maudsley Hospital in London (Wykes 1982; Wykes and Wing 1982).

It is expected that the form of care provided by a hostel ward should be in addition to the services of a psychiatric unit of a DGH. Indeed, it is clear from this study that some 'long-stay' patients could not be cared for in this setting, and that from time to time some patients required the services of the hospital for brief periods.

It should be noted that the monetary effects of the hostel ward are not compared with the costs of caring for patients in a large mental hospital. It is likely, however, that the costs of providing care in a hostel ward will be more expensive than this alternative, since the average costs of keeping patients in mental hospitals would be very much lower. Moving patients to a hostel ward should nevertheless make it possible to use the released resources more effectively, for example, by offering additional places to patients who would benefit from short-term treatment.

Finally, it is not possible to generalise from the results reported for two reasons: first, the number of 'long-stay' patients in the DGH who were eligible to take part in the evaluation was small; second, the data refer only to the first 2 years since the Hostel Ward opened, which makes it impossible at this stage to predict what the non-monetary effects will be in the long term. As it is important that health care policies should not be based on the evidence of a single study, it is important that further evaluations are carried out using similar instruments and methodology so that data can be compared.

References

Folstein MF, Folstein SE, McHugh PR (1975) Mini-Mental State: a practical method for grading the cognitive state of patients for the clinician. J Psychiatr Research 12: 189–198

Glass NJ, Goldberg D (1977) Cost-benefit analysis and the evaluation of psychiatric services. Psychol Med 7: 701–707

Goldberg D, Jones R (1980) The costs and benefits of psychiatric care. In: Robins L, Clayton P, Long J (eds) The social consequences of psychiatric illness. Brunner/Mazel, New York, pp 55–70

Goldberg DP, Bridges K, Cooper W, Hyde C, Sterling C, Wyatt R (1985) Douglas House: a new type of hostel ward for the chronic psychotic patient. Br J Psychiatry 147: 383–388

Hyde C, Bridges K, Goldberg D, Lowson K, Sterling C, Faragher B (1987) The evaluation of a hostel ward: a controlled study using modified cost-benefit analysis. Br J Psychiatry 151: 805–812

Jablensky A, Schwarz P, Tomov T (1980) WHO collaborative study of impairment and disabilities associated with schizophrenic disorders. Acta Psychiatr Scand [Suppl] 285: 152–159

Jones R, Goldberg D, Hughes R (1980) A comparison of two different services treating schizophrenia: a cost-benefit approach. Psychol Med 10: 493–505

Krawiecka M, Goldberg D, Vaughan M (1977) A standardised psychiatric assessment scale for rating chronic psychotic patients. Acta Psychiatr Scand 55: 299–308

Williams A, Anderson R (1975) Efficiency in social services. Blackwell, Oxford

Wing JK, Cooper JE, Sartorius N (1974) The measurement and classification of psychiatric symptoms. Cambridge University Press, Cambridge

Wykes T (1982) A hostel ward for new long-stay patients: an evaluation study of a ward in a house. Psychol Med [Monogr Suppl] 2: 55–97

Wykes T, Wing JK (1982) A ward in a house: accomodation for new long-stay patients. Acta Psychiatr Scand 65: 315–330

The Cost of Long-Term Psychoses in a Scottish Psychiatric Hospital

A. A. McKechnie and J. May

Introduction

In Europe and the United States of America inpatient care and treatment in hospital has become increasingly expensive in recent years. In the U.S.A., for 15 years, costs have risen at 2.5 times the rate of inflation (Faith 1985). In the United Kingdom, National Health Service inpatient treatment, particularly in general hospitals, remains the largest and fastest-growing component of total expenditure (Glass and Goldberg 1977).

Within the U.K. less is spent on "health" than in other EEC countries, but most governments are increasingly anxious about the effects of inflation in relation to health and welfare. In social democratic states monopolies may be created which provide compulsory education, transport, health and social welfare, etc. In the U.K., most educational, health and welfare services are funded by direct or indirect taxation, the former based on the value of occupied property. Even where there is local control of services, the bulk of money is collected, allocated and controlled by central authority.

In the U.K., psychiatric services were formerly based upon large inpatient institutions, but policy for the past 25 years has been to reduce or abolish them and to replace them with community resources. These plans have had support on financial and humanitarian grounds. But this has to be qualified; much stigma is still attached to severe mental illness. It is therefore a naive and speciously logical approach to assert that abolition of institutions will in itself solve most of the problems.

A common feature in EEC countries is the growing need for services for the elderly. In the U.K. the elderly account for a high proportion of primary care resources and for approximately 50% of all admissions to medical, surgical and orthopaedic units of general hospitals. Nationally, in England and Wales it is estimated that 50% of orthopaedic facilities, 55% of general medical beds and 40% of psychiatric facilities are blocked by the elderly (Hunt 1984), largely due to the lack of more appropriate care facilities.

The overall picture in the U.K. is of substantial increases in services with increased manpower directly involved in patient care but with a declining number of beds.

Scotland is to a certain extent a separate region within the U.K. The Scottish Health Service (SHS) receives a separate total fund from the rest of the U.K. and its form is in some ways different, with a higher dependence on institutional care. In psychiatry we have retained more hospital beds than has been the case in England and Wales.

Separate financial statements are available for the SHS. Costs are available for the 15 Health Boards, each of which serves a discrete sector of the population. There are also detailed costings for each type of hospital. It is possible, using national and local data, to determine overall costs and to relate these to a specific defined population, to a hospital, or to a speciality in a district general hospital.

Such refinements of costing have not been available for specific psychiatric wards. McKechnie et al. (1982) did publish data relating to one such hospital and its constituent wards, and this information has been updated, in relation to later financial years, in this paper.

In an annual review of NHS resources, Hunt (1984) identified four areas of major concern:

1. Management budgets and the need to identify budget decision-makers and to sustain activities within predetermined budget levels
2. Clinical costing data to enable appropriate management budgets to be drawn up and to involve clinicians in the planning and budgeting process, including priority rating
3. Activity data to illustrate utilization of resources and to enable results of transferring resources to be identified
4. Data on the outcomes and quality of service provided so that the public is able to judge the appropriateness and adequacy of the Health Services

However, alongside these studies there must also be some attempt at defining quality of life. This is of particular relevance where scarcity of resources may have profound effects on decision-making (Maynard 1985).

Hunt's four areas of concern provide a good framework applicable to all services, including psychiatry, and form the basis of this paper.

Management Budgets and the Need to Identify Budget Decision-Makers and to Sustain Activities Within Predetermined Budget Levels

There is a need to identify total costs of services provided, and whilst it is customary to do so in relation to total communities or to hospital units it is of greater value to identify these costs in relation to each individual in a given catchment area. This gives an overall figure against which the relative allocation of budgets may be determined; at the same time, the cost to a community can be extrapolated. An attempt has been made to identify for each individual, that is on a per capity basis, the net cost of health care and of local authority regional/district services (Table 1). The cost of health services were obtained for the financial year to April 1984 from the Scottish Home and Health Department, and those for the local authority were taken from estimated *net* budgets for the same financial year. The per

Table 1. Net expenditure on provision of local authority services in Lothian Region and of Health Services - £ sterling per capita 1983/1984

	Local authority (£)	Health Service expenditures including capital expenditures	
		Lothian (£)	Scotland average (£)
S) Education	253		
E) (regional)			
L)			
E) Social work	69		
C) (regional)			
T)			
E) Housing	17		
D) Leisure and recreation	19		
All services (regional and district)	576	350	(328)

capita figures for health care were then calculated by dividing total expenditure (estimated net and actual costs including capital expenditure) divided by the total population utilizing Health Board facilities. Selected local authority figures give the net cost of provision of social work services and state education (primary, secondary and further education but excluding centrally funded institutions such as universities). Housing costs exclude rental charges which are derived from Wages, state pensions, etc. Again, per capita expenditure was calculated by dividing total net budgets by the population in receipt of these services. A total of £ 926 was spent on all these facilities, *the two largest individual costs being education (£ 253) and health (£ 350).* The overall cost of health services within the Lothian Health Board is greater than the Scottish average.

The total cost of all medical services can thus be identified for each individual. There is no loading in this simplistic calculation for age - children and the elderly are the greatest consumers of Health Service facilities. Similarly, with regard to local authority services, no division, for example within education, has been attempted. Of particular importance are those costs identified with education, social and recreational facilities, and housing. People with psychiatric illness who are in an institution should receive these elements as a part of their total programme. In a community setting it is vital that an appropriate proportion of the resources available be made accessible to those who are psychiatrically disadvantaged. Redistribution of health resources may not be the best way of dealing with other social necessities.

Comparisons Within the Health Service of Related Categories of Hospital - General, Psychiatric and Geriatric

The SHS issues costing information for individual hospitals within Health Boards. In Scotland there are 15 Health Boards. To assist in the comparison of individual

Table 2. Cost per week (pounds per week per bed) for financial years 1974/1975 and 1983/1984

General hospital			Psychiatric			Geriatric assessment			Index of consumer goods and services	
1975	1984	Change	1975	1984	Change	1975	1984	Change	1974/1975	1983/1984
(£)	(£)	(%)	(£)	(£)	(%)	(£)	(£)	(%)	(£)	(£)
150	537	+258	33	199	+503	54	256	+374	100	+198

hospitals, these have been classified into 50 categories which provide broadly similar treatment facilities. Using this information average running costs per week have been compared between large general hospitals (non-teaching), large psychiatric hospitals (non-teaching), and geriatric assessment and long-stay units (Table 2).

During the period 1975–1984 hospital costs rose considerably, the greatest percentage increase being in psychiatry. The rate of increase in hospital costs substantially exceeds the index of retail prices, which rose by 198% (1974/1975 = 100).

During this period there was a 20% reduction in staffed occupied beds in psychiatric hospitals. There was an *increase* in *occupied* beds in both *general* and *geriatric hospitals* in the categories examined. Discharges were slightly increased for psychiatry and substantially so for general hospitals.

During this time the local hospital (Bangour Village Hospital) costs rose from £57 to £214 per patient, bed occupancy fell by 10% and discharges remained the same. The increase was less than the Scottish average and by 1984 the cost of hospital-based psychiatric services per bed was nearer to the average figure. In fact, major changes took place in relation to care of the elderly and the development of community-based services (McKechnie and Corser 1984, McKechnie 1985), but the way in which the budget is presented fails to give any measure of change in allocation of resources.

Clinical Costing Data to Enable Appropriate Management and Budgets to be Drawn Up and to Involve Clinicians in the Planning and Budgeting Process, Including Priority Rating

Earlier tables have demonstrated overall budgets. Within general hospitals some speciality costing has been achieved, but in relation to psychiatry at a national (U.K.) level all beds are grouped together. Although information is available about age it is not related to actual bed utilization; neither are there separate costs for different types of bed; e.g. short-stay, care of the elderly, chronic psychoses. McKechnie et al. (1982) showed that short-stay units were almost twice as costly as long-stay and that long-stay beds for the elderly were more expensive than those beds allocated to the units serving rehabilitation and long-stay units (Tables 3 and 4).

In this study hotel (or service) costs were fairly uniform; it is treatment and care costs which vary most. In general terms no significant difference is apparent

Table 3. A comparison of inpatient costs at Bangour Hospital 1979/1980, per bed per week

	Short-term/assessment beds		Mental illness		Psycho-geriatric
	Mental illness (age 16–64)	Psychogeriatric (65+)	Rehabilita-tion	Long-term	Long-stay elderly
Average cost per bed per week (£)	206	199	116	107	121

Table 4. Staffing and drug costs per week in selected units expressed as a percentage of total care and treatment costs (1979/1980)

	Short-stay		Mental illness		Psycho-geriatric
	Mental illness	Psycho-geriatric	Rehabilitation	Long-term psychosis	Long-stay elderly, severely mentally infirm
All nursing	74	81	77	85	88
Medical	14	8	3	2	4
All other staff	9	9	16	9	2
Drugs and dressings	3	2	4	4	6
Total cost (to nearest £)	131	116	52	46	61

between the costs of short-term and long-term care for mental illness and psycho-geriatric patients. In this hospital separate units for those aged 65 and over have been developed along the lines advocated by Robinson (1969). In general terms, lower costs reflect poorer staff/patient ratios (Table 4).

The major cost – that of providing nursing care – varied between 74% and 84% of total treatment costs. Except in short-stay units, medical costs were very low. Paramedical staff (principally occupational therapists) were deployed to mental illness beds and in assessment units. Drugs in real terms accounted for a small proportion of total costs. This latter point is of great relevance, given the current preoccupation in the U.K. with reducing expenditure on medicines.

In general, costs were influenced by a number of factors:

1. Occupancy rates: The greater the occupancy the lower the cost.
2. Actual ward size: Service costs may be disproportionately increased especially when, in upgrading, bed numbers in the nurse/patient group are reduced.
3. Staffing ratios: The single highest cost is that of providing nursing care. An important variable is the ratio of trained to untrained staff.
4. Dependency needs: Units built for one purpose and staffed accordingly may not be appropriate for other categories of patient. In particular, as the resident population becomes older and frailer, physical dependency increases. The attri-

tion rate for a graduate (i. e. elderly patient with functional psychosis) does not appreciably affect numbers except over a lengthy time span.

5. Empty beds: Calculations on the basis of official bed complements can be particularly misleading. Such calculations should be based on the number of staffed (properly resourced) beds (Scottish Home and Health Department 1979).

6. Changing demands for treatment: The concept of intensive psychiatric care units is uncommon in psychiatry. Furthermore, staffing norms are not usually available for guidance (compared with general hospital units). Yet there is a clear need for high staff levels for small groups of patients who present with particular management problems on account of disturbed behaviour.

The long-term cost implications of residual cohorts of long-stay patients cannot be overemphasized and is of particular importance where catchment-area boundaries have been altered. In this context it is important to remember that for certain employees salaries are related to bed numbers or bed complement. A reduction of these, even if it means a redeployment of resources to alternative community projects will result in a downgrading of salary for those individuals and may delay rational planning of financial allocation. It is also clear that a reduction in bed numbers or an increase in staff/patient ratios will increase costs. Programmes of return to the community must be accompanied by increased costs, some of which will be spurious and will not reflect an increase in quality of care. Changes in staffing – in particular, a reduction in working hours – will have the effect of increasing costs and may not be adequately budgeted for.

Activity Data to Illustrate Utilization of Resources and to Enable Results of Transferring Resources to Be Identified

It has already been established that the cost of treatment (care) accounts for the largest part of the budget, with that of nursing care being the largest single component. By utilizing Scottish returns it is possible to look at nursing ratios in the three categories of hospital selected and to identify total ratios as well as a breakdown by trained staff, those in training, and untrained nursing assistants. "Trained" in this context means that they are registered nurses and have undergone professional tuition and examination.

Table 5 shows a comparison between 1975 and 1983. In 1984 a change was made and an index for the "Weighted Patient Week Analysis" was adopted. This is a composite measure taking into account inpatients, day patients, and day cases as well as accident and emergency attendances. There has been a marked increase in both general and psychiatric hospitals in the number of trained staff. The overall increase in staff is greater in psychiatry than in either of the other two groups. In general hospitals, staff in training continue to represent a high proportion of total staff. The Weighted Patient Index is of value because a reduction in staff in general hospitals implies an increased measure of community or alternative care (Table 6). No such reduction is as evident either in hospitals for the elderly or in

Table 5. Average number of nurses per 100 inpatient beds

	Year	Training	Change (%)	In training	Change (%)	Other	Change (%)	Total	Change (%)
General hospital	1975	55		49		38		142	
	1983	81	+47	56	+14	40	+ 5	177	+25
Geriatric assessment	1975	38		10		38		86	
and long-stay	1983	43	+13	14	+40	49	+29	106	+23
Psychiatric	1975	21		9		15		45	
	1983	32	+52	13	+44	25	+67	70	+56
Bangour Village	1975	20		6		21		48	
Hospital	1983	35	+75	11	+83	28	+33	74	+54

Table 6. 1984 Weighted Patient Week, a composite measure of nurse staffing per 100 patients, taking into account inpatient/outpatient attendance, day patients, day cases, accident and emergency attendance

	Training	In training	Others	Total
General hospital	67	48	32	147
Geriatric	43	12	43	98
Psychiatric	33	14	24	71

psychiatric hospitals. General hospital psychiatric units are few in number in Scotland and would not substantially alter the figures. Furthermore, the non-teaching units compared usually serve a defined population. The inference must therefore be that, particularly in psychiatry, there has been little redeployment into the community. But is this strictly true? The increased number of long-term elderly in hospital will heavily influence this, in that they absorb a high proportion of total care.

Based on the findings at Bangour Village Hospital (Table 3) the total hospital costs were found to be higher in assessment units; the cost per week for other units where *relative overcrowding* had been eliminated was about 60% of acute assessment units. The estimated costs in the study were found to be within 4% of the SHS costs for the hospital in 1980. Allowing for a 50% increase in costs, and adjusting units depending on bed occupancy, a cost was identified for each category of psychiatric bed. The total estimation for each category of psychiatric bed. The total estimation was found to be within 2% of the published SHS returns for the year 1983/1984. Table 7 shows the distribution of costs by type of bed. It also identifies a major source of distortion.

The hospital was originally built as an asylum for the city of Edinburgh and has continued to offer long-stay beds for the elderly with dementia. Since 1974 Bangour has served only West Lothian, yet today *50%* of the budget remains committed to a population who came from Edinburgh. As this elderly population becomes frailer it makes heavier demands on staff resources. Earlier work (McKechnie 1984) has demonstrated that very few patients were being treated as inpatients other than in the catchment hospital particularly those in long-stay beds. On this basis the resources identified with the care of inpatients with chronic

Table 7. Total annual expenditures, Bangour Village Hospital, 1983/1984

	Occupied beds	£	%
Care of the elderly[a]	384	4514000	(67)
Acute assessment	76	808000	(12)
Rehabilitation and long-stay psychotics	120	1145000	(17)
Intensive psychiatric care unit	20	269000	(4)
Total	600	6736000	(100)

[a] Including elderly with long-term psychoses

Table 8. Actual cost to defined population ($n = 140000$) based on percentage occupancy of specific units by residents from local catchment area

	Percent of occupied beds	Total (£)	Cost per head of population (to nearest pound)
Care of elderly	39	1761000	12
Assessment	100	808000	6
Rehabilitation and Long-stay Psychotics	48	550000	4
Intensive psychiatric care unit	100	269000	2
Total		3388000	24

psychoses can be estimated. To this can be added a proportion of short-stay beds, in that 50% of admissions are readmissions. (The phenomenon of blocked beds is not seen exclusively in general hospitals; it is a feature of psychiatric units as well.)

The actual cost of providing care per head of the population (Table 8) was £24 per annum. Care of the elderly accounted for half of this, and that for rehabilitation and long-term care was only £4 per head. A community-based service could not be accurately costed and is within the total budget – in crude terms, for nursing services alone, it was the equivalent of a 25-bed short-stay or assessment unit.

The psychiatric services to this defined population have recently been described (McKechnie 1985). They include a relatively large community-based service and, together with the hospital resources, it is possible to demonstrate that a nursing unit serving day hospital, domiciliary and depot clinics, can function as an effective service. This would be supported by Fenton et al. (1979) as a more efficient use of expertise. Further support has been found for this in Scotland by McCreadie et al. (1985). They found that if there were more chronic day patients there were fewer misplaced "new" chronic inpatients and more day patients with adequate alternative services. They found that almost all such facilities were *hospital based* – with a *dearth* of staffing, accommodation, occupational or social facilities – and support services being provided either by local authorities or voluntary agencies.

Data on the Outcome and Quality of Services Provided so that the Public Is Able to Judge the Appropriateness and Adequacy of the Health Service

Unfortunately, there is not enough information available for professional groups to begin to inform the public about services for psychotic 1 patients. The first comprehensive report on these services concluded: "The Mental Health Services in Scotland are a deprived area of care" (Mental Health in Focus 1985). It is important to stress that 90% of admissions to psychiatric services are now informal and that 95% of inpatients at any one time are in this category – i.e. compulsory admission in the U.K. to psychiatric hospitals is the exception rather than the rule.

In Britain the generic bed concept prevalent in psychiatric hospitals militates against either the identification of special needs or changing patterns of demand on care facilities.

Whilst there has been a reduction in bed numbers, an increasing proportion of the long-stay population are elderly and physicaly frail. Inadequate accommodation and staffing levels are put under even greater strain by the ageing nature of the population. In Scotland, the elderly with dementia depend for this provision of services on the psychiatric hospital.

A simple categorization of inpatient beds by age-group, broad diagnostic categories, psychiatric and physical dependency needs and a subdivison into short, medium or long-stay would help considerably in planning services. The existence of overcrowding in units for the mentally ill needs to be openly acknowledged. The proportion of money spent on psychiatric inpatient accommodation has definitely increased over the past decade, but it is still substantially less than that spent on general and geriatric units within the Health Service, and staffing levels reflect this.

Planning must take account of the existence of residual cohorts and the continuing demands they place on services. For quality of life to be enhanced there needs to be local planning, integrating health services with those available from local authority and voluntary bodies. Planners need to ask about:

1. Overcrowding
2. Pattern of care for the elderly with dementia
3. Effectiveness of community services, particularly in regard to housing, activities, occupation and leisure
4. The development of strong links between primary health and specialist psychiatric services
5. The extent to which Community Social Work Services are utilized in helping the mentally ill and their families

The costs of inpatient treatment including nursing, medical care, drug or medicine costs, and costs of other services (particularly occupational therapy) have been demonstrated. Over a period of years these become considerable in relation to individual or small group aggregations. No comparable data is available with regard to the identified groups of patients attending day hospitals, receiving domiciliary support from community-based psychiatric nurses, or from depot neuroleptic clinics and lithium clinics. The inference in terms of comparison with nursing personnel based on inpatients would support this on economic grounds. But this whole area of community care is neglected with regard to real outcome and to quality of life. Many patients have been attending these facilities for many years, the tacit assumption being that this is more acceptable and better than inpatient care. These assumptions need careful and urgent examination.

Using data demonstrated earlier in this paper community deployment, particularly of nursing staff, in day hospitals, domiciliary support, and depot neuroleptic clinics would seem a viable alternative to custodial care. It is too easy to become polarized into one extreme of care, either institutional or community based. What is needed is a *spectrum of care* against which the requirements and quality of life of individuals can be assessed. It is vital to consider separately the needs of the elderly from those with mental illness in younger age-groups. Quality of life in relation to services becomes of great importance. For disabled groups, attention must be paid to sheltered employment, recreation and leisure pursuits, aids to daily living, and special housing needs. The extent to which welfare, housing, education and leisure are funded is clear from local authority financial information. What is needed is a concerted effort to identify an appropriate proportion of these services for the psychiatrically disabled. Those of us in professional groups presently responsible for their care need to change our own perceptions in order to utilize these considerable resources and also to further encourage voluntary bodies to participate. This will ensure a more equable distribution of resource and of – equal importance – will alter the present poor image, thus enabling services for chronic psychotic patients to become other than second best.

References

Faith N (1985) The dollar transplant. Financial Times, August 17

Fenton FR, Tessier L, Struening EL (1979) A comparative trial of home and hospital psychiatric care. Arch Gen Psychiatry 36: 1073–1079

Glass NJ, Goldberg D (1977) Cost-benefit analysis and the evaluation of psychiatric services. Psychol Med 7: 701–707

Hunt P (1984) Annual economic review of NHS resources. NAHA, Birmingham

McCreadie RG, Affleck JW, Robinson AD (1985) The Scottish survey of psychiatric rehabilitation and support services. Br J Psychiatry 147: 289–294

McKechnie AA (1984) Integrated mental health services in a Scottish Health District. Health Bull (Edinb) 42/1: 14–24

McKechnie AA (1985) The development of an integrated psychiatric service in a Scottish community. Acta Psychiatr Scand 103: 72–97

McKechnie AA, Corser CM (1984) The role of psychogeriatric assessment units in a comprehensive psychiatric care service. Heath Bull (Edinb) 42/1: 25–35

McKechnie AA, Rae D, May J (1982) A comparison of inpatient costs of treatment and care in a Scottish psychiatric hospital. Br J Psychiatry 141: 602–607

Maynard A (1985) The economic evaluation of mental health policies. In: Manger SP (ed) Mental health care and the European Community. Croom Helm, Dover

Mental Health in Focus (1985) Report on the Mental Health Services for adults in Scotland. SHHD, Edinburgh

Robinson RA (1969) The prevention and rehabilitation of mental illness in the elderly. In: Lowenthal MF, Zilli A (eds) Interdisciplinary topics in gerontology, vol 3. Karger, Basel, pp 89–102

Scottish Health Service Annual Costs 1975–1984. HMSO, Edinburgh

Scottish Home and Health Department, Scottish Education Department (1979) Report on services for the elderly with mental disability in Scotland. HMSO, Edinburgh (Timbury Report)

Management of Schizophrenia: Cost-Benefits, Time-Budget, Better Treatment? Which Time Frame Are We in?

L. Barrelet and W. Fischer

We address here three issues:

1. The wide variability of the main traits of chronic schizophrenics, as illustrated by an outpatient cohort of chronic schizophrenics in Geneva (Switzerland) and by a time-budget analysis of a group of young chronic schizophrenics
2. Contradictions in definitions of treatment benefits and difficulties in establishing correlations between them and treatment goals
3. Analyses of cost components of management of chronic schizophrenics which strongly suggest the importance of occupational rehabilitation for young schizophrenics

How to Define Chronic Schizophrenics

Although chronic schizophrenia is customarily recognized as a subcategory of schizophrenia, one of the chief technical difficulties in defining this group lies in obtaining a truly representative sample population. Nevertheless, follow-up and prospective research of the clinical course of schizophrenia indicate that there is indeed a chronic subgroup of this disease entity (Owens and Johnstone 1980; WHO 1979; Strauss and Carpenter 1981).

In a review of the literature, Stephens (1978) noted that fair- and favourable-outcome schizophrenia was observed to range from 32% to 53%, depending on the particular study in question. In the larger follow-up studies favourable outcome was found to be 20% by Bleuler (1978) and 22% by Huber et al. (1979). The remainder of the patients were considered chronic schizophrenics. As a first approximation, based mainly on retrospective studies, chronic schizophrenics have been categorized into three principal types of clinical course:

1. Recurring schizophrenia with symptom-free intervals between relapses
2. Recurring schizophrenia with stable deficits in the intervals between acute phases
3. Recurring schizophrenia with progressive deterioration following each acute phase

In order to obtain and unbiased group one must identify all schizophrenics within a given catchment area. This is rarely possible. In a recent study, a British research team (Watt et al. 1983) determined the ratios of four subtypes of clinical course in a highly representative population. This group found that the clinical course following the first hospitalisation was:

1. No relapse for 32% of female patients and 15% of male patients
2. Relapse and return to premorbid level of functioning for 36% of female patients and 35% of male patients
3. Relapse and persistent deficit between acute phases in 14% of female patients and 4% of male patients
4. Relapse and progressive deterioration between acute phases in 18% of female patients and 46% of male patients

One of the most striking and least exploited findings of this study is the great dissimilarity of clinical course according to sex: indeed unfavourable outcome occurred in only one of five women, as opposed to one of two men. It has been postulated that in the past half century the prognosis for schizophrenic women has improved dramatically, that for schizophrenic men only slightly. Chronic schizophrenics are to be found in groups 2, 3 and 4. An alternate method of identifing chronic schizophrenics consists in selecting a large sample from a treatment center where they usually receive care. A number of cohorts selected in this manner, mainly from hospital populations and more recently from outpatient treatment centers, have been studied. Study of the cohort selected in this manner has furnished much information on the characteristics, behaviour and needs of chronic schizophrenics.

As the literature contains a limited number of studies of outpatient cohorts (Engelhardt et al. 1982; Cheadle et al. 1978; Glazer et al. 1980), it is worth describing the characteristics of the schizophrenic population treated at the outpatient services of community mental health centers in Geneva in 1981 and comparing them with data available on other psychotic and non-psychotic patients treated at the same facilities. Subsequently, the institutional cost of managing this cohort will be given in detail.

Characteristics of Schizophrenic Patients Treated at the Outpatient Services in Geneva

The results presented in this cross-sectional study were drawn from a representative sample of patients (one of two patients) consulting the outpatient services of community mental health centers (Department of Psychiatry of the University of Geneva, Switzerland). The survey was begun in 1981 and includes 361 patients who consulted the outpatient services at least once during a 2-month period (FNSRS Project No: 4.343.079.08). Our special focus of interest is the group of 69 patients diagnosed as schizophrenics[1]; an additional 63 patients were diag-

---

[1] ICD 295

nosed as having other psychoses,[2] and 229 patients were diagnosed as neurotic or borderline, or were given other non-psychotic diagnoses.[3]

Sociodemographic Description

There are no significant differences regarding the *sexual distribution:* 50.7% of the schizophrenics are men and 49.3% are women. These ratios are similar to those found in the other diagnostic categories, as well as to those of the overall population in Geneva for persons between the ages of 20 and 64 years (48.5% men, 51.5% women in 1981). However, from the standpoint of *age,* significant differences can be demonstrated. Thus, although the age of male schizophrenics is similar to that found in the male population in Geneva, female schizophrenics are clearly older (Table 1).

Significant differences are also observed with regard to *marital status.* Generally speaking, schizophrenics are often unmarried; only 8.6% of men, somewhat more women: 23.5%; this is a considerable underrepresentation compared with the population at large. This underrepresentation is also observable for the other category of psychotic patients although not to the same degree: more than a third of these patients are married. Conversely, unmarried individuals are very much overrepresented (Table 1). This absence of close marital ties in the schizophrenic

Table 1. Distribution by sex, age, civil status, professional activity and socioprofessional level of schizophrenics and the resident population in Geneva

	Schizophrenics			Resident population in Geneva aged 20–64 years		
	Men	Women	Total	Men	Women	Total
Age: <40	51.5	11.8	31.9	51.6	51.7	51.7
40–49	17.1	41.2	29.0	23.8	22.4	23.0
⇒ 50	31.4	47.0	39.1	24.7	25.9	25.3
Civil status:						
Single	77.1	50.0	63.8	25.0	23.7	24.3
Married	8.6	23.5	15.9	68.5	64.1	66.2
Divorced widowed	14.3	26.5	20.3	6.5	12.2	9.5
Unemployed	77.2	67.6	72.5	10.0	43.6	27.3
Actively employed	22.8	32.4	27.5	90.0	56.4	72.7
Profession:						
Middle and upper class	3.1	2.9	3.0	27.4	22.2	24.6
Shopkeepers and tradesmen	6.3	2.9	4.5	8.9	3.7	6.2
Qualif. white-collar workers	9.4	29.4	19.7	19.3	39.3	29.7
Unqual. white-collar workers	12.5	26.5	19.7	11.1	27.7	19.8
Qualif. blue-collar workers	12.5	2.9	7.6	16.4	1.4	8.7
Unqual. blue-collar workers	56.3	35.3	45.5	16.9	5.7	11.0

---

[2] ICD 290–294, 296–299
[3] ICD 300–316

group is further accentuated by the high separation and divorce rates characteristic of this group, which are more than double (20.3%) those for the general population (9.5%). This is especially true for female schizophrenics. It should also be noted that the divorce rate for the non-psychotic group is slightly higher (24.2%); it is higher still for the other psychotic category (30.6%), in which nearly half of the women (42.9%) are either divorced or separated.

The instability associated with this type of *social environment* is a finding which can be applied generally to the psychiatric population at large, but it is also related to an additional particularity which is characteristic of the schizophrenic group: one sixth of them live in institutional settings, and this is especially the case for men: 26.5%. This state of affairs is applicable to only a small minority of other patients: 6.3% of those in the other psychotic category and 3.1% of those with a non-psychotic diagnosis. Furthermore, the proportion of individuals living alone is also elevated: 37.9% of schizophrenics, a proportion similar to that found in the other diagnostic categories. For the psychiatric outpatient groups, the proportion of individuals living alone is almost double that found in the overall population, where only 19.3% are single dwellers. Another significant pattern is that schizophrenics rarely live in households comprised of three or more persons (only 12.1%), and this is slightly more frequent for women than for men. For the other psychotic category in this survey, 22.2% live in larger households, as do 33% of those having a non-psychotic diagnosis. The figures for the general population is 45.3%.

Gainful Employment

Another crucial factor for schizophrenic patients is the *employment rate*. The majority are excluded from the work arena (Table 1). This is similar for other psychotics, only 30.2% of whom are gainfully employed. Non-psychotic patients are more often gainfully employed: 67.3% of men and 54.7% of women. For women, this is a very high percentage compared with the overall professional activity of women in the general population (56.4%: Table 1). By and large, the psychiatric population, and more specifically schizophrenics, are characterised by a very low socioprofessional degree of integration. The exclusion from the employment market has increased over the past 15 years, particularly since the onset of the economic crisis, which heightened the competition for jobs. Thus, many patients were invalidated and assigned a psychiatric disability status. While in 1967 only 3.6% of the ambulatory psychiatric population were classified as disabled, by 1981, at the time of this study, the proportion of the population considered disabled had risen to 36.4%, and since then these figures have continued to climb (Fischer 1981). Another 16.1% of this population were unemployed although they were not disabled. This employment pattern is even more frequently the case for men (68.6%) than for women (52.9%); in addition, 8.6% of the men are currently receiving unemployment benefits and 14.7% of the women are not presently working, be it by choice or by circumstance. The number of disabled workers is slightly less among other psychotics (47.6%), although only 30.2% are employed, but 60.8% of the non-psychotic patients are employed and 22.9% are considered disabled.

The findings indicating the level of socioprofessional functioning reached by patients at the time of the survey, or at the time when their professional activities were discontinued, give a first indication concerning *the mechanisms leading to eviction from the labor market*. In fact, the socioprofessional level of psychiatric patients is clearly and systematically inferior to that of the general population. A closer comparison between the latter and the schizophrenic patients demonstrates certain sex-related differences. Typically, male schizophrenics tend to have very low social positions; 56.3% are unqualified workers. This is more than three times the number found in the overall male population, where non-qualified workers represent only 16.9% of the total (Table 1). Of male schizophrenics, 68.8% are employed as unskilled laborers. This is the case for only 28% of the active male population. On the other hand, male schizophrenics are underrepresented in skilled occupations: 21.9% versus 35.7% in the overall population, and they are virtually absent form the higher socioprofessional levels (technicians, teaching professions, middle management and the medical and legal professions): 3.1% versus 27.4% of economically active males, i.e. nearly nine times fewer. Similar findings can also be observed for female schizophrenics. However, the socioprofessional downgrading of women is based more frequently on the distinctions between blue- and white-collar workers rather than on skilled and unskilled occupations. In fact, 38.2% of the schizophrenic group are female blue-collar workers. The majority are unskilled; in the economically active female population, blue-collar workers represent only 7.1% of the total. Thus, female schizophrenics occupy the lowest rungs on the socioprofessional ladder, more than five times more frequently than can be observed in the population at large. On the other hand, skilled white-collar workers (clerical, commercial) are underrepresented: 29.4% of the schizophrenic group and 39.3% of the economically active female population. Finally, 22.2% of the latter group hold middle or superior socioprofessional status; this is the case for only 2.9% of the female schizophrenic patients, i.e. nearly eight times less frequently (Table 1).

Education, Occupational Training, and Careers

The *socioeconomic downgrading* described above may be explained in part by the events which intervened and disrupted the professional training and careers of this group of patients. At this point, we will not consider the data concerning the lack of family integration, although these factors may have been very influential. In examining patterns of education and occupational training more closely, one is struck by a series of findings which, when taken individually, might seem minor; however, when they are grouped together, they draw a very specific picture of the history of schizophrenic patients. Unfortunately, we have no comparative data for the general population and will thus limit ourselves to a comparison among the three categories of patients already defined.

Schooling: Generally, the educational level of psychiatric patients is low. Of the schizophrenics 71.2% have only completed compulsory education; 15.2% continued their education without obtaining a diploma, and 13.6% have acquired a secondary or university level education.

Occupational training of schizophrenics is comparable to that observed in other groups of patients: 13.6% have completed long-term formal professional training or other advanced training; 21.8% have completed a non-manual apprenticeship and 30.8% have completed a manual apprenticeship, whereas 33.8% have had no occupational training. This is mainly the case for women, more than half of whom (51.6%) have no professional qualifications as opposed to 17.6% of the men (Table 2).

Occupational trajectory: Schizophrenics tend to show consistent downgrading, from the first occupation they choose for training to the last job. Among male schizophrenics, 50% obtained a manual qualification but only 12.5% are employed as skilled blue-collar workers (Table 2); 20.6% have completed professional training or superior education, but only 3.1% still hold a middle or superior occupational position. The same pattern holds true for female schizophrenics.

Several factors may be considered to explain this downgrading phenomenon. The first is the *entry into the labour market,* once training has been completed. In fact, the step taken between training and first employment for approximately a third (30.6%) of the schizophrenic patients is characterised by a total change in the field of professional activity from that for which they were trained. This professional re-orientation, which occurs more frequently for the men (35.5% versus 25.8% for the

Table 2. Distribution by sex and level of professional qualification of schizophrenics

	Professional qualification			Last employment		
	Men	Women	Total	Men	Women	Total
Unqualified	17.6	51.6	33.8	75.0	64.8	69.7
Qualified blue-collar workers	50.0	9.7	30.8	12.5	2.9	7.6
Qualif. white-collar workers	11.8	32.2	21.8	9.4	29.4	19.7
Superior qualification	20.6	6.5	13.6	3.1	2.9	3.0
Total ($n=100\%$)	34	31	65	32	34	66

Diff. men: $x^2 = 19.78$ $P < .001$
Diff. women: $x^2 = 2.09$ n.s.
Diff. total: $x^2 = 18.54$ $P < .001$

Table 3. Distribution by sex, interruptions in professional training, change of profession at the time of entry into the labour force, and changes in employment level between first and last employment held by schizophrenics and other patients

	Schizophrenics			Other patients		
	Men	Women	Total	Men	Women	Total
Interruptions during professional training	60.0	50.0	55.0	30.8	27.7	29.2
Change of prof. at time of entry into labour force	35.5	25.8	30.6	14.6	9.2	11.8
Significant changes between first and last employment	53.6	36.4	44.3	47.7	35.0	41.2

women) almost invariably entails a loss of acquired skills and capacities (Table 3). The second factor which characterises schizophrenics is the high frequency of *interruptions and switches* in educational and occupational training. This finding applies especially to men, 60% of whom have gone through more than one reorientation after having experienced a failure. The same process affects 50% of the women in the schizophrenic group (Table 3). As a third factor, the pattern of "downward drift" continues throughout the entire span of their *work careers*. Thus, 44.3% end up working in a completely different field than the one in which they began after training. Again, men are more frequently confronted with this situation (53.6%) than women (36.4%; Table 3). In addition, for more than half of this population, the shift in employment spheres is a clear professional disqualification and increases their vulnerability to the mechanisms excluding them from the labor force, as will be demonstrated shortly. Whereas the first two factors are typical for schizophrenics, the latter is prevalent among all psychiatric patients.

The downgrading already observed during the course of their professional life is a forerunner of other disparities, especially the divergency in achieved socioeconomic status of the patient and his family of origin. More than half (54%) of the schizophrenic patients occupy lower socioeconomic positions than did their fathers. Other evidence exists that these *intergenerational differences* contribute to the weakening of family ties and add to the stresses already accumulated in the socioprofessional sphere.

The factors described above are linked not only to the socioprofessional trajectory of schizophrenics, but also to their position either as gainfully employed workers or as occupationally disabled persons. Among the male schizophrenics who moved completely out of the employment field for which they received training, nearly three quarters (72.7%) were considered disabled at the time of the survey; in addition, 9.1% were on sick leave or receiving unemployment compensation (Table 4). For women, the relative proportions are similar: 75% receive disability compensation, and another 12.5% are not gainfully employed, but for other reasons. Consequently, only 18.2% of the men and 12.5% of the women have been able to continue a professional activity despite the strong downward pressures which were operating at the time they entered the employment market. By comparison, economic activity rates are higher for schizophrenics who have been able to continue to work in the field for which they were trained (25% of men and

Table 4. Distribution of schizophrenics according to employment level in the labour force, level of professional training, and sex

	Employed at level for which trained			Employed in field unrelated to training		
	Men	Women	Total	Men	Women	Total
Actively employed	25.0	30.0	27.9	18.2	12.5	15.8
Sick, at home	10.0	17.8	14.0	9.1	12.5	10.5
Disabled	65.0	52.2	58.1	72.7	75.0	73.7
Total ($n=100\%$)	20	23	43	11	8	19
Diff. total: $x^2=3.05$	n.s.					

30% of women), and the proportion of disabled is less (65% of men and 52.2% of women). The relationship of these findings to other indices of intergenerational or intragenerational factors influencing professional careers demonstrate some deviations which, although not highly significant, point up two interesting findings.

Generally speaking, the professional *careers of men,* and especially their current situation with regard to the employment market, seem to be more strongly influenced by the events which occurred during educational training and the progressive loss of socioeconomic status while they were exercising their professional career. Thus, of male schizophrenics who were not able to get professional training or who dropped out before the end of training, only a small proportion (9.5%) are working; the rest have been eliminated from the employment market and are classified as disabled (76.2%). On the other hand, of those who are professionally qualified, 42.9% hold their ground in the employment world (Table 5). This figure is four and a half times larger than that cited for the previous group. The consequences accruing to progressive career downgrading for those actually exercising a professional activity follow the same pattern as for the group mentioned above, albeit to a lesser degree. The same phenomenon is observed when one takes into account the discrepancy between the level of socioprofessional functioning of the patient and that of his or her father. The interesting part of this relationship is the following: it is the degree of stability or congruence between father's and patient's occupational status which is associated with remaining in the employment market or not. Exclusion from the labor force is more frequent for patients who have a different socioeconomic position than that held by their father (be it upward or downward mobility).

A last interesting observation concern the *higher economic activity rates for women* who have had psychiatric treatment. This pattern also holds for female schizophrenics. Their employment situation is less directly related to the vicissitudes they may have encountered during educational training and/or during the course of their professional career. They are more affected by their life situation in general. As they are often divorced or separated and also frequently have parental responsibilities, they work for reasons of economic necessity. This economic constraint (which would not be adequately met through alimony payments, widow's pension or public assistance) forces them to accept employment even on the lowest rungs of the economic ladder. They therefore accept jobs not requiring professional qualifications that are monotonous as well as comparatively badly paid.

Table 5. Distribution of labour force status by interruption in professional training and sex

	Interruptions during training			No interruptions		
	Men	Women	Total	Men	Women	Total
Actively employed	9.5	30.0	16.1	42.9	33.3	36.8
Sick, at home	14.3	0	9.7	0	30.8	13.2
Disabled	76.2	70.0	74.2	57.1	45.9	50.0
Total ($n=100\%$)	21	10	31	14	24	38
Diff. total: $x^2=6.31$	$0.02 > P > 0.01$					

The consequences linked to these working conditions are highly detrimental for both physical and mental well-being; soon or later the burden becomes too great and this aggravates their psychological state. It is equally probable that the increased stresses which these patients experience mobilise personal resources which are, indirectly, perhaps beneficial for them.

Treatment Patterns

As compared with other diagnostic categories, schizophrenics treated in the public sector are far more frequently institutionalised. Several factors may explain this: hospitalisation, place and duration of outpatient care, psychiatric assessment.

- *Hospitalisation:* With the exception of only two women, all schizophrenics had had at least one psychiatric hospitalisation (this is the case for 87% of other psychotics and for 55% of those with another diagnosis). In addition, they were hospitalised more frequently. Nearly two-thirds of male and female schizophrenics have had four or more psychiatric admissions (Table 6). Lengthy hospitalisations are common among schizophrenics: 62.4% of men and 40.6% of women had hospital stays of 1 year or longer (Table 7). In comparison, the proportion is 30% for the men and 32.3% for the women suffering from other psychoses, 23.7% for men and 15.5% for women with non-psychotic diagnoses. For women in general, and in all three diagnostic categories, the total length of hospital stays is less than for men, despite the fact that they are hospitalised more often; i.e. on the average, women's hospitalisations are briefer than those of men. Schizophrenics were determined to have spent more time in hospital: on an average a total of 781 days, as compared with 384 days for other psychotics and 330 days for non-psychotic patients (Table 8).
- *Place of treatment:* Another feature distinguishes schizophrenics from the other patients. In analysing the outpatient treatment patterns more closely, we observed that other psychiatric services, as well as psychiatrists who practise in the

Table 6. Distribution of the total number of hospitalisations by sex and diagnostic category

	Men				Women			
	Schizo-phrenia	Other psychoses	Other diagnoses	Total	Schizo-phrenia	Other psychoses	Other diagnoses	Total
None	0	15.4	62.3	43.0	5.9	11.1	48.7	33.5
1	12.1	23.1	12.3	13.9	2.9	19.4	16.5	14.6
2–3	24.2	34.6	12.3	18.2	26.5	27.8	15.7	20.0
⇒4	63.7	26.9	12.3	24.9	64.7	41.7	19.1	31.9
Total (*n*=100%)	33	26	105	164	34	36	115	185

Diff.: male schizophrenics – other psychoses	$x^2 = 16.93$	$P < 0.001$
Diff.: male schizophrenics – other diagnoses	$x^2 = 51.11$	$P < 0.001$
Diff.: female schizophrenics – other psychoses	$x^2 = 5.92$	$0.02 < P < 0.05$
Diff.: female schizophrenics – other diagnoses	$x^2 = 36.34$	$P < 0.001$

Table 7. Distribution of the duration of hospitalisation according to sex and diagnosis

	Men				Women			
	Schizo-phrenia	Other psychoses	Other diagnosis	Total	Schizo-phrenia	Other psychoses	Other diagnoses	Total
% No hosp.	0	14.8	63.5	43.3	5.9	11.4	49.1	33.7
<4 months	21.9	43.5	57.8	42.0	18.8	29.1	45.6	34.7
4–12 months	15.7	21.7	18.4	19.4	40.6	38.8	37.9	38.9
1–2 years	28.1	13.0	13.2	18.3	15.6	22.6	8.6	14.1
>2 years	34.3	17.4	10.5	20.4	25.0	9.7	6.9	12.4
Total ($n=100\%$)	32	23	38	93	32	31	58	121

Comparison of duration of hospitalisation
Diff.: male schizophrenics – other psychoses $x^2 = 4.60$ $P>0.05$
Diff.: male schizophrenics – other diagnoses $x^2 = 12.24$ $0.01 > P > 0.001$
Diff.: female schizophrenics – other psychoses $x^2 = 3.34$ $P>0.05$
Diff.: female schizophrenics – other diagnoses $x^2 = 11.25$ $0.02 > P > 0.01$

Comparison of presence/absence of hospitalisation
Diff.: male schizophrenics – other psychoses $x^2 = 3.29$ n.s.
Diff.: male schizophrenics – other diagnoses $x^2 = 30.69$ $P<0.001$
Diff.: female schizophrenics – other psychoses $x^2 = $ n.s.
Diff.: female schizophrenics – other diagnoses $x^2 = 19.51$ $P<0.001$

Table 8. Hospitalisations before and after the start of outpatient treatment by sex and diagnosis

	Hospitalisations before the first outpatient treatment			Hospitalisations after the start of outpatient treatment		
	% of Hospital-isations	Absolute interval	Median (days)	% of Hospital-isations	Absolute interval	Median (days)
Men						
Schizophrenics	51.4	28 days–19 years	152	74.3	8 days–9 years	350
Other psychotics	44.5	5 days– 2 years	42	70.4	20 days–4.8 years	128
other diagnoses	17.3	7 days– 6 years	47	24.8	7 days–2.2 years	91
Women						
Schizophrenics	61.8	15 days–14 years	95	88.2	30 days–10 years	189
Other psychotics	44.4	10 days–6.9 years	91	72.2	12 days–2.3 years	213
Other diagnoses	26.7	8 days–259 days	61	37.7	2 days–22 years	114

private sector, preferentially oriented these patients towards the outpatient services in the public sector: more than half of both men (51.6%) and women (54.9%). Forty-four percent of the schizophrenics had been treated by psychiatrists in the private sector before their outpatient treatment. These findings demonstrate that schizophrenic patients are major consumers of psychiatric treatment and that they have successively utilized multiple services and therapists. It can be seen that treatment continuity frequently poses problems.
– *Outpatient treatment:* As has been shown with hospitalisations, outpatient psychiatric treatment also extends over considerably longer periods for schizophrenics: 84.1% had their first psychiatric consultation at least 5 years before

the study. This is the case for 58.7% of other psychotics and for 31.8% of patients with other diagnoses. Patients receiving outpatient treatment for less than a year represent only 7.2% of the schizophrenics, 23.8% of other psychotics and 54.1% of patients with other diagnoses. Outpatient treatment in the university psychiatric services in Geneva is especially long for women; 91.2% of female schizophrenics have been treated in the outpatient services for more than 5 years, and for a substantial proportion treatment has extended over a period of more than 10 years.

- *Psychiatric treatment:* One last specificity related to schizophrenics is the frequency of requests for psychiatric evaluation to determine eligibility for disability compensation. It was requested for 68.7% male and 67.6% female schizophrenics and, from this point of view as well, the professional difficulties described earlier play an important role. For other psychotics, the frequency of requests for psychiatric evaluation is also elevated (66.7% for men and 61.1% for women) but it is less prevalent for patients with other diagnoses: 31.8% for men and 28.5% for women. The degree of institutionalisation for schizophrenic patients extends even further when one considers the number of these patients who are also treated in day hospitals and brief therapy centers, as well as in sheltered workshops. A large majority of these patients have spent time in one or another of these two types of services.

Psychiatric Treatment Patterns and Social Characteristics

Up to this point we have observed a close relationship between the psychiatric treatment patterns and the social career characteristics of schizophrenic patients: the deterioration in socioprofessional activity and the breakdown of family ties goes hand in hand with increasing psychiatric institutionalisation and dependency on a number of public and private social services. The details of the interactions between these two factors will be described elsewhere.

Time Budget: Preliminary Study of a Group of Young Chronic Schizophrenics Who Maintain Close Ties with Their Families

At the WHO meeting in Mannheim in May 1983, participants were confident that different ways of managing chronic schizophrenics could be validly compared. At the time, the difficulties involved in establishing comparable groups and estimating benefits were underestimated. Consequently, we planned to study the burden that chronic schizophrenics represent for their families (Platt 1985). With this in view, we intended to collect time-budgets (TB) of patients and their families. During the interviews we questioned the patient about the preceding day and one day of the weekend, by asking questions about every quarter of an hour of this day. In addition, we held the same interview with one family member, usually the mother. We asked additional questions about meeting people during the week, about feeling lonely and the wish to have more contacts with others. In a preliminary study we took a sample of chronic schizophrenics who maintain close ties with their families but who have various living arrangements: most live with their families; some work, some attend a day care center, still others work in highly sheltered settings, and some are without any scheduled day activity at all. Some had recently had a psychotic relapse, some had been stabilized for a few months. Our goal was to determine the extent of the burden schizophrenics constitute for their families and to ascertain whether TB could be used as indicators of this burden. Here we describe the interpersonal contact time on one test weekday and the weekly contacts. In our group, some patients work or hope to return to work, some attend a day care center or a patients' social club with a view to ultimate reinsertion into the community.

The time patients spent socialising with others was broken down into four categories according to involvement and importance of subject discussed, as suggested by Lawson et al. (1985): concentrated social contacts (or intimate), continuous social contacts (or close), available social contacts (or near), separate (or absent). On average, patients had concentrated social contacts with someone on weekday test days for 1 h and 20 min and were involved in an uninterrupted joint activity with this person, or had close social contacts with someone (generally entailing verbal communication), for 4 h and 45 min, available social contacts (usually sharing lodgings) for 4 h and 30 min, or remained alone (separate) for 4 h and 30 min. These averages are comparable to those for other family members interviewed (Table 9). Analysis of TB for Sundays shows a similar distribution of the durations of social contacts: here, too, there is no quantitative difference between patients and parents. Table 10 presents the comparison of the number of persons

Table 9. Young chronic schizophrenics: time-budget analysis of social contacts

| Types of contacts | Duration per weekday | | Difference[a] |
	Mean per patient	Mean per family member	P
1. Concentrated social contacts	1 h 20 min	1 h 05 min	0.33
2. Close social contacts	4 h 45 min	3 h 05 min	0.09
3. Available social contacts	4 h 30 min	6 h	0.31
4. Alone	4 h 30 min	5 h 10 min	0.61

[a] Wilcoxon matched-pairs test

Table 10. Young chronic schizophrenics: comparison of weekly contacts with those of family members

Persons met weekly	Median per patient	Median per family member	P[a]
Members of the immediate family	5	4	0.55
More or less close friends	1	3	0.61
Other personal acquaintances	7[b]	8	0.58

[a] Wilcoxon matched-pairs test
[b] Five of the seven persons were encountered in a therapeutic or a sheltered setting

with whom the parents or the patients had contact during a week. Patients met five members of their immediate family, one more or less close friend, two other personal acquaintances and five other persons encountered in a therapeutic setting (median value). Parents' and patients' values do not differ significantly. The subjective judgements of patients and parents about their social contacts and their feeling of loneliness are also similar: most patients responded affirmatively to the question "Do you often feel lonely?" (8 yes, 2 no). Six patients would have liked to have more interpersonal contacts and four would not. Six stated they felt lonely even in the company of others and four not. The interviewed parents answered five times 'yes' and five times 'no' to the first two questions and four times 'yes' and six times 'no' to the third question.

The sociability of this group is also manifested by the fact that time spent on leisure activities is as long as that for the parental group. On the other hand, the employed patients work an average of 2 h less per day than the employed parents. The remainder of the patients perform no work, whereas the remaining parents are all active housewives. In addition, the patient group averaged about the same number of waking hours as the parent group. This is interpreted to mean that there is no particular attempt to withdraw by sleeping.

Analysis of the TB of our sample population revealed that schizophrenics spend relatively little time with their families – taken as a group, a median time of 1 h and 30 min per weekday. Most patients share their weekend with their families, meeting parents but also brothers, sisters or other relatives. Therefore, patients' scheduling of time did not appear to be a significant factor in the putative burden they constitute for their relatives. Quite on the contrary, we gathered the impression that relatives considered the time spent with patients as a welcome relief from loneliness. Two clinical observations illustrate this point: A 22-year-old schizophrenic girl living with her 47-year-old divorced mother and her 19-year-old brother spent one or two 30- to 45-min periods per day in very close interpersonal contact with her mother. The working mother was socially isolated. The relation with her daughter was the only regular daily contact of this type, although she did get together with some close friends on weekends. A 28-year-old schizophrenic man visited his mother and father almost every evening after work. His father worked, but his mother was a housewife with little contact outside home. Her son's visits provided a welcome opportunity to have regular detailed conversation with someone besides her husband.

A second finding was contrary to expectation. Schizophrenics who maintain close family ties showed only a few of the signs of withdrawal and isolation usually associated with chronic schizophrenics. As a matter of fact, we found that these patients may be quite sociable. As the above comparison of the TB shows, patients and family members seem to have interpersonal contacts of similar lengths. In fact, they usually spend not more than 30% of their time alone, and most of them seek more interpersonal contacts. One may ask if their sociability is the result of better treatment, whether this sociability can be maintained in the future, and what are the best means to maintain this sociability. As has been shown (Isele et al. 1985), the social network of schizophrenics is restricted. One way to maintain their sociability may be to enable them to keep up other relations, even while they are actively attending day centers or clubs. This seems to have been the case for many of their social contacts in sheltered settings. For these reasons, we did not find it advisable to subdivide social contacts into different types in our TB. Our observations seem to indicate that patients tend to prefer sociability to seclusion.

Benefits of Treatment

In the first section, we attempted to show how difficult it is to define chronic schizophrenics as a group. Because there are few outpatient studies, it appeared useful to describe the characteristics of the cohort treated in the outpatient services of community mental health centers in Geneva. The study of the interpersonal contacts of a subgroup of chronic schizophrenics who maintain ties with their families led us to believe that the majority remained highly sociable. In addition to the wide variability of the characteristics of chronic schizophrenics, there is an other methodological problem in estimating costs and benefits of treatment: the definition of 'benefits'.

Benefits Connected with Hospitalisation

Indications (Engelhardt et al. 1967) and goals of hospitalisation (Goldberg et al. 1965) have changed greatly over the past 30 years (Mann and Cree 1976). Reasons for the hospitalisation of chronic schizophrenics (Caton 1982; Rosenblatt 1984) are multiple (Rosenblatt and Mayer 1974). In addition to current relapses, other reasons are (Barrelet 1984):

1. Adjustment of medication
2. Reduction of symptomatology to a point where outpatient care is feasible
3. Wherever they can be identified, modification of factors responsible for relapse

Many functions formerly handled through hospitalisation (Erickson 1975) are now performed by alternative structures within the community (Barrelet 1985; Test and Stein 1978; Goldstein and Caton 1983): halfway houses provide lodging on a medium- or long-term basis; social rehabilitation (Falloon and Marshall 1983), training in coping skills (Paul and Lentz 1977), and participation in group activities, even minimal, take place in sheltered workshops (Black 1977), day hospitals (Linn et al. 1979; Pryce et al. 1983), or social clubs for patients. Additional care is provided by various agencies which make home visits (Ozarin 1976). For this reason, the measurements of hospitalisation (duration and frequency) are no longer a good indication of clinical course and quality of treatment. Nevertheless, they cannot simply be replaced by another standard measuring the new structures used by patients (McCreanie and Mizell 1978). Indications for using these structures depends, like hospitalisation, on multiple other criteria besides the condition of patient (Pai and Roberts 1983). We cannot forget, for example, the need of the treating staff to distribute the burden of caring for chronic schizophrenics between the different treatment structures.

Benefits Related to Working Capacity

The clinical course of the schizophrenics – which is extremely irregular – is in contradiction to the rules existing in the business world and tends to force schizophrenics out of the mainstream of life (Cheadle et al. 1978; Lorei and Gurel 1973). This removal from the social mainstream is detrimental. Even when working capacity is fully recuperated, employers hesitate to hire schizophrenics because of the high risk of relapse (Dohrenwend et al. 1983). Everyone hopes that "these people" will sooner or later get disability benefits (Huffine and Clausen 1979). The measure of the effectiveness of work became the result of complex interactions between the real working capacity of the patient and the characteristics of the possibility of being hired (Strauss et al. 1981). Clinicians know that the quality of the social network is a complementary dimension which is comportant for the success of going back to work (Beck 1978). Occupational performance is a poor measure of the benefits of treatment because it depends on other, still unknown factors (Carpenter and Stephens 1982; McCreadie 1982).

Benefits Related to the Course of Symptoms

A small group of patients live with sustained psychotic symptoms, such as hallucinations, in spite of different kinds of treatments. With most schizophrenics, the psychotic symptoms disappear after the acute phase (Bland and Orn 1980). The reappearance of the psychiatric symptomatology occurs in episodes that we call 'relapses' (Falloon and Marshall 1983; Herz and Melville 1980). The course can be described by taking into consideration the symptomatology during relapse. In between these relapses we observe periods or phases of fewer symptoms or even a lack of psychotic symptomatology. During the non-psychotic phases we observe a more neurotic symptomatology (Johnson 1981), social isolation, bizarre behavior, depression (Hirsch 1982), deficit of language, or minor behavior problems. The clinical course can be described in different ways (Bleuler 1978). For the relapses we measure the type, frequency, time, and intensity of the symptomatology. Between two relapses we measure the presence and the intensity of the different symptoms. These measures need to be better correlated with treatments (medication and psychosocial therapies; May 1976; Goldberg et al. 1977). Some facts are already established. For instance, we know that neuroleptic medication (Davis 1975; Woggon 1979) helps to reduce the frequency and intensity of relapses (Falloon et al. 1978; Davis et al. 1980), while rapid initiation of a full and adequate treatment program at the moment when the patient relapses is certainly very important; psychosocial treatment is certainly important during the phases between relapses (Johnson et al. 1983; Hogarty 1984). On the other hand, important factors still need to be determined (van Putten 1983; Buckley 1982). For example, it has still not been sufficiently demonstrated that the quality of life and long-term outcome are essentially improved (Mosher and Keith 1979; Gaebel and Pietzcker 1985; Boker et al. 1984) when we reduce the frequency and intensity of relapses by administering high doses of neuroleptics (Kane 1979; Herz 1982) or by other therapeutic measures (Goldberg 1980) like ECT, or when we risk relapses by using the

stimulation of psychological or psychosocial approaches aimed at the improvement of social adjustment between acute phases (McGlashan 1984; Liberman et
al. 1983; Williams 1983; May et al. 1981; Karon 1984).

Benefits from Interpersonal Relationships

Schizophrenics gradually have fewer social contacts (Beck 1978; Beels and Gutwirth 1984). This may already happen before the first period of hospitalisation.
The social network of the schizophrenic has a tendency to be poor (Sokolovsky et
al. 1978; Hammer 1981); this fact is difficult to explain. Some authors think that
this has to do with their difficulty in adapting themselves to the external world
(Linn et al. 1985; Sommer and Osmond 1984). Some studies show that forcing
schizophrenics to establish social contacts leads to an increase in symptoms and a
deterioration in social adjustment (Schooler and Spohn 1982). On the other hand,
the improvement of social relationships can be related to a global improvement
and a reduction of symptomatology (Spencer et al. 1983; Wallace et al. 1980). Because of these contradictory facts, the measures of interpersonal relations cannot
be used as a straightforward standard of benefits. The effects of medication and
psychosocial treatment on social relatedness have to be better understood (Goldstein and Caton 1983; Wallace and Boone 1984).

Benefits Connected with Quality of Life

Many authors have attempted to measure the quality of life of schizophrenics
(Kunze 1985). Their studies show that such measurements are fraught with methodological difficulties (Lehmann et al. 1982). The quality of life needs to be observed in its objective and subjective aspects (Platt 1985). The patient can perceive
every aspect of his life as being a benefit or not. For instance: watching TV can be
considered pleasant or unpleasant, a tiresome pastime. As for symptomatology
and social relatedness, it is very difficult to interpret what is beneficial and what is
not.

Benefits Associated with Independence from Family and Friends

One of the very important criticisms concerning deshospitalisation is that the
whole burden of a patient's difficulties is on the parents' shoulders. Independence
from the social environment can be measured in different ways (Runions and Prudo 1983). Here too, it is not clear if different ways of being more independent
from the family can be seen as something desirable (Liem 1980). Family therapy
(McFarlane 1983) and systemic approaches have shown the different interrelations between different family members (Goldstein 1981; Leff and Vaughn 1985;
Falloon et al. 1984). Becoming more autonomous can be perceived either as a relief or as a threat (Doane et al. 1985). For example, it is not unusual for parents to
get depressed when their offspring become independent and less of a burden to
the family.

Generally, some additional precautions must be cited when benefits of treatments for schizophrenics are evaluated:

- There is even less information available on long-term benefits (Capstick 1980; Rifkin and Siris 1983). Before the era of community mental health, schizophrenics remained in psychiatric hospitals, and we believe that their quality of life was not very good (Gruenberg 1967; Test and Stein 1980). Many other institutions were opened for chronic schizophrenics in order to improve their quality of life (Beiser et al. 1985; Barrowclough and Terrier 1984; Barrelet 1985). Only a few studies have shown improvement and benefits on a short-term basis (Braun et al. 1981; Test and Stein 1978; Bockoven and Solomon 1975; Mollica 1983). For example, Weisbrod et al. (1980) compared a good standard treatment program in a psychiatric hospital with follow-up treatment in a day-care center or a sheltered workshop with an experimental treatment program in which they included a team of clinicians who were doing some outreach work in the community. This comparative study tries to incorporate the dimension of cost and benefits: during the 12 months of the study, the community program resulted in a gain of US $ 1200 per patient for an additional outlay of US $ 800 per patient. The authors note that after the termination of the program there was a significant amount of relapse. It could therefore be supposed that no economic benefit derived from the community program after its termination. Thus, long-term benefits of the various treatments for schizophrenics have practically never been investigated (Lamb 1979; Scheper-Hugues 1981; Strauss et al. 1985).
- Since the late 1970s, Strauss and Carpenter (1977, 1978) have postulated the idea that the different factors in the clinical course of schizophrenics (hospitalisation, work activity, course of symptoms, interpersonal relationships, quality of life, etc.) are partly correlated and partly independent of each other (Strauss and Carpenter 1981; Carpenter and Stephens 1982). Such assumptions inevitably entail research methods which are difficult to manage. While the many findings of individual studies may be quite valid for the group and conditions concerned, it is very difficult to draw general conclusions applicable to a broader schizophrenic population or even to another group of schizophrenics. Therefore, results of research efforts might be improved by the selection of more homogeneous subgroups of schizophrenics for investigation. For instance, patients living with their family; young, gainfully employed patients, who might be further divided according to sex; patients presenting special problems such as communication and language impairments. Correlating these more homogeneous subgroups with their response to various treatment modalities should provide the hard data we need to understand at least some schizophrenic populations more thoroughly and, more importantly, to devise more effective treatment leading to a better quality of life.

In conclusion, there is general agreement that it is preferable to have a competitive job producing a decent income, to have a family and to have interesting activities. If this life style involves decompensation and despair brought on by the tremendous efforts needed to recuperate from relapses, it might be wise to think about adopting a different life style. In this case, it might be preferable to withdraw socially so as to avoid insecurity and tension. How is it possible to reach a decision on this important issue?

As we have not yet arrived at a point where benefits can really be evaluated, it is not yet possible to correlate them with programme costs. For the time being it would therefore seem advisable to concentrate our efforts on the improvements of treatment, on understanding better the effects on patients of what we do, and on determining what we should be doing. For this, additional funds will be needed. In this connection, it should be mentioned that the means allocated to research in this field are very limited, compared with the overall cost of the management of chronic schizophrenics.

Cost Analysis of the Management of Chronic Schizophrenics

Although the difficulty of establishing comparable groups of chronic schizophrenics and of defining benefits as they correlate with treatment, analysis of cost components may nevertheless indicate weak points in the management of chronic schizophrenics. A wareness of such points may provide clues as to where efforts may be most fruitfully expended.

A survey (Gunderson and Mosher 1975) carried out in the United States during the fiscal year 1974–1975 estimated that the global annual cost of schizophrenia to the national economy ranged between 11.6 and 19.5 thousands of millions of dollars. These costs can be broken down as follows:

Treatment	17.5%–20.5%
Loss of productivity	58.5%–73.0%
Public assistance	8.5%–20.5%

Loss of productivity is calculated as representing 7%–8.5% of the overall figure during hospitalisation and 51.5%–64% when patients reside in the community.

An Australian study (Andrews et al. 1985) carried out in the 1980s gives a cost analysis for schizophrenia in one Australian state. Indirect costs – mainly loss of earning capacity – were assessed at 80% of total costs for women and 84% for men. By way of comparison, indirect costs due to myocardial infarction have been calculated to range from 80% to 90% of total costs for both sexes, in Australia as well as in the United States.

A third study (Müller 1983), carried out in one catchment area of the Manhattan West Side in the late 1970s, shows a breakdown of costs for a cohort of 119 chronic schizophrenics during the year following index hospitalisation. In this study loss of earning capacity represented 50% of total costs for men and 37% and 45% respectively for women, depending on whether or not housekeeping is counted as gainful employment. The direct-cost ratio between inpatient care (rehospitalisation only) and aftercare was estimated at 60:40 for women and 80:20 for men.

Basis of the Calculation of Costs

For the totality of the cost components of the Geneva schizophrenic outpatient cohort (from the beginning of April 1981 until the end of March 1982), we have used mean values relative to different services of the community mental health centers (Department of Psychiatry of the University of Geneva), as well as the disability pensions, complementary allowances and salaries. Unit costs have been defined as follows:

Direct Costs
- Cost of a day spent in a hospital - real cost in 1981: US $ 189; in 1982: US $ 217. These amounts were obtained from the Financial Director of the Department of Psychiatry of the University of Geneva (IUPG).
- Cost of a day spent in a day hospital - real cost in 1981: US $ 217; in 1982: US $ 179. This amount has been calculated on the basis of the accounts of the IUPG Carouge day hospital (the only one to have functioned regularly throughout the year) and the total number of days during the year.
- Cost of an outpatient consultation - real cost in 1981: US $ 148.

The third amount was obtained by taking into consideration the accounts for the year 1981 of the outpatient consultation services, of the halfway house, and of the sheltered workshop, as well as the total number of consultations (doctors, psychologists, social workers, but not other therapists). The inclusion of the halfway house and the workshop in the total costs was imperative, as psychotics in general are the principal users of these two facilities, and the outpatient treatment of schizophrenics frequently has recourse to the concomitant intervention of these professional facilities. We were not able to take into account the duration of a consultation on an outpatient basis, and we cannot furnish differentiated unit costs. Schizophrenics had on average shorter consultations (modal duration 20–30 min), but given that schizophrenics mobilised therapists much more frequently for other purposes than consultations as such, the mean cost per consultation can be considered a justified approximation. This mean cost can also be considered valid for other groups of patients who, needing less additional aid, had consultations which were of longer duration on the average.

Indirect Costs
- *Disability pensions and complementary local authority allowances:* Given the low socioprofessional level of the majority of schizophrenics and the limited duration of their professional activity, pensions are also on the lower end of the benefits scale, and this necessitates the local authority granting complementary allowances in most cases. The total amount of these two payments takes into account the minimum living wage fixed by the social welfare services: US $ 631 a month for a single person and US $ 947 a month for a couple during 1981. (This amount was communicated to us by the Hospice Général.) It is this amount that we have used as a general reference, whilst probably underestimating the costs of pensions. But this underestimation is low; the fact of taking into account the lower end of the scale is compensated for as some patients - even though they have the right to - do not ask for any complementary allowances.

- *The lack of gainful employment of patients* who are not professionally active: we have singled out 1981 salaries in Geneva as expressed in terms of sex and level of professional qualification ("Vie Economique", August 1982: Average salaries by local authority and by urban centers in 1981, pp. 577–582). These amounts have been increased by 10%, which represents, on average, the employers' part of social deductions.

Analysis of Cost Components

Initially we will examine the structure of costs of treatment of schizophrenic patients. We will then compare this with the costs for other psychotic patients, as well as with those for a non-psychotic group.

Costs of Schizophrenics

Calculated on the basis already specified, the total cost of the cohort of schizophrenics described above comes to US $ 1936961 per annum, i. e. US $ 28073 on average, per patient. As Table 11 shows, the preponderant part is represented by indirect costs (72.39%) and amongst these, above all, the lack of gainful employment (52.8%), whereas disability pensions and other allowances (above all, social welfare payments) total only 19.54% of total costs.

Direct costs (altogether 27.61%) are strongly influenced by hospitalisation and generate 17.63% of total costs, to a lesser degree by outpatient consultations (8.89%), and very little by care in a day hospital (1.09%).

Further analysis shows that these mean costs vary considerably according to certain characteristics of the patients.

- On the basis of distribution according to *sex,* the costs of male patients are more than a third higher than those of female patients (Table 11). Total mean costs for men are US $ 32074 whilst for women they total only US $ 23954 annually. For

Table 11. Averages of direct and indirect costs (US $) and their distribution for the cohort of schizophrenic patients followed up by the psychiatric institutions of Geneva University during a 1-year period (1981–1982), by sex

	Men ($n=35$)		Women ($n=34$)		Total ($n=69$)	
	Costs	%	Costs	%	Costs	%
Averages of direct costs						
Hospitalisation costs	6496	20.25	3359	14.02	4950	17.63
Costs for consultations	2722	8.49	2261	9.44	2495	8.89
Day hospital costs	155	0.48	460	1.92	305	1.09
Total averages of direct costs	9373	29.22	6080	25.38	7750	27.61
Averages of indirect costs						
Disability pensions	6276	19.57	4672	19.50	5486	19.54
Earning losses	16425	51.21	13202	55.12	14837	52.85
Total averages of indirect costs	22701	70.78	17874	74.62	20323	72.39
Averages of total costs	32074	100.00	23954	100.00	28073	100.00

$x^2 = 1258,40$ $P < .001$

all costs studied except those of periods spent in the day hospital, male schizophrenics cost distinctly more. This is above all true of hospitalisation, the mean
cost of which (US $ 6496) is about double that for female schizophrenics
(US $ 3385); of lack of gainful employment: 24% higher; and of pensions and
other social welfare benefits: 34% higher. It is on the consultation level that
costs for male patients come nearest to those for female patients; however, they
are still 20% higher.

A second aspect of the differentiation of costs lies in the *age factor*. Contrary to
expectations, the younger the patient the more expensive the costs (Table 12).
Patients aged under 40 are responsible for mean costs of US $ 35630; those
aged between 40 and 49: US $ 25551, and the over-50 group is responsible for
mean costs of US $ 23781.

Even when indirect costs are basically the same (the greatest difference being on
the order of 4%), margins are much greater when one considers direct costs.
These are US $ 15194 for the youngest category (under 40), who are responsible
for the highest hospitalisation costs (US $ 11277 on average), i.e. nearly three
quarters of their direct costs, and nearly eight times more than hospital costs of
patients aged 50 and over. This last group has the lowest direct costs, US $ 3847
on average, whilst patients between 40 and 49 total US $ 4830. Expressed in
terms of growth index of costs from the oldest to the youngest group, the index
(100 for the oldest), of direct costs moves from 126 for patients in the
40–49-years-old group to 395 for the under-40 group. As for hospital costs, the
index (100 for the oldest group) is 183 for the 40–49 group and 768 for the
youngest group.

– When these two factors – *sex and age* – are combined (Table 13) it can be observed that the different composition of costs gradually and regularly dimin-
ishes from the high mean total cost for men under 40 (US $ 36071) to that for
female patients over 50 (US $ 19674). This tendency can also be noted, in gener-

Table 12. Averages of direct and indirect costs (US $) and their distribution for the cohort of
schizophrenic patients followed by the psychiatric institutions of Geneva University during a
1-year period (1981–1982), by age

	<40 years (n=22)		40–49 years (n=20)		⇒ 50 years (n=27)	
	Costs	%	Costs	%	Costs	%
Averages of direct costs						
Hospitalisation costs	11277	31.65	2689	10.53	1469	6.18
Costs for consultations	3670	10.30	2141	8.37	1799	7.57
Day hospital costs	247	0.69	–	–	579	2.43
Total averages of direct costs	15194	42.64	4830	18.90	3847	16.18
Averages of indirect costs						
Disability pensions	5853	16.43	6249	24.46	4621	19.43
Earning losses	14583	40.93	14472	56.64	15313	64.39
Total averages of indirect costs	20436	57.36	20721	81.10	19934	83.82
Averages of total costs	35630	100.00	25551	100.00	23781	100.00

$x^2 = 17780,48$ $P < .001$

Table 13. Averages of direct and indirect costs (US $) and their distribution for the cohort of schizophrenic patients followed up by the psychiatric institutions of Geneva University during a 1-year period (1981–1982), by age and sex

| | <40 years | | | | 40–49 years | | | | ⇒50 years | | | |
| | Men (n=18) | | Women (n=4) | | Men (n=6) | | Women (n=14) | | Men (n=11) | | Women (n=16) | |
	Costs	%	Costs	%	Costs	%	Costs	%	Costs	%	Costs	%
Averages of direct costs												
Hospitalisation	10523	29.17	14669	43.60	3209	11.09	2467	9.46	1699	6.24	1311	6.66
Consultation	3251	9.01	5555	16.51	2494	8.62	1989	7.62	1970	7.23	1676	8.52
Day Hospital	301	0.84	–	–	–	–	–	–	–	–	976	4.96
Total average	14075	39.02	20224	60.11	5703	19.71	4456	17.08	3669	13.47	3963	20.14
Average of indirect costs												
Disability pension	6312	17.50	3787	11.26	6312	21.82	6222	23.85	6197	22.75	3551	18.05
Earning losses	15684	43.48	9630	28.63	16910	58.47	15413	59.07	17373	63.78	12160	61.81
Total average	21996	60.98	13417	39.89	23222	80.29	21635	82.92	23570	86.53	15711	79.86
Averages of total costs	36071	100	33641	100	28925	100	26091	100	27239	100	19674	100

Diff.: men $x^2 = 142.07$ $P < 0.001$
Diff.: women $x^2 = 377.38$ $P < 0.001$

Table 14. Averages of direct and indirect costs (US $) and their distribution for the cohort of schizophrenic patients followed up by the psychiatric institutions of Geneva University during a 1-year period (1981–1982), according to employment

	Gainfully employed ($n=12$)		Without gainful employment ($n=57$)	
	Costs	%	Costs	%
Averages of direct costs				
Hospitalization	2611	35.17	5442	16.79
Consultations	2383	32.09	2518	7.77
Day hospital	904	12.18	179	0.55
Total averages	5898	79.44	8139	25.11
Averages of indirect costs				
Disability pensions	–	–	6641	20.48
Earning losses	1527	20.56	17639	54.41
Total averages	1527	20.56	24280	74.89
Averages of total costs	7425	100.00	32419	100.00

x^2 Averages of direct costs $=2196.74$ $P<.001$

al, for hospital costs as well as for consultations. As far as indirect costs are concerned, it would appear that those for male patients are systematically higher than those for females for all three age-groups. These margins are particularly accentuated for patients in the under-40 age-group (mean cost for men is 64% higher than that for women) and in those in the over-50 group (50% higher), whilst the margins are much less pronounced for the intermediate age-group (40–49 years: 7% higher).

Thus, a differential study of costs confirms the findings drawn from the analysis of sociodemographic and sociocultural characteristics of young male schizophrenics and older female schizophrenics already highlighted above. Men are clearly overrepresented in the younger age-groups (82%), whilst this is the case for female patients over 40 (64%). Young men have a mean total cost 83% higher than that for women over 50. These margins are particularly pronounced with regard to the mean cost of hospitalisation, which is nearly eight times higher for young men than for older women; the global cost of treatment for the first group is 3.6 times higher than that for the second.

- The most significant differences are related to *professional activity and inactivity* (Table 14). Those patients who are not employed represent costs 4.4 times higher than those for patients who work: US $ 32419 as against US $ 7425. It goes without saying that this margin is explained by indirect costs above all. But those who are not employed also have higher direct costs (US $ 8139) than the active population (US $ 5898), i.e. an increase of 38%. It is principally hospital costs that account for this margin (US $ 5442, more than twice as high as that of the active population: US $ 2611).

Table 15. Direct and indirect costs (US $) for the patients followed up by the psychiatric institutions of Geneva University during a 1-year period (1981–1982), by diagnosis

	No. of patients	Direct costs				Indirect costs			Total costs
		Hospital-isation	Consul-tation	Day hospital	Total	Disability pensions	Earning losses	Total	
Schizophrenics	69	341537	172138	21048	534723	378510	1023728	1402238	1936961
Other psychotics	63	186266	151545	20506	358317	311813	830183	1141996	1500313
Non-psychotics	227	251655	612848	6510	871013	681696	1778870	2460566	3331579
Total	359	779458	936531	48064	1764053	1372019	3632781	5004800	6768853

Table 16. Distribution of direct and indirect costs for the patients followed up by the psychiatric institutions of Geneva University during a 1-year period (1981–1982), by diagnosis

	% of patients	Direct costs				Indirect costs			Total costs
		Hospital-isation	Consul-tation	Day hospital	Total	Disability pensions	Earning losses	Total	
Schizophrenics	19.2	43.8	18.4	43.8	30.3	27.6	28.2	28.0	28.6
Other psychotics	17.6	23.9	16.2	42.7	20.3	22.7	22.8	22.8	22.2
Non-psychotics	63.2	32.3	65.4	13.5	49.4	49.7	49.0	49.2	49.2
Total	100.0	100.0	100.0	100.0	100.0	100.0	100.0	100.0	100.0

A Cost Comparison of the Three Cohorts
From data concerning detailed costs of the groups of psychotic patients and non-psychotics we have taken only results which permit a comparison with the costs of the cohort of schizophrenic patients.

Comparison of Mean Costs. Tables 15–17 clearly show that schizophrenics are responsible for markedly higher costs than other psychotics and non-psychotic patients.

- Schizophrenics represent 19.2% of all patients, but their total cost represents 28.6% of total costs. On the other hand, non-psychotic patients represent 63.2% of all patients, but are responsible for only 49.2% of costs.
- It is direct costs (above all hospitalisation and day hospital care) which are particularly high amongst schizophrenics, who alone are responsible for 43.8% of these two cost factors.
- In terms of mean costs per patient it can be noted that, with one notable exception (cost of consultations), all costs are higher for schizophrenics.

Comparison of the two extreme cohorts shows that costs for schizophrenics in relation to non-psychotics are:

- 346% higher for hospitalisations
-   8% less for consultations
- 102% higher for direct costs
- 83% higher for pensions
- 89% higher for lack of gainful employment
- 87% higher for indirect costs
- 91% higher for the average total cost

Table 17. Averages of direct and indirect costs (US $) and their distribution for the cohort of schizophrenic patients followed up by the psychiatric institutions of Geneva University during a 1-year period (1981–1982), by diagnosis

	Schizophren-ics ($n=69$)	Other psycho-tics ($n=63$)	Non-psycho-tics ($n=227$)	Total ($n=359$)
Averages of direct costs				
Hospitalisation	4950	2957	1109	2171
Consultations	2495	2405	2700	2609
Day hospital	305	326	29	134
Total averages	7750	5688	3838	4914
Averages of indirect costs				
Disability pensions	5486	4950	3003	3730
Earning losses	14837	13177	7836	10119
Total averages	20323	18127	10839	13849
Averages of total costs	28073	23815	14677	18763

$x^2 = 2220.42$ $P < .001$

Table 18. Averages of direct and indirect costs (US $) and their distribution for the cohort of schizophrenic patients followed up by the psychiatric institutions of Geneva University during a 1-year period (1981–1982), by diagnosis and sex

	Schizophrenics		Other psychotics		Non-psychotics		Total	
	Men	Women	Men	Women	Men	Women	Men	Women
Averages of direct costs								
Hospitalisation	6496	3359	3283	2712	1229	995	2623	1755
Consultations	2722	2261	2365	2436	2104	3260	2270	2920
Day hospital	155	460	201	419	28	29	82	183
Total averages	9373	6080	5849	5567	3361	4284	4975	4858
Averages of indirect costs								
Disability pensions	6276	4672	4816	5050	3420	2611	4220	3455
Earning losses	16425	13201	12632	13587	7485	8167	10112	10126
Total averages	22701	17873	17448	18637	10905	10778	14332	13581
Averages of total costs	32074	23953	23297	24204	14266	15062	19307	18439

x^2 of total $= 650.34$ $P < .001$

As can be seen, costs for other psychotic patients (mean total cost US $ 23815) are in between, but they are appreciably nearer those for schizophrenics than for non-psychotics.

Comparison of Costs as a Function of Selected Parameters. We have noted that amongst schizophrenics, male patients are responsible for a higher mean total cost (around one third more) than female patients. Table 18 clearly shows that this is specific for the schizophrenic group, as these cost differences are not found in the other patient categories.

Nonetheless, two facts stand out clearly. In the first place, no matter what the diagnosis, hospital costs for men are on average systematically higher than those for women: 93.4% for schizophrenics, 21% for other psychotics, 23.5% for non-psychotics, and finally 49.4% for all patients. For other psychotics and non-psychotics, these higher costs for men are relatively compensated for by their lower costs with reference to outpatient consultations. In the second place, the most perceptible difference that can be observed amongst non-schizophrenic patients lies in the costs for outpatient treatment among non-psychotic women, who, compared with men with the same diagnosis, represent 55% higher costs. As we will see, it is a question of either young women (psychotherapy) or of women over 50 (long-term treatment).

No matter what the age, non-psychotic women represent proportionately the most important part of direct costs (in consultation costs) and the least important in hospitalisation.

The differentiation of costs as a function of age shows an inverse correlation between age and costs amongst schizophrenics: young patients have direct and total costs markedly higher than those for the others. This result is not confirmed amongst other patients: other psychotics do not present any variation in costs according to age (Table 19).

Among non-psychotics the total amount of costs increases with age, i.e. an inverse phenomenon to that seen in schizophrenics. Here also, differences are statis-

Table 19. Averages of direct and indirect costs (US $) and their distribution for the cohort of schizophrenic patients followed by the psychiatric institutions of Geneva University during a 1-year period (1981–1982), by diagnosis and age

	Schizophrenics			Other psychotics		
	<40 years	40–49 years	⇒ 50 years	<40 years	40–49 years	⇒ 50 years
Averages of direct costs						
Hospitalisation	11 277	2 689	1 469	985	3 667	3 602
Consultations	3 670	2 141	1 799	3 167	2 588	1 846
Day hospital	247	–	579	983	–	170
Total averages	15 194	4 830	3 847	5 135	6 255	5 618
Averages of indirect costs						
Disability pensions	5 853	6 249	4 621	3 945	4 983	5 500
Earning losses	14 583	14 472	15 313	12 185	12 977	13 881
Total averages	20 436	20 721	19 934	16 130	17 960	19 381
Averages of total costs	35 630	25 551	23 781	21 265	24 215	24 999

	Non-psychotics			Total		
	<40 years	40–49 years	⇒ 50 years	<40 years	40–49 years	⇒ 50 years
Averages of direct costs						
Hospitalisation	935	570	2 124	2 362	1 647	2 350
Consultations	2 883	2 136	2 874	3 019	2 229	2 324
Day hospital	42	26	–	165	15	194
Total averages	3 860	2 732	4 998	5 546	3 891	4 868
Averages of indirect costs						
Disability pensions	2 235	3 673	4 141	2 904	4 486	4 627
Earning losses	5 867	8 975	11 389	7 697	10 953	13 062
Total averages	8 102	12 648	15 530	10 601	15 439	17 689
Avrages of total costs	11 962	15 380	20 528	16 147	19 330	22 557

x^2 of total $= 2548.54$ $P < .001$

tically significant, but they are rather imputable to indirect costs, whilst amongst schizophrenics they are the result of the margins between direct costs.

Lastly, cost differences according to economic activity are completely generalised (Table 20). What has already been observed in relation to schizophrenics can also be verified in the other two groups of patients: the inactive sector has higher mean direct costs than do patients employed in the labour market. Thus, the inactive group is responsible for the surplus of the following costs, compared with the active group:

Schizophrenics:	38% more for direct mean costs	108% for hospital costs
Other psychotics:	187% more for direct mean costs	490% for hospital costs
Non-psychotics:	62% more for direct mean costs	240% for hospital costs
Total for all patients:	99% more for direct mean costs	375% for hospital costs

It should be added that, over and above the particularly high costs related to hospitalisation, the inactive population also generates more important consultation costs than the active population. Without doubt the margin is less accentuated; however, it varies in the same direction, and this over all diagnostic groups.

Table 20. Averages of direct and indirect costs (US $) and their distribution for the cohort of schizophrenic patients followed up by the psychiatric institutions of Geneva University during a 1-year period (1981–1982), according to employment status

	Schizophrenics		Other psychotics		Non-psychotics		Total	
	GE ($n=12$)	WGE ($n=57$)	GE ($n=19$)	WGE ($n=44$)	GE ($n=138$)	WGE ($n=89$)	GE ($n=169$)	WGE ($n=190$)
Averages of direct costs								
Hospitalisation	2611	5442	669	3945	572	1941	727	3455
Consultation	2383	2518	1801	2666	2497	3014	2411	2785
Day hospital	904	179	–	466	22	39	82	180
Total averages	5898	8139	2470	7077	3091	4994	3220	6420
Averages of indirect costs								
Disability pensions	–	6641	–	7087	–	7659	–	7221
Earning losses	1527	17639	133	18811	183	19704	273	18878
Total averages	1527	24280	133	25898	183	27363	273	26099
Averages of total costs	7425	32419	2603	32975	3274	32357	3493	32519

GE, Gainfully employed; *WGE*, without gainful employment

As far as indirect costs of patients exercising an economic activity are concerned, two findings are noteworthy. The costs are relatively minor: only US $ 273 on average per case. Here again, it is the active group of schizophrenics who account for the most: US $ 1527 on average.

Obviously, it is the indirect costs which primarily determine the considerable difference of mean total cost between inactive patients (above all the disabled) and those who are employed. Amongst schizophrenics, the relationship between the mean total cost of an employed patient as opposed to an unemployed patient is 1:4.4. This divergence, already considerable, is even more accentuated in the other diagnostic groups: amongst the other psychotics it is 1:12.7 and amongst non-psychotics 1:9.9. The general average calculated for all patients is around US $ 3493 for the employed group and US $ 32519 for the unemployed group. This means that the latter are responsible for costs 9.3 times higher than those for the employed group.

Differential Costs According to the Hospitalisation of Patients

The analysis of costs up to now has been based on mean costs per patient, taking into account all patients in each diagnostic group. thus, mean hospital costs have been calculated on the basis of all patients, whether they have been hospitalised or not.

In this last part, we propose to examine the costs of patients actually in treatment, differentiating between direct costs of hospitalised patients and of those who have been treated exclusively in outpatient consultations. We will leave a side the cost of day hospital care, which intervenes in only a minority of cases.

As shown in Table 21 the mean direct cost for a hospitalised patient is US $ 16739. Other psychotics have the highest direct costs, at US $ 21709, followed by schizophrenics, US $ 19622, and non-psychotics, US $ 12254. Amongst hospitalised patients, these direct costs represent 58.27% of total costs; this pro-

Table 21. Averages of direct and indirect costs (US $) and their distribution for the patients hospitalised during the year followed up by the psychiatric institutions of Geneva University during a 1-year period (1981–1982), by diagnosis

	Schizophrenics (n=21)		Other psychotics (n=14)		Non-psychotics (n=64)		Total (n=99)	
	Costs	%	Costs	%	Costs	%	Costs	%
Averages of direct costs								
Hospitalisation	16264	39.67	18884	46.69	8678	44.07	13399	46.64
Consultations	3358	8.19	2825	6.99	3576	18.16	3340	11.63
Total averages	19622	47.86	21709	53.68	12254	62.23	16739	58.27
Averages of indirect costs								
Disability pensions	5771	14.08	4869	12.04	1775	9.02	3061	10.65
Earning losses	15602	38.06	13863	34.28	5662	28.75	8930	31.08
Total averages	21373	52.14	18732	46.32	7437	37.77	11991	41.73
Averages of total costs	40995	100.00	40441	100.00	19691	100.00	28730	100.00

$x^2 = 2634.20$ $P < .001$

Table 22. Averages of direct and indirect costs (US $) and their distribution for the patients without hospitalisation during the year followed up by the psychiatric institutions of Geneva University during a 1-year period (1981–1982), by diagnosis

	Schizophrenics (n=48)		Other psychotics (n=49)		Non-psychotics (n=163)		Total (n=260)	
	Costs	%	Costs	%	Costs	%	Costs	%
Averages of direct costs								
Consultations	1735	8.03	2216	10.99	2554	17.34	2371	13.90
Total averages	1735	8.03	2216	10.99	2554	17.34	2371	13.90
Averages of indirect costs								
Disability pensions	5361	24.82	4972	24.65	3485	23.66	4112	24.11
Earning losses	14502	67.15	12982	64.36	8690	59.00	10572	61.99
Total averages	19863	91.97	17954	89.01	12175	82.66	14684	86.10
Averages of total costs	21598	100.00	20170	100.00	14729	100.00	17055	100.00

$x^2 = 1448.85$ $P < .001$

portion is highest for non-psychotics (62.23%) and lowest for schizophrenics (47.86%).

On the other hand, for patients who were not hospitalised during the year, direct costs were only 13.90% of the total, which directly expresses the crucial repercussion of hospitalisations and the economy of costs realised in their absence (Table 22).

In fact, by far the most important part is made up of hospital costs (Table 21): each patient hospitalised during the year is responsible for costs of US $ 13399. Here also, psychotics are responsible for the highest amount, US $ 18884; the mean cost of hospitalised schizophrenics is US $ 16264 and that of non-psychotics US $ 8678. Consultation costs of the same hospitalised patients (on average US $ 3340) vary little according to diagnosis: the highest is amongst non-psychotics (US $ 3576) and the lowest amongst other psychotics (US $ 2825). Generally speaking, hospitalised patients are responsible for direct costs seven times higher than those of persons treated exclusively in outpatient services. The most important difference is found for schizophrenics, where hospitalised patients account for direct costs 11 times higher than those for patients treated exclusively on an outpatient basis.

It is not solely the surplus of hospital costs which brings out these differences. Outpatient costs of hospitalised patients are systematically higher than those of patients treated exclusively in outpatient consultation services (Tables 21 and 22). Thus, it can be noted that outpatient costs of hospitalised patients are 40.9% higher than the same costs occasioned by patients treated solely on an outpatient basis. This cost surplus is more marked for men (56.6%) than for women (29.5%). It is particularly high for schizophrenics (93.5%), and in this group for women (145.1%).

This significant accumulation of outpatient costs with other treatment modalities is corroborated by the fact that patients who have had to be hospitalised and/or have frequented a day hospital give rise to the highest mean outpatient costs. They are over 50% higher than outpatient costs for patients treated exclusively on a consultation basis.

Mean hospital costs for patients hospitalised during the year show important variations according to age. They are far and away greater for schizophrenics younger than 40 (US $ 27 565 for each case of hospitalisation); this is followed by other psychotics aged between 40 and 49 (US $ 21 119), whilst the lowest costs are for schizophrenics over 50 (US $ 6610) and for non-psychotics 40–49 years of age (US $ 5222).

It can also be noted that the cumulative effect of hospitalisations and/or attendance at a day hospital on outpatient costs is most marked for young patients, and very clearly so for schizophrenics and non-psychotics. Thus, schizophrenics under 40 who have been treated exclusively in outpatient consultation have a mean outpatient cost of US $ 2074. This cost rises to US $ 5266 (an increase of 154%) when they have been treated either in a hospital or in a day hospital, or in both. For schizophrenics in the 40–49 age-group this cumulative effect is on the order of 63.2% and for those over 50, 58.6%.

As for non-psychotics, amongst whom the same tendency prevails, the cumulative effect on outpatient costs is 53.3% for the youngest group (less than 40 years), 48.3% for those between 40 and 49 years, and 12.4% for the oldest age-group.

Likewise, considerable differences exist in direct costs, according to whether the hospitalised patients are professionally active or inactive. Even though, given the small numbers in certain categories, results must be interpreted with prudence, several salient facts can be mentioned. Amongst all cases, hospitalised patients who have no professional activity are responsible for more than double the direct costs (US $ 18 604, an increase of 113.1%) for those who have not been hospitalised during the year (US $ 8732). This margin is particularly marked amongst the other psychotics (increase of 348.7%). It is less marked amongst schizophrenics (increase of 98.7%) as well as amongst non-psychotics (52.3%). Professional inactivity is thus associated, even amongst hospitalised patients, with a considerable increase in total direct costs.

A second important fact is that the growth effect on outpatient costs by hospi-talisation or treatment in a day hospital is noticeable above all amongst unemploy-ed patients. For all cases, unemployed patients, whether hospitalised or in care in a day hospital, are responsible for outpatient costs 57% higher than those for pat-ients who have been treated solely by outpatient services. On the other hand, for those patients who are gainfully employed, this growth effect of outpatient costs by other forms of care is only 20%.

The analysis of costs - direct and indirect - of treatment for three groups of patients, that has been presented is a first attempt to show the economic conse-quences of psychiatric illness in figures. It is necessarily incomplete: direct costs refer only to medical acts and care within the institution. It would be necessary to complete them with costs of medical acts and, in the private sector in particular of psychiatry. The amounts of pensions are estimates based on official scales. Finally, we have no trustworthy information concerning the economic cost of psychiatric illness of the family members or environment of patients. Other elements con-cerned with costs have not been tackled.

It is true that if other components were taken into account total costs would without doubt be modified. However, it appears that the differences in costs, as well as in their structure, according to diagnosis, sex, age, and professional activity would not be fundamentally altered.

Conclusions

As a general conclusion we underline three main points:

1. Our results with an outpatient cohort confirm what had been found in the litera-ture. Indirect costs, mainly wage loss, represent the largest portion of the costs. In addition, in our cohort costs decrease with age, and men tend to cost more than women.
2. Probably the best way to control the costs of chronic schizophrenics is to sup-port programs which help schizophrenics to recover a wage-earning capacity. A young schizophrenic patient who is maintained even intermittently at his job will both cost less and, probably, have a better quality of life.
3. The great variability in the characteristics of chronic schizophrenics and the dif-ficulty to give definitions of benefits comprehensively related to treatment re-duce the possible validity of cost-benefits comparison between cohorts of chronic schizophrenics.

This leads us to conclude that we are still at the stage where we should seek to de-vise better treatment modalities for chronic schizophrenics.

Acknowledgement. The authors thank M. Davies, D. Didisheim, J. Favrod, S. Gubler, A. Hooton, G. Pellizer and D. Ypsilantis for their helpful assistance in collecting the data, analysing the results and preparing the English version of the original text.

References

Andrews G, Hall W, Goldstein G, Lapsley H (1985) The economic costs of schizophrenia – implications for public policy. Arch Gen Psychiatry 42: 537–543

Anthony W, Farkas M (1982) A client outcome planning, model for assessing psychiatric rehabilitation interventions. Schizohr Bull 8: 13–38

Barrelet L (1984) Le traitement des psychotiques et des schizophrènes dans une psychiatrie de secteur. Praxis 37: 1109–1112

Barrelet L (1985) Traitement institutionnel et traitement de famille: spécificité thérapeutique ou thérapeutique spécifique? Des références psychanalytiques aux références systémiques dans le traitement institutionnel de jour. L'information psychiatrique 61: 809–814

Barrelet L (1986) Le devenir de la bouffée délirante: évolutions cliniques et conséquences diagnostiques. L'information Psychiatr 62: 353–358

Barrowclough C, Tarrier N (1984) "Psychosocial" interventions with families and their effects on the course of schizophrenia: a review. Psychol Med 14: 629–642

Beck JC (1978) Social influences on the prognosis of schizophrenia. Schizophr Bull 4: 86–101

Beels CC, Gutwirth B (1984) The measurement of social support in schizophrenia. Schizophr Bull 10: 3

Beiser M, Shure JH, Peters R, Tatum E (1985) Does community care for the mentally ill make a difference? A tale of two cities. Am J Psychiatry 142: 104–152

Black BJ (1977) Substitute permanent employment for the deinstitutionalized mentally ill. J Rehabil Res Dev 39: 32–35

Bland RC, Orn H (1980) Prediction of long-term outcome from presenting symptoms in schizophrenia. J Clin Psychiatry 41: 85–88

Bleuler M (1978) The schizophrenic disorders – long-term patient and family studies. Yale University Press, New Haven, London

Bockoven J, Solomon H (1975) Comparison of two five-year follow-up studies: 1947 to 1952 and 1967 to 1972. Am J Psychiatry 132: 796

Boker W, Brenner HD, Gerstner G, Keller F, Muller J, Spichtig L (1984) Self-healing strategies among schizophrenics: attempts at compensation for basic disorders. Acta Psychiatr Scand 69: 373–378

Braun P, Kockansky G, Shapiro R, Greenberg S, Gudemann JE, Johnson S, Shore MF (1981) Overview: deinstitutionalization of psychiatric patients, a critical review of outcome studies. Am J Psychiatry 138: 736–749

Buckley P (1982) Identifying schizophrenic patients who should not receive medication. Schizophr Bull 8: 429–432

Capstick N (1980) Long-term fluphenazine decanoate maintenance requirements of chronic schizophrenic patients. Acta Psychiatr Scand 61: 256–262

Carpenter W, Stephens J (1982) Prognosis as the critical variable in classification of the functional psychoses. J Nerv Ment Dis 170: 688–691

Caton C (1982) Effect of length of inpatient treatment for chronic schizophrenia. Am J Psychiatry 139: 856–861

Cheadle AJ, Freeman HL, Korer J (1978) Chronic schizophrenic patients in the community. Br J Psychiatry 132: 221–227

Curran JP, Monti PM (1982) Social skills training with schizophrenics. Guilford, New York

Davis JM (1975) Overview: maintenance therapy in psychiatry. 1. Schizophrenia. Am J Psychiatry 132: 1237–1245

Davis JM, Shaffer CB, Killian GA, Kinard C, Chan C (1980) Important issues in the drug treatment of schizophrenia. Schizophr Bull 6: 70–87

Doane J, Falloon IRH, Goldstein MJ, Mintz J (1985) Parental affective style and the treatment of schizophrenia. Arch Gen Psychiatry 42: 34–42

Dohrenwend BS, Dohrenwend BP, Link B, Levai I (1983) Social functioning of psychiatric patients in contrast with community cases in the general population. Arch Gen Psychiatry 40: 1174–1182

Engelhardt DM, Rosen B, Engelhardt JOZ, Cohen P (1982) A 15-year follow-up of 646 schizophrenic outpatients. Schizophr Bull 8: 493–503

Engelhardt DM, Rosen B, Freeman D, Margolis R (1967) Phenothiazines in the prevention of psychiatric hospitalization. Arch Gen Psychiatry 16: 98-101

Erickson GC (1975) Outcome studies in mental hospitals: a review. Psychol Bull 82: 519-540

Falloon IRH, Marshall GN (1983) Residential care and social behavior: a study of rehabilitation needs. Psychol Med 13: 341-347

Falloon IRH, Boyd J, McGill CW (1984) Behavioral family management of mental illness: enhancing family coping in community care. Guilford, New York

Falloon I, Watt DC, Shepherd M (1978) A comparative trial of pimozide and fluphenazine decanoate in the continuation therapy of schizophrenia. Psychol Med 8: 59-70

Fischer W (1981) La crise économique et ses effets sur la population psychiatrique. Med Hyg 39: 3117-3122

Gaebel W, Pietzcker A (1985) One-year outcome of schizophrenic patients - the interaction of chronicity and neuroleptic treatment. Pharmacopsychiatry 18: 235-239

Glazer MW, Aaronson H, Prusoff B, Williams D (1980) Assessment of social adjustment in chronic ambulatory schizophrenics. J Nerv Ment Dis 168: 493-497

Goldberg SC, Klerman GL, Cole JO (1965) Changes in schizophrenic psychopathology and ward behaviour as a function of phenothiazine treatment. Br J Psychiatry 111: 120-123

Goldberg SC, Schooler NR, Hogarty GE, Roper M (1977) Prediction of relapse in schizophrenic outpatients treated by drug and sociotherapy. Arch Gen Psychiatry 24: 171-184

Goldberg SC (1980) Drug and psychosocial therapy in schizophrenia: current status in research needs. Schizophr Bull 6: 117-121

Goldstein M (ed) (1981) New developments in interventions with families of schizophrenics. Jossey-Bass, San Francisco

Goldstein JM, Caton CLM (1983) The effects of the community environment on chronic psychiatric patients. Psychol Med 13: 193-199

Gruenberg E (1967) The social breakdown syndrome - some origins. Am J Psychiatry 123: 1481-1489

Gunderson J, Mosher L (1975) The cost of schizophrenia. Am J Psychiatry 132: 901-906

Hammer M (1981) Social supports, social networks and schizophrenia. Schizophr Bull 7: 1

Herz M, Melville Ch (1980) Relapse in schizophrenia. Am J Psychiatry 137: 801-806

Herz MI, Szymanski HV, Simon JC (1982) Intermittent medication for stable schizophrenic outpatients: an alternative to maintenance medication. Am J Psychiatry 139: 918-922

Hirsch SR (1982) Depression "revealed" in schizophrenia. Br J Psychiatry 140: 421-424

Hogarty G (1984) Depot neuroleptics: the relevance of psychosocial factors - a United States perspective. J Clin Psychiatry 45: 36-42

Huber G, Gross G, Schuttler R (1979) Schizophrenia, eine verlaufs- und sozial-psychiatrische Langzeit-Studie. Springer, Berlin Heidelberg New York

Huffine CL, Clausen JA (1979) Madness and work: short and long-term effects of mental illness on occupational careers. Soc Forces 57: 1049-1062

Isele R, Merz J, Malzacher M, Angst J (1985) Social disability in schizophrenia: the controlled prospective Burghölzli study. II. Premorbid living situation and social adjustment - comparison with a normal control sample. Eur Arch Psychiatr Neurol Sci 234: 348-356

Johnson DAW (1976) The expectation of outcome for maintenance therapy in chronic schizophrenia. Br J Psychiatry 128: 246-250

Johnson DAW (1981) Studies of depressive symptoms in schizophrenia. I. The prevalence of depression and its possible causes. II. A two year longitudinal study of symptoms. III. A double blind trial of orphenadrine against placeb IV. A double blind trial of nortriptyline for depression in chronic schizophrenia. Br J Psychiatry 139: 89-101

Johnson DAW, Pasterski G, Ludlow JM, Street K, Taylor RDW (1983) The discontinuance of maintenance neuroleptic therapy in chronic schizophrenic patients: drug and social consequences. Acta Psychiatr Scand 67: 339-352

Kane JM, Rifkin A, Quitkin F, Nayak D, Saraf K (1979) Low-dose fluphenazine decanoate in maintenance treatment of schizophrenia. Psychiatr Res 341-345

Karon B (1984) The fear of reducing medication, and where have all the patients gone? Schizophr Bull 10: 613-621

Kunze H (1985) Rehabilitation and institutionalisation in community care in West Germany. Br J Psychiatry 147: 261-264

Lamb RH (1979) The new asylums in the community. Arch Gen Psychiatry 36: 129–134

Lawson A, Robinson I, Bakes C (1985) Problems in evaluating the consequences of disabling illness: the case of multiple sclerosis. Psychol Med 15: 555–579

Leff J, Vaughn C (1985) Expressed emotion in families: its significance for mental illness. Guilford, New York

Lehman AF, Ward NC, Linn LA (1982) Chronic mental patients: the quality of life issue. Am J Psychiatry 139: 1271–1276

Liberman RP, Falloon IRH, Wallace CJ (1983) Drug environment interactions in schizophrenia. In: Moratis M (ed) The chronically mentally ill: research and service. Springer, Berlin Heidelberg New York

Liem J (1980) Family Studies of Schizophrenia: An Update and Commentary. Schizophr Bull 6: 429–455

Linn MW, Caffey EM, Klett CJ (1979) Day treatment and psychotropic drugs in the aftercare of schizophrenic patients. Arch Gen Psychiatry 36: 1055–1066

Linn M, Gurel L, Willifurd W, Overall J, Gurland B, Laughlin P, Barchiesi A (1985) Nursing home care as an alternative to psychiatric hospitalization. Arch Gen Psychiatry 42: 544–551

Lorei T, Gurel L (1973) Demographic characteristics as predictors of posthospital employment and readmission. Journal of Consulting and Clinical Psychology 40: 426–430

Mann SA, Cree W (1976) "New" long-stay psychiatric patients: a national sample survey of fifteen mental hospitals in England and Wales 1972–1973. Psychol Med 6: 603–616

May P, Tuma A, Dixon W (1981) Schizophrenia – a follow-up study of the results of five forms of treatment. Arch Gen Psychiatry 38: 776–784

May PRA (1976) When, and why? Psychopharmacotherapy and other treatments in schizophrenia. Compr Psychiatry 17: 683–693

McCreadie RG (1982) The Nithsdale schizophrenia survey 1. Psychiatric and social handicaps. Br J Psychiatry 140: 582–586

McCreanie EW, Mizell TA (1978) Aftercare for psychiatric patients: does it prevent rehospitalization? Hosp Communit Psychiatry 29: 584–587

McFarlane W (ed) (1983) Family therapy in schizophrenia. Guilford, New York

McGlashan TH (1984) The Chestnut Lodge follow-up study. Arch Gen Psychiatry 41: 573–601

Mollica RF (1983) From asylum to community: the threatened disintegration of public psychiatry. N Engl J Med 30: 367–373

Mosher LR, Keith S (1979) Research on the psychosocial treatment of schizophrenia: a summary report. Am J Psychiatry 136: 623–631

Müller C (1983) Economic costs of schizophrenia: a postdischarge study. Med Care 21: 92–104

Owens C, Johnstone E (1980) The disabilities of chronic schizophrenia – their nature and the factors contributing to their development. Br J Psychiatry 136: 384–395

Ozarin LD (1976) Community alternatives to institutional care. Am J Psychiatry 133: 69–72

Pai S, Roberts EJ (1983) Follow-up study of schizophrenic patients – initially treated with home care. Br J Psychiatr 143: 447–450

Paul GL, Lentz RJ (1977) Psychosocial treatment of chronic mental patients: milieu versus social learning programs. Harvard University Press, Cambridge

Platt S (1985) Measuring the burden of psychiatric illness on the family: an evaluation of some rating scales. Psychol Med 15: 383–393

Pryce IB, Baughan CA, Jenkins TDO, Venkatesan B (1983) A study of long-attending psychiatric day patients and the services provided for them. Psychol Med 13: 875–884

Rifkin A, Siris SG (1983) Long-term drug treatment of schizophrenia. In: Rifkin A (ed) Schizophrenia and affective disorders. London

Rosenblatt A, Mayer JE (1974) The recidivism of mental patients: a review of past studies. J Orthopsychiatry 44 (5): 697–706

Rosenblatt A (1984) Concepts of the asylum in the care of the mentally ill. Hosp Community Psychiatry 35: 244–250

Runions J, Prudo R (1983) Problem behaviours encountered by families living with a schizophrenic member. Can J Psychiatry 28: 382–386

Scheper-Hugues N (1981) Dilemmas in deinstitutionalisation: a view from inner-city Boston. J Operational Psychiatry 12: 90–99

Schooler C, Spohn HE (1982) Social dysfunction and treatment failure in schizophrenia. Schizophr Bull 8: 85

Sokolovsky J, Cohen C, Berger D, Gerger J (1978) Pensional networks of ex-marital patients in a Manhattan SRO Hotel. Human Organization 37: 5-15

Sommer R, Osmond H (1984) The schizophrenic no-society revisited. Psychiatry 47: 181-191

Spencer PG, Gillespie CR, Ekisa EG (1983) A controlled comparison of the effects of social skills training and remedial drama on the conversational skills of chronic schizophrenic inpatients. Br J Psychiatry 143: 165-172

Stephens JH (1978) Long-term prognosis and follow-up in schizophrenia. Schizophr Bull 4: 25-47

Strauss JS, Carpenter WT (1977) Prediction of outcome in schizophrenia: III. Five-year outcome and its predictors. Arch Gen Psychiatry 34: 159-163

Strauss JS, Carpenter WT Jr (1978) The prognosis of schizophrenia: rationale for a multidimensional concept. Schizophr Bull 4: 56-67

Strauss JS, Loevski L, Glazer W, Laef P (1981) Organizing the complexities of schizophrenia. J Nerv Ment Dis 169: 120-126

Strauss JS, Carpenter WTJ (1981) Schizophrenia. Plenum, New York

Strauss JS, Hafez H, Liberman P, Harding CM (1985) The course of psychiatric disorder. III. Longitudinal principles. Am J Psychiatry 142: 3

Tessler RC, Manderscheid RW (1982) Factors affecting adjustment to community living. Hosp Community Psychiatry 33: 203-207

Test MA, Stein L (1978) The clinical rationale for community treatment: a review of the literature. In: Stein L, Test MA (ed) Alternatives to mental hospital treatment. Plenum, New York, 3-22

Test M, Stein L (1980) Alternative to mental hospital treatment: social cost. Arch Gen Psychiatry 37: 409-412

van Putten Th (1983) Adverse psychological (or behavioral) responses to antipsychotic drug treatment of schizophrenia. In: Rifkin A (ed) Schizophrenia and affective disorders. Wright, Bristol, pp 323-341

Wallace CJ, Boone SE (1984) Problem solving training for chronic schizophrenics. Proc Nebraska Symposium on Motivation. University of Nebraska Press, Boston

Wallace CJ, Nelson CJ, Liberman RP, Atchison A, Lukoff D, Elder JP, Ferris C (1980) A review of critique of social skills training with schizophrenic patients. Schizophr Bull 6: 42-64

Watt DC, Katz K, Shepherd M (1983) The natural history of schizophrenia: a 5-year prospective follow-up of a representative sample of schizophrenics by means of a standardized clinical and social assessment. Psychol Med 13: 663-670

Weisbrod B, Test M, Stein L (1980) Alternative to mental hospital treatment, II. Economic benefit-cost analysis. Arch Gen Psychiatry 37: 400-405

Williams P (1983) Factors influencing the duration of treatment with psychotropic drugs in general practice: a survival analysis approach. Psychol Med 13: 623-633

Woggon B (1979) Neuroleptiki - Absetzversuche bei chronisch schizophrenen Patienten. 1. Literatur-Zusammenfassung. Int Pharmacopsychiatry 14: 34

World Health Organiation (1979) Schizophrenia - an international follow-up study. Wiley, New York

Methodological Approaches

Methodological Problems of Comparing the Cost-Effectiveness of Different Mental Health Institutions

J. Sabatini and J. M. Elchardus

From an economic point of view, it is generally considered that the resources we can devote to medical care are limited and that, consequently, their allocation within the health system must be carried out in the most optimal way. Therefore, the decisions in this matter should be guided by considerations on the costs of strategies and on the benefits we can expect from them.

Within the psychiatric field, there is a growing interest in minimizing costs for the community or/and improving the quality of mental health care. The reason for this interest can be found in the importance of the costs and expenditures related to mental illness in industrialized countries. It manifests itself, among others, in the search for more cost-effective models of health care services delivery.

Why Compare Institutions?

In the past several years the deinstutionalization movement, promoted by the discovery of psychotropic drugs, has changed the morphology of the supply of care. It has given us a range of new ways of treating mental illness. At the beginning the asylum was the only possibility. Now people can receive treatment in various structures; the asylum still exists, but renovated, more modern, and with an enlargement of outpatient services, along with psychiatric units in general hospitals, crisis centers, day hospitals, therapeutic flats, etc.

This is real progress, but what we do not know exactly is the performance of these institutions and, more particularly, their efficiency in relation to their cost. And this is an important question for public authorities. They are not prepared to support anything new, especially since they have a natural tendency for disliking experiments. So they politely listen to the proposals of health-care providers, but their aim is really to try to cut down expenditures without always taking into consideration the positive effects of innovations, both on costs and on patients.

The psychiatric world has not really been explored from a medical and economic point of view. It is true that evaluations are particularly difficult in this field, due to the characteristics of mental illness, the specific features of institutions, and the interrelations between psychological and social levels. And these are just some of the obstacles one needs to overcome. Methodological care is more essential here than anywhere else, for studies must not be fictions, or worse, justifications for policy orientations already implicitly taken.

It is no secret that psychiatrists are rarely involved in evaluating the services they are delivering. One of the reasons for this lack of concern can probably be found in their qualitative approach to mental illness, which is more pronounced here than in the rest of medicine.

This is now changing with the difficulties psychiatrists have to face in protecting what they do and promoting new projects. But the intersubjective relation and the analogical way of thinking cannot alone explain the hostility we sometimes find toward attempts made at appraising the delivery of mental health care. Practitioners do know, perhaps, that what they do is not always very efficient and, consequently, they can be uneasy about any comparison.

But the crucial question is that of the specific effects of each institutional model. For some people, institutions have specific influences on the evolution of mental illness, and this quite independently from the nature and quality of treatments, techniques, or personnel. If asylums were denounced it was, without any doubt, because they were outdated but also because it became clear that they were reproducing the mental illness they were trying to care for. And all the institutions can potentially have the same negative impact. They constitute an answer to psychological needs, they model themselves on mental pathology but, at the same time, they also shape their clientele's future. They reflect the mental needs and simultaneously reproduce these needs identically.

The patients, especially the psychotic ones, who do not move from one institution or type of service to another, in spite of the practitioner's wishes, are not wrong. Such institutions restrain the populations in their charge, and these patients are only capable of conforming to these restraints. So the capacity of health-care models to treat seems to be one of the main points to resolve in the future, and this question is very characteristic of psychiatry compared with the other medical fields.

However, this question neglects a fundamental problem, i.e., what is the main function of mental institutions? Is their essential end to satisfy collective goals (such as social control, for instance) or is it effectively to treat? Even if the medical actions taken obtain positive results on both levels, it is not possible to elude the question and to confuse the levels, even if only one of them interests us here.

This general remark can also be made with regard to the evaluation of the institutions themselves. These do not have exactly the same objective, because of the tasks assigned to them. Emergency services, for instance, treat mental disorders but their essential function is to take over the care of people in crisis states. The nature of this activity makes the comparison with other institutions difficult, because they aim to treat mental diseases in the long term. In addition, the criteria of evaluation within this type of service can be specific (duration of the waiting period, rapidity of the disappearance of symptoms, etc.).

What to Compare?

Cost-effectiveness analysis requires the assessment of two components: cost and effectiveness. Each of these elements involves difficulties which are particular to mental health care institutions.

At first it is necessary to evaluate the most exhaustive set of costs. But what, exactly, are the relevant costs? In the case of a cost-effectiveness analysis, it seems that indirect costs are superfluous. Production losses, in particular, are generally associated with cost-benefit analyses. They are, in addition, very difficult to evaluate because psychosis is not only an illness but also a handicap affecting the working capacity differently, according to the degree of handicap and the periods of remission. In addition, in its search for efficiency, the market economy marginalizes the patients, and an improvement of their health state is not necessarily followed by a recovery of their professional activity. So, all things considered, this sort of evaluation is complex and highly uncertain.

The various direct costs are those involved in the delivery of health care. They correspond to the use of sanitary resources on behalf of patients. The listing of these costs is not always easy because the sick can utilize several care institutions simultaneously.

Furthermore, their measurement raises problems. In principle, the quantification must relate to the resources effectively used by the patient in terms of personnel, consumable goods, and various equipment. This evaluation is difficult because it requires precise bookkeeping of an analytical type, which is not always available due to the archaic accounting systems of some institutions. It also supposes that one can assign these cost data to the different types of pathologies.

Sometimes, because of the lack of precise information, one takes the hospital day price as a reference. But this is a financial indicator which does not adequately reflect the costs, so it should not be used.

In general, the psychiatric work is very different from one institution to another. As a matter of fact, institutions have several types of patients (psychoses, neuroses, geriatric disorders ...) in charge, and the clientele therefore varies between structures. Some cater to a large range of pathologies (by public necessity or by philosophy); others take an interest in restricted samples of mental disorders. This concerns not only the nature of illness but also the degree of morbidity. The extent, the scope of intervention has an important consequence. This is a real limit to the use of average costs per patient in institutions, but it is also an advantage, because it is a good reflection of the real activity of the institution. The global cost of the institution, and consequently the cost per patient, can be higher or lower because of the illness alone.

As far as medical care is concerned, it is necessary to note that treatment success leads to the discharge of the patient to his or her home. A new problem arises here: the patient, the relatives, or the social services will now have to bear new costs which must also be evaluated. Some are easy to define because they often express themselves in monetary terms; others are difficult to quantify (additional work for the family, for instance). Obviously, only costs which are additional to those of a non-sick subject should be considered in such an evaluation.

The measure of effectiveness, on the other hand, is not short of problems. It depends, first of all, on the assumptions on which the study is based. For instance, the way in which one views psychosis (i.e., whether it is considered a curable disease or a lifetime handicap) will influence the measurement.

Concerning the global effectiveness of an institution, it is generally appropriate to use many variables at the same time. This is important because, from a medical point of view, we do not know what criterion is adequate for assessing the evolution of patients. It can range from clinical criteria, at a purely psychological level, to considerations concerning the social adaptability. And all the variables used are probably not sufficient to give a real account of the evolution of the psychosis. As far as possible, it is better to use existing scales so as to make comparisons possible between one study and another. One can never be sure that a patient is completely cured, and it is well known that relapses are frequent. So the follow-up of the sick in the long term has to be carried out, using special parameters. Cohort studies seem to be essential but they are not very easy, either to conduct (on account of the complex pathways of patients, for instance) or to link-up with the calculation of costs (patients treated in several institutions, introduction of time in the calculation, etc.). In this hypothesis two alternatives can be envisaged: (a) to consider for the costs a given time period corresponding to the care received and to follow the subjects after that period for the evaluation of effectiveness, or (b) to consider an entire period of time (which is bound to finish one day) for both the cost and the effectiveness. None of the two methods is perfect and each of them raises empirical problems. In addition, they can generate very different results. Consequently, the choice is important here and not neutral.

How to Compare?

The first difficulty in comparing two things is to make sure that the samples used are identical. The classic way to ensure this is the method of controlled trials. But an experimental situation is used when different treatments are compared, and it is very difficult to apply it to the activities of the institutions. As a matter of fact, a large degree of freedom exists: each medical structure has its own way of recruiting patients, who also have, in most countries, the freedom to choose where they want to be treated. So there is no real way of building perfect samples.

Another possibility, which is not so precise, is to use what is concretely available, i.e., the population effectively treated by institutions. This choice requires the definition of subsamples within the population considered. A minimum number of criteria is necessary: clinical characteristics of the mental disease (with exclusion, if possible, of the deviant behaviors which complicate the evaluation somewhat), age, sex, marital status, social variables (social class, ethnic differences, professional activity, quality of social and family support).

We must point out that clinical criteria are very controversial: problems of nosology, differences in diagnosis, and the use of subgroups are often matters of debate. It is not certain that the more subtle criteria are able to give a faithful account of the clinical reality and of the subjective reasons for sending a patient to a particular institution. What is more, some people argue that morbidity can change from one place to another because patients are able to present different facets of their personality in different institutions.

If comparing institutions requires similar samples, it also imposes that the sick receive homogeneous treatments. For instance, if an institution prescribes many electroshocks to patients and has good results, it may be because of the electroshocks or because of the institution's own functioning. So it is better to collect precise information concerning quality, quantity, and chronology of the different treatments.

Finally, and we have kept for the end the most difficult problem, one generally considers that the patient's future is largely influenced by his or her treatment career. Some even put forward the fact that the first contact with the caregiver is a determinant of the future development of the mental illness. So the most perfect study would select only new patients. One of the problems in this case is that they are not very numerous because the incidence of psychosis is low. Another is that new patients sometimes choose special, e.g., new or unusual, treatments.

After the definition of samples and the data collection comes the time for comparisons. The basis of the evaluation of results is constituted by the costs necessary to derive the effectiveness under study. Taking into consideration the methodological difficulties involved in the deriving of pertinent evaluation criteria, it seems logical to avoid restricting the comparison elements and to use a range of effectiveness indicators so as obtain a good prediction.

The comparison must also consider, not simply the average costs but also the marginal costs, which are the additional costs necessary to obtain the effectiveness increase. And this requires clarity about the nature of the change.

All these considerations lead us to conclude that the evaluation of the cost and effectiveness of different institutions is not an easy process. The main limitation we could point out is the distortion of the size of the sample and the large number of variables to be taken into account. These requirements may make the study impossible. In fact, it may be argued that it is better to do nothing than to obtain controversial results. From another point of view, however, the economic appraisal of mental health care is a real requirement which must be satisfied. In pointing out the methodological flaws we hope to contribute to their progressive elimination in evaluation studies.

Time-Budget Analysis for Chronic Patients. Towards a Cost-Effectiveness–Oriented Indicator System for Comparing Inpatient and Outpatient Psychiatric Care

P. Potthoff, R. Leidl, W. Bender, and D. Schwefel

Introduction

The career of a person supposed to be suffering from chronic psychotic disturbances is markedly influenced by his/her country of residence. An Italian has a
higher chance of living with the family at home; a French patient is likely to be institutionalized; in the case of a German it depends where and with whom he/she
lives. Whether and on the basis of what criteria such differences are justified, and
whether they constitute opportunities for saving costs (not only savings in fees and
funds, but also the prevention of suffering for the patient and his/her family can
be regarded as a saving) are important questions to be posed before a rational
choice can be made between treatment alternatives.

The comparison of patterns of care which occur in drastically different social
processes and places, such as ambulatory care, hospital care or living in a therapeutic home community – while not neglecting the contributions by relatives, a
partner, neighbours or, in extreme cases, even the services of the police – touches
very different economies: individuals, households, municipalities, or the national
economy. Each of these economies comprises different monetary interactions as
well as quite different forms of non-monetary exchange of resources. How can, for
comparative purposes, common attributes of cost and effectiveness be identified,
without overlooking crucial elements?

Cost-effectiveness analyses are economic tools for coping with such questions.
But there is no standard cost-effectiveness analysis. What is needed first is a relatively comprehensive indicator system that reveals information about the life and
the daily routines of psychotic patients and the resources (housing, time, personnel, materials, drugs, neighbourhood assistance, police, etc.) required for their cure
and care. Resources are then – not necessarily in monetary terms only – to be
added up and compared with the impact of treatment or of the pattern of care
used (e.g. improvement, stationary conditions, deterioration).

Our contribution discusses some methodological aspects of indicators for costs
and effects of psychiatric care and some approaches towards their aggregation to
more comprehensive indexes. For this purpose, theoretical considerations and
proposals from the literature were supplemented by an analysis of existing routine
data on psychiatric care and by our own exploratory, empirical approach.[1]

---

[1] Upper Bavaria, in the Federal Republic of Germany, including the city of Munich and the sur-
rounding region, forms the institutional background of psychiatric care for the empirical part of
the study. A short description of the system is given below

Costs in Psychiatric Care

Costs can be looked upon as a result of the (monetarily or non-monetarily defined) consumption of resources, or, in terms of opportunity cost (i.e. the best alternative utilization of resources), of a loss of gains in terms of effectiveness. The distinction between costs and ineffectiveness (or deficient effectiveness) is frequently an arbitrary one. The literature on the cost-effectiveness of mental health care assumes a variety of cost elements to be important and operationalizes them in different ways. Hardly one cost-effectiveness analysis is comparable with another; almost all select a few cost categories from a universe of possible cost categories.

One first step of cost-effectiveness analysis is the identification of cost elements (for a list, see Appendix A). A next step is their operational definition and the use of appropriate methods to assess them empirically. One should consider:

- Institutional costs, as documented in routine accounting files of the institutions
- Nation-wide or regional costs, where appropriate estimates based on official statistics may have to be used
- Living costs (per household), which can be collected by surveys that measure income and consumption, as well as e.g. 'irrational' expenditures
- Social costs understood in terms of externalities, which can be explored by surveys, estimates, or analytic fantasy
- Costs incurred in the care of a patient, based on activity surveys of patients, family members, relatives, or health workers
- "Rare" costs derived from information on the number of ambulance rides, suicides, or police services; official statistics and routine data are the sources.

When institutional data can be used, or where accounting and budgeting systems – for example, per diem rates of psychiatric hospitals – are available, interorganizational comparisons of cost indicators are feasible. However, difficulties arise if intraorganizational and supraorganizational comparisons of, for example, outpatients with inpatients, psychotic with non-psychotic patients, are made, or if an identification of individual patient costs, or an evaluation of costs arising from services in kind by a cooperation among patients, or visits of relatives, or outdoor activities should be performed. Thus, an institutional perspective alone is hardly sufficient to analyze cost and effectiveness in the treatment of chronic psychotic patients.

To compare, for example, the costs of outpatients with those of inpatients, no single instrument will do. Only a comprehensive research strategy relying on several approaches will provide information for a relatively comprehensive assessment of costs. A single research approach captures only segments in the various economies of individuals, households, the community, an institution, or the whole nation. Also, a comprehensive approach towards the assessment of costs will offer information on the particularity of a constrained approach.

Therefore, we will highlight costs of psychiatric care from two different viewpoints: from an institutional and from an individual viewpoint. The first approach is a description of indicators for structures, processes and costs of psychiatric care in Upper Bavaria by means of routine data. The second approach – and this is the main part of our contribution – is an example of how information about the consumption of resources can be assembled in different therapeutic settings by a detailed time-budget analysis of chronic patients. While, also from an individual viewpoint, resource-oriented patient classification systems like the diagnosis-related groups split up a heterogeneous population to identify groups homogeneous in respect to resource use, the time-budget approach tries to cumulate resource consumption for each individual seperately.

Structures, Processes and Costs of Psychiatric Care in Upper Bavaria

Among all types of care,[2] the most information is available on hospital care for psychiatric patients. For a population of about 3.6 million people in Upper Bavaria, about 4500 beds are provided in 16 hospital units for psychiatric care, most of them in public hospitals (see Table 1). Of these beds, some 13% are designated for long-term psychiatric care. Almost all beds – with the exception of about 2% – are included in the Bavarian Hospital Plan and thus subject to public grants for their investment financing. The operating costs for the beds are to be raised by the hospital patients or their insurance in a lump-sum daily-rate payment according to a full-cost reimbursement principle. (This follows the hospital financing scheme valid at the time of our research. Meanwhile, the full-cost reimbursement has been changed to a negotiation of prospective budgets.)

Table 1. Structure of and costs for inpatient psychiatric care, Upper Bavaria,[a] 1985[b]

Indicators	Public hospitals	Other non-profit hospitals	Proprietary hospitals	All hospitals
	– Inpatient departments –			
Number of hospitals	8	1	7	16
Number of beds	4077	107	342	4526
Daily rate[c] (DM)	141.00	250.00	137.00	144.00
	– Day or night clinic –			
Number of hospitals[d]	6	1	–	7
Number of beds	164	20	–	184
Daily rate (DM)	84.00[e]	120.00	–	90.00

[a] Population about 3.6 million
[b] Source: Bayerisches Staatsministerium für Arbeit und Sozialordnung (own calculations)
[c] Rates for 1984, weighted per bed
[d] Four hospitals provide beds in inpatient departments and day or night clinics, as well
[e] Rates were available for two units only

---

[2] A detailed description of the West German mental health care system is given by Mangen (1985)

Table 1 also shows the average daily rates for hospitals, which are weighted per bed. However, they are calculated on an average basis for the whole hospital. As a consequence, the (high) average rate of a large-scale hospital with a small psychiatric unit can hardly be compared with the (low) average rate of a large psychiatric hospital. Also, the rates are not controlled for the teaching status of the hospital. In spite of this, the overall average might still give some idea of the average daily price.

The different financing sources of patients are described for a large psychiatric hospital in Table 2. This financing includes neither the (publicly granted) investment expenditures nor the deficits, which in that year also reached about 1.4% of the operating costs. While in other hospitals most patients are covered by the sick funds, in psychiatric hospitals a large portion of costs are paid by public authorities (see Table 2). In addition, considerable out-of-pocket payment is found, as well as a 3% share of unpaid bills.

Both the out-of-pocket payments and the high share of social-welfare financing (in which case the same public authorities pay for low-income patients as well as for the deficits remaining with the publicly owned hospital) show that long-term care for psychiatric patients is not included in the comprehensive scheme of compulsory health insurance in the Federal Republic of Germany, which insure approximately 95% of the population. In fact, the rule that the sick funds have to finance cure but not care (especially in the case of chronic diseases) has led to an arrangement whereby the sick funds pay for 1 year (or, after an examination of the curability, for a longer period), but after that, the patient, his relatives, or in the case of no income or poverty social welfare have to pay for further hospital stays. Thus, long-term illness may imply impoverishment.

Day or night clinics are considerably lower in their price (for half the time of care). In comparison with full inpatient treatment, there are only very few beds provided for this type of care (see Table 1). A survey of all psychiatric inpatients in Bavaria in 1983 revealed that only a very small number of hospital patients were considered suitable for admission to this type of care; this may, however, depend on the small capacity of day or night clinics.

Table 2. Financing of operating costs in a large psychiatric hospital in Upper Bavaria, 1983[a]

Financing party	Percentage of operating cost
Sick funds	43.9
Social welfare[b]	37.4
Judical authorities	7.7
Out-of-pocket	6.2
Private insurance	1.0
Unknown	3.0
Other	0.8
Total	100.0

[a] Source: Information from the *Bezirksverwaltung, Oberbayern*
[b] Is identical with the hospital owner

The ambulatory physicians in Upper Bavaria comprised 158 neurologists and psychiatrists in 1984; another 177 were listed for psychotherapy. However, an exact differentiation of psychiatric care from activities not concerned with the mentally ill cannot be given. Very roughly, the average number of all cases for neurologists can be estimated at about 575 for each quarter of a year, and the average costs per case (only those listed in the fee schedule) at about DM 120. (The estimates are based on internal MEDIS panels and routine data analyses among ambulatory physicians in Bavaria.) As another method of estimating the costs of ambulatory treatment, items from the fee-for-service schedule can be useful to describe the physician's remuneration for standard treatments (see Table 3). For example, such a standard treatment – similar to the ones reported in our survey – could comprise a checkup and two therapeutic consultations per month, resulting in a total remuneration of about DM 56. Following this method of estimating treatment costs, the costs for typical service combinations can be deduced from the fee schedule.

Community Services and Non-medical Care. Care outside the professional medical care sector is supplied by a broad variety of institutions, which, to a great extent, are publicly funded; some are also financed by charitable funds or belong to privately organized psychiatric care. Because of the institutional, organizational, and financial variety of this part of the care system, a list of several types of care and services can be given rather than a comprehensive description of all care and money involved.

A major institution providing psychiatric care in the communities are the so-called *Sozialpsychiatrischen Dienste,* providing services like counselling or support for social rehabilitation. In 1985 there were 19 of these services; of these about 90% were funded by public authorities, the remaining 10% by their owners, mostly charitable funds. For Upper Bavaria, the costs of these services can be estimated

Table 3. Examples of standard items of ambulatory treatment of psychiatric patients in a fee schedule, F. R. G., 1985[a]

Item in fee schedule	Service	Fee (in DM)[b]
1	General counselling	7.30
801	Psychiatric examination	25.50
804	Psychiatric counselling	15.30
806	Psychiatric treatment by exploration and counselling, at least 20 min, also in acute situations	25.50
812	Psychiatric emergency treatment (e.g. suicide)	51.00
833	Bringing the patient to a hospital and writing the referral documents	29.00

[a] Source: *Bewertungsmaßstab für kassenärztliche Leistungen (BMÄ)*

[b] Rounded; the figures were calculated on the basis of the fee schedule (which gives point figures as relative prices for each item), using the point value of 10.2 pfennig (which was used in the Bavarian system until June 1985)

at around 5 million marks, which, however, cannot be split up for chronic psychotic patients and the rest of patients adequately.

An overview of some other institutions providing care outside the medicotherapeutic system is presented in Table 4. The capacities of the units listed for outpatient care or care in intermediate institutions are considerably low compared with the number of hospital beds for psychiatric patients. While this list of institutions complementing hospitals cannot claim to be fully complete – these units are not listed in routine statistics – it comprises only about 10% of the number of places for inpatients in the same region. Table 4 also shows the daily rates per patient, which are lowest in therapeutic homes (flats shared by, on average, eight patients) and about half the cost in a working center compared with an intermediate home (which charges almost standard hospital rates).

Conclusions for Cost Calculations Based on Institutional Cost Data. The prices charged or the budgets allotted for the treatment of psychiatric patients in the different institutions of care – hospitals, ambulatory physicians, community services – may be the most readily available or sometimes the only source of information on the costs of treatment. However, as the preceding short survey of the financing of psychiatric care in Upper Bavaria shows, there are some problems interfering with the estimation of treatment costs on the basis of institutional data:

– Some of the data are not comprehensive in terms of institutional costs (e.g. hospital costs did not include investment costs or funds raised by the hospital owner), and of course expenditure calculations can be far from an analysis of the 'social' resource consumption.
– It is in general not possible to attribute cost data to a specific patient group, such as the chronic schizophrenics, because of lump-sum calculations in the institutions. In addition, the multiple utilization of more than one institution by the same patient (group) cannot be determined.

As a result, when seeking the treatment costs of a specific patient group, a patient-oriented approach has to be employed. This approach is to be supplemented by

Table 4. Institutions providing non-medical care for psychiatric patients in the region of Munich, 1982[a]

Institution	Number of institutions	Number of patient units	Average rates (in DM)
Therapeutic homes	12	100	22.00[b]
Working center	1	45	58.00
Intermediate home for psychiatric patients	1	122	
– full time		72	133.00
– daytime		20	
– nighttime		30	91.00

[a] Source: *Bezirk Oberbayern* (ed) (1983) Einrichtungen im Stadt- und Landkreis München, 4th edn.
[b] cost for care only

the information on institutional costs. Some of the institutional cost data can be used as proxy measures for the monetarization of quantities of institutional resource consumption specified individually per patient (group).

Resource Consumption in Psychiatric Care Derived from Time-Budget Analyses

The Purpose of Time-Budget Analyses

Activities (as well as the inactivity) of psychotic patients and the persons interacting with them can be considered common descriptors of the processes in different therapeutic settings and their economies. An analysis of where and with whom these activities are undertaken and how long they last is an individually based, patient-oriented approach toward the identification of the elements of resource utilization, which later can be valued monetarily.

To inquire into the feasibility, usefulness and limitations of a patient-centered approach to the assessment of costs and effects, we studied the time budgets of 18 chronic psychotic patients living in different settings. This exercise was aimed at collecting data on resource consumption and functional health status as basic material for constructing indicators of the costs and effects of care.

Time-budget analysis (TBA) is well known as an efficient instrument for registering comprehensively the temporal activity patterns of people within their spatial, material, monetary, social and other contexts. In the context of this pilot study, the purpose of TBA was manifold, since time can be looked upon both as a resource and as a unit of measurement (As 1982; Harvey et al. 1984):

- TBA is a means of describing the actions, social interactions and institutional processes that are involved in the (self-)management of patients. By applying TBA the stream of actions and social processes is broken down into 'time-atoms' or 'actons', which can be reported or recorded in detail.
- TBA is a means of recording material and cost of professionals, relatives and significant others (of patients) devoted to the process of care, i.e. resources spent for cure and care. TBA can be considered to be a check-list procedure which tries to guarantee a comprehensive recording of these 'expenditures'. By taking the cost of time into consideration, one specially important cost element of health care can be estimated. However, this approach may necessitate making assumptions on the attribution of resources which are not consumed in direct interactions between patients and providers of care (an example of such an 'overhead' would be a physician's time spent for, but not together with the patient). Besides, the impact of rare events (e.g. suicide attempts involving high rescue costs) and very general factors (e.g. the creation of a federal commission on psychiatry) on treatment costs is unlikely to be satisfactorily documented by this method, even if one tries to identify all activities of all psychotic patients over a long period of time. Thus, a necessary supplement is the generation and comparison of highly aggregated data about such overall supportive services

and the overhead costs. Institutional analyses, as discussed above, are needed to complement a patient-oriented approach and vice versa (see also Appendix A).

- As the active (self-)organization of daily life may be seen as a goal of psychiatric treatment, the TBA of patients may provide information on their functional health status. It can thus be interpreted as a measure of the health status of the patients and as an outcome dimension of psychiatric care.
- With the information collected by TBA, one can compare (or try to make comparable) the actions and social processes of patient management in a variety of different institutions, health care systems and nations: Time and the temporal structure of behaviour patterns are dimensions common to them all, and time consumption can be a comparable unit of measurement.

The Pilot Study

The present feasibility study on the TBA of chronic psychotics concentrated on two groups of patients. The first were inpatients from two wards of the *Bezirkskrankenhaus Haar,* a 2100-bed municipal hospital near Munich. The second group were outpatients, previously treated in this hospital, who lived at home but still used outpatient nursing services of the clinic.

To achieve comparability between inpatients and outpatients with respect to psychiatric diagnoses and acuteness of psychopathological disturbances, patients were selected by several psychiatrists. The criteria were met by patients who had suffered for at least 3 years from a schizophrenic disorder which was not paranoid or accompanied by hallucinations (for a specific period of time prior to the interview). By this specification, patients in extremely agitated stages of schizophrenia or with delusions were to be excluded from the study.

Inpatients and outpatients who matched this definition were selected by psychiatrists of the clinic. The interviews were carried out by (female and male) nurses of the clinic who had been instructed on how to administer the questionnaire. This procedure was chosen in order to gain experience as to whether such an interviewing procedure could be carried out in the daily routine of the institution, a major prerequisite for an extension of the study to larger groups of patients or hospitals.

The preliminary results reported below stem from two small patient groups interviewed so far: nine inpatients and nine outpatients.

Structure and Variables of the Interviews

TBA can be performed for different time windows: for days, weeks, years or even for the whole life cycle of a person. For our study we have chosen a short-term approach: daily, weekly and, for some variables, monthly periods of reference. The core question of the TBA approach can be put as follows: "What did the patient do, where was it done, who was involved and at what costs (in terms of money, material, etc.)?" This question was repeatedly posed for several variables that describe the situation and treatment of the patients.

Information was gathered by a semi-structured questionnaire. TBA, the major part of the questionnaire, was performed in two ways: firstly, by using the course of the day as a structuring device to register all the events that occurred in that day; secondly, by establishing a list of predefined activities, institutional processes, etc. and by inquiring whether, when and how many times these activities took place and how long they lasted. The first approach leads to a comprehensive picture of (small) time intervals, the second is a cross-check suitable for identifying events that happen less frequently. The TBA questionnaire contained both approaches, in that it supplemented a diary with a check list of activities. In addition to TBA, the questionnaire referred to some other variables which are useful for deriving cost estimates from time budgets, or which are important in themselves for cost analyses.

Starting point for the development of the questionnaire was a 'comprehensive' list of cost elements (see Appendix A). Using a draft of a questionnaire, several interviews were conducted. In this phase, which preceded the 18 interviews, it was important to find out whether the method of data collection was feasible in different therapeutic institutions and whether the time schedules and lists of activities, therapies and cost elements in the draft questionnaire were complete. Some pilot interviews were conducted in a psychiatric hospital and in a day-and-night clinic with psychiatrists, nurses, social workers, patients and their relatives. After six revisions, the questionnaire was completed.

An overview of the content and structure of the final questionnaire is given in Table 5. In more detail, the following information was collected:

- *Diary:* From 6 a.m. until 1 a.m., all active or passive behaviour, i.e. the 'time-behaviour units' or 'actons', (e.g. working, shopping, hanging around) as phrased by the patient himself. This also included data on the place of the event, the persons involved, and the amount of time and money spent.

Table 5. Structure and content of the questionnaire

Part of questionnaire	Time period relative to the day of interview
Diary	last day
Activity check list	last month
Institutional care	at present
Therapies	last week
Drugs	at present
Personal and social situation	
– marital and social status	at present
– care by relatives, friends and others	at present
– housing	at present
– job situation	last month and year
– social security	at present
– income	last month
– expenditures paid by patient	last month
– expenditures for patient by relatives and others	last month

- *Check list of activities:* 33 predefined activities; information on when they were last performed, how long they went on, who was involved, how much money was spent, and how many times they were performed.
- *Institutional care:* 18 categories; information about the last contact with each institution and its duration, about the persons who cared for the patient, the amount of money spent, and the frequency of these care activities during a month.
- *Therapies:* 12 items describing therapies; information about the last event of each type of therapy, where it took place, how many other patients participated, which therapists were involved, how much money was spent, and how often this therapy was performed.
- *Drug therapy:* Names of drugs, dose, frequency of intake.
- *Life situation, income and expenditures:* Information on the patients' life situation and household (including such items as number of household members, rent paid, etc.), on regular non-financial support given to them by professional and non-professional care, on their income situation (including social welfare, pensions, or support by relatives), and on their consumption patterns (according to the market basket of the consumer-price index of the Federal Bureau of Statistics).

The Interviews

Interview Procedure and Checks for Reliability. For each patient, interviews were planned with three informants:

- The patient him/herself
- A nurse who knew the patient well
- Relatives or other significant contacts of the patient

Comparison of the reports of the professionals (or relatives) with those of the patients on the same activities was intended to serve as a reliability check for the patients' reports. The interviews with relatives and other significant persons were to produce additional data on their expenditures (in terms of money or time) for the patient. This triple concept was not very successful. In the case of outpatients, the nurses did not know the patients well enough to be able to assess their time and other resource budgets independently of the interviews with patients. For approximately half of the patients no relatives or friends were found to answer the questionnaire.

Problems of Implementation. In conducting the survey we encountered the following problems:

- Not all the patients met the diagnostic definition of the sample.
- One interview was incomplete, one was completely missing.
- In one case, a patient was interviewed both as an inpatient and, after discharge, as an outpatient.

- In some cases, differences occurred between the activities, expenditures, and therapies within one questionnaire as reported by the patients, by relatives or nurses.
- Sometimes, the patient and his/her relatives reported together; hence, their information could not be separated and no independent reports were available.
- For only one patient did we succeed in gathering all three types of interviews as planned.
- On the other hand, in most cases two of the three sources were available, but different answers raised a reliability problem, where one would have to decide either to rely on only one informant or to accept the fact that different informants report on different 'realities'. Still, one has to keep in mind the different perspectives of the interviewees, which places in question the notion of a unique consistent reality.

Descriptive Results

Tentative results of our study will be presented in two steps: At first, an overview of the elements of the patients' time budgets, activities, therapies, living conditions and consumption patterns is given. This material is taken directly from the interviews. In the second part a still more programmatic outline will be discussed, that shows how we plan to aggregate and value the elements of the patients' lives by different methods (e. g. with regard to different cost elements or to health status).

Personal and Social Data. Incidentally, all nine outpatients but one were women, whereas among the same number of inpatients men were in the majority. The male patients were significantly younger than the female patients. As to their civil status, nearly all the patients were single; only five had children. Only two patients had no family support at all; the rest were being looked after, in some way or the other, by their mother, brothers or sisters, children, partners or close friends. Eight of them lived alone; only one inpatient had no home of his own. The rents they reported indicated that most interviewees were relatively poor. Only four of them had some kind of occupation (such as gluing of bags, caretaking, printing, kitchen work); four were pensioners, two jobless, and all the rest were officially labelled as ill and incapable of work.

Diaries. The time and behaviour patterns, seen in a daily perspective, are displayed in the diaries of the patients. On the right side, Table 6 gives an overview of the timetables of two inpatients of roughly the same age. The time schedule of both of them is rigidly structured by the framework of routine life in a clinic: getting up at the same time, breakfast, lunch, dinner, going to bed early in the evening. Within this framework the two behave quite differently: the one (patient N) is actively engaged in work and therapies, the other spends most of his time hanging around in the ward. In the upper part of Table 6, a female inpatient is compared with a female outpatient. In this case the outpatient is more active and 'consumes' more social contacts than the inpatient; this is, however, not the case with every outpatient.

From the diaries of all patients we derived a comprehensive list of so-called time-behaviour units, or actons (Appendix B), which can be used as a basis for the assessments and aggregations.

Activities. The diaries were complemented by a list of active and passive behavioural units, which had been recorded for the time period of 1 month before the interview (see Appendix C). In the diaries as well as in the lists of activities the incidence of behavioural elements (e.g. 'shopping'), contact and support by other

Table 6. Time – use patterns of two inpatients (same ward) and of an inpatient and an outpatient

Patient J (female, 46 years) outpatient		Patient B (female, 24 years) inpatient	
		6.30	wakes up, dresses
7.00	wakes up, dresses	7.00	breakfast
		7.30 ⌐	
8.00 ⌐	breakfast, housework		
9.00 ⌐			walks on the ward, smokes,
9.00 ⌐	goes shopping		talks with patients, at 10.00 a 10-min visit by a doctor
10.00 ⌐			
10.00 ⌐	visit at the labor office		
		11.30 ⌐	
		11.30	lunch
12.00 ⌐		12.00 ⌐	
12.00 ⌐	lunch, has a rest, is brooding		
13.00 ⌐			
13.00 ⌐			spends some time in bed, smokes,
	housework		walks on the ward
16.00 ⌐			
16.00 ⌐	adult education course	16.30 ⌐	
		16.30	supper
		17.00 ⌐	
18.00 ⌐			
18.00 ⌐	supper		walks on the ward, smokes
19.00 ⌐		19.00 ⌐	
19.00 ⌐		19.00	in bed, sleeps
	adult education course		
22.00 ⌐			
22.00 ⌐	watches television, is brooding		
23.00 ⌐			
24.00	in bed, sleeps		

Table 6 (continued)

Patient N (male, 32 years) inpatient		Patient M (male, 24 years) inpatient	
6.30	wakes up, dresses	6.30	wakes up, dresses
7.10	breakfast	7.00	breakfast
7.45	works in the kitchen	7.30 ⌐	
8.00 ⌐			plays piano 10 min, reads a book, hangs around in the ward, at 9.50 a 10-min visit by the doctor
	works in the printing office		
10.30 ⌐			
10.30 ⌐			
	musico – therapy	11.30 ⌐	
11.30 ⌐			
11.30	lunch	11.30	lunch
12.00 ⌐	works in the	12.00 ⌐	
12.30 ⌐	kitchen		
13.00 ⌐			
	works in the printing office		spends time in bed
16.30 ⌐		16.30 ⌐	
16.45 ⌐	supper	16.45 ⌐	supper
17.00 ⌐		17.00 ⌐	
17.00 ⌐	works in the kitchen	17.00	goes to bed, falls asleep sometime
17.30 ⌐			
17.30	goes to bed, reads a book, falls asleep sometime		

persons (professionals, relatives or other significant persons) and the duration of these elements were registered.

Institutional Care. As a consequence of the sampling procedure, the patterns of institutional care for the 18 patients were rather homogeneous. Institutional care for the outpatients was delivered mainly by office-based physicians and psychiatrists, as well as by nurses of the clinic. For patients who are subject to other forms of care, e.g. day clinics, different institutional patterns can be expected.

Therapies. Therapies for outpatients were mainly individual counselling by ambulatory physicians, psychiatrists and nurses, and drug therapy. The time of counseling varies between half an hour and 4 h per week by physicians and between 2 and 7 h per week by nurses. Therapies for inpatients were of a greater variety than for outpatients. Most patients received individual as well as group counseling. Five patients were engaged in one kind of social therapy or another.

Drug Therapy. The kinds of drugs consumed – in terms of patent medicines as well as generics – varied considerably. With respect to the types used, there was no 'homogeneity' between patients, or patterns, or types of care. The monetary amount spent for the drug therapy of inpatients, however, exceeded that for the outpatients by far: Depending on whether the respective quantities of the drugs reported were also known or not (in the latter case, a mimium dose was calculated), inpatients on average were treated with drugs at a two- to threefold higher cost than outpatients.

First Steps of Aggregation

TBA and the other parts of the questionnaire deliver a descriptive picture of the daily life of the patients. Whereas selected comparisons of inpatients and outpatients can be done on this level of analysis, the intention of comparing costs and effects requires aggregation of the multitude of single pieces of information to global indexes of costs and effects, e.g. health status. Aggregation of descriptive indicators to indexes implies the well-known problems of weighting the indicators and elaborating an appropriate arithmetic model. At present, such models have

Table 7. Duration of inpatients' and outpatients' contacts with relatives and professionals

		Patient D (female, 46 years) inpatient		Patient K (female, 54 years) outpatient
Diary (hours per day)	??[a]	Counselling (20 other patients)	4	A relative (visit)
Activities (hours per month)	75	Other patient (shopping)	30	A relative, friend (visit)
	10	Other patient (restaurant)	¼	A relative, friend (taking pictures)
	2	Four other patients (doing the dishes)	28[b]	Visit
	1	A relative (visit)		
	6	A psychiatric nurse (tasks)		
Therapy (hours per month)	3[c]	Two doctors, two nurses, student (individual counselling)	½	A general practitioner (individual counselling)
	1½[d]	Two doctors, two nurses, student (counselling, 20 other patients)	¼	A neurologist (individual counselling)
	32[e]	A working therapist (50 other patients)	3	A psychiatric nurse (individual counselling)
	6	A musicotherapist (10 other patients)		
	1⅓	An occup. therapist (10 other patients)		
Life situation (hours per month)	1	A relative (general support)	24	A relative (visit)
	3	Friends (general support)	12	A relative (visit)
	3	A relative (general support)		

[a] Hours and personnel unknown
[b] Person unknown
[c] Patient and relatives report ½ h, doctor only
[d] Patient and relatives report 6 h, two doctors and two nurses
[e] Patient and relatives report 60 h

not yet elaborated. The first steps of aggregation data with respect to time spent in social contacts and income and expenditure patterns are reported below.

Time of Caring Activities and Contacts of Patients with Others. As a first step, we cumulated the total amount of time for caring activities and for contacts of patients with others. Major differences between the groups of patients were that outpatients received less care and contact time by doctors and nurses than inpatients (see Table 7), and that inpatients participated more in therapeutic programmes (work, music, activities, and balneal therapy). The time and care devoted to a patient by non-professionals (relatives and friends) was not obviously related to the (inpatient or outpatient) type of care. Some inpatients had many, some outpatients only very few contacts, and within each type of care the variation in non-professional time spent with the patient was remarkable. For variations in the total amount of caring activities, the social environment of the patient seems to be more important than the type of care. However, before the time of care devoted to a patient can be evaluated in terms of resource consumption, it has to be distinguished from periods of time just spent with somebody incidentally; this is particularly necessary in the case of outpatients who live together with other people.

Income and Expenditure Patterns. Although in many of our cases it was not possible to determine income and expenditure exactly, our findings provide some information on the patients' standards of living, income sources and consumption patterns (see Table 8). In general, the budgets – or budget elements – clearly show

Table 8. Income and expenditures of two inpatients (in DM, rounded)

Income/expenditures	Patient A (male, 45 years)	Patient D (female, 46 years)
Rent (inclusive)	166	553
Food		
Drinking, tobacco	100	200[a]/250[b]
Clothing		
Hygiene	10	40
Culture, leisure		20
Transportation	10	33
Communication	30	50
Restaurant	20	–[c]
Total expenditures	336	916/946
Wages, salary	60	
Social welfare	105	
Pension		1100
Unemployment benefits		
Pocket money by hospital		
Support from relatives		
Total income	165	1100
Savings or deficits	− 171	+ 184/154

[a] Reported by patient and relative
[b] Reported by personnel
[c] Regular restaurant visits were reported

that the patients were extremely poor. Roughly estimated, most of them belong to the lowest 5%–8% of the income-distribution scale. A very small part of their income was based on wages or salaries (outpatients reported no such income at all). Other sources include low-level incomes from social welfare, pensions, unemployment benefits, support from relatives, and pocket money from the hospital for inpatients. Probably, however, not all income sources were discovered by the survey; occasionally, a gap remained between income and expenditure. In addition, some economic activities may have been hidden in the interviews with the nurses. To a great extent, differences in the budgets of inpatients can be traced back to whether or not rent has to be paid. Not only for institutional reasons, but also as a result of their low budgets, the consumption activities reported by the patients concentrated on drinking and smoking, restaurantvisits or communication rather than on furniture, clothing or travelling.

Valuation of Indicators in Terms of Effects and Costs

As mentioned earlier, the comparison of costs and effects requires the weighting and aggregation of indicators. A hypothetical example of an evaluation of actons and activities for two patients displays the logic of this exercise (Table 9). The time atoms of the diary can be classified by cost categories (e.g. use of time of staff care, use of physicians' time, hotel costs) or by dimensions of effectiveness (e.g. implications of patient's autonomy, or 'social' activities). The course of the patient's day could also be assessed in terms of the quantity, diversification, contents, etc. of the activities performed. Taking two (groups of) patients as an example for demonstration, the following results could be gained:

Table 9. Evaluation of actons in terms of different weighting dimensions (fictitious example)

Acton	Weighting dimensions[a] for actons					Actons performed by patient	
	a	b	c	d	e	X	Y
Wakes up	−	−	80	−	−	yes	yes
Washes himself	0	−	−	0	−	no	yes
Waits	−	−	−	−	−	no	yes
Has breakfast	0	−	10	0	−	yes	no
Balneal therapy	+	−	25	0	0	yes	no
Talks to neighbours	−	−	−	+	+	no	yes
Reads a book	−	−	−	+	+	no	yes
Visit by doctor	+	+	20	0	0	no	yes

[a] Dimensions: a, intensity of care by personnel; b, intensity of care by psychiatrist; c, costs according to hotel prices (DM); d, involvement of self-reliance; e, involvement of social contacts
Comparison of the time budgets of the two patients (X and Y):
- Patient Y is more active than patient X
- Patient X involves a higher intensity of care by personnel than patient Y
- Both patients range about the same in terms of self-reliance
This exercise could be modified by taking the duration and/or intensity of the actons into account

- On average, patient (group) A uses more staff time for care than patient (group) B
- In terms of hotel costs, patient A consumes less than patient B
- Both patients are in a similar position regarding their degree of autonomy
- If autonomy is considered a dimension of effectiveness, and if hotel costs are regarded as an indicator of costs, then patient A is treated more cost-effectively than patient B.

This procedure is based on only some of several possible assumptions for interpreting and evaluating the diaries, and the evaluation of diaries is only one method of estimating resource consumption.

When these evaluations are performed systematically some open issues arise: for example, how can the diaries be evaluated as a whole, or how can cost categories be aggregated? The transformation of costs into monetary values can rely on the usual techniques of valuation, such as the use of market prices, shadow prices or oppportunity costs. For the following estimations and aggregations different assumptions in various scenarios must be performed:

- The (social) cost of therapy and care, which is rendered by persons of different qualifications (professionals and non-professionals)
- The total consumption of non-staff resources in different institutions
- The costs of living for chronic psychotic patients
- The overhead costs (computed from additional data sources) that are involved in the living and care of chronic psychotic patients, or in the provision of treatment.

In addition to these problems, elements of the time budgets might be viewed in a different perspective. The time 'atoms' of behaviour in the diaries – e.g. sleeping, having breakfast, talking with neighbours, drowsing, playing piano, counseling by a physician, working therapy with 20 other patients – imply aspects of resource consumption (as an indicator of cost) as well as autonomy and diversity of behaviour (as indicators of functional health and outcome of treatment).

To deal with the problem of weighting and valuing the information from TBA with respect to costs and effects, some exploratory work of the above-mentioned type was also performed with the empirical material of the pilot study. Concerning effectiveness dimensions, the following points were touched upon:

- In a first step, the (unweighted) frequencies of the activities reported were compared for inpatients and outpatients. The basic activities of life, such as sleeping and eating, were of course reported regularly for all patients. As a restriction imposed by the small sample size, all activities reported for just one or two patients are omitted here. Differences between patient groups occurred in the activities with a medium-range frequency: Outpatients pursued more household work like cleaning or cooking, but also had more contact with friends. Inpatients reported more therapeutic activities and more contacts with other patients. The results offer an intuitively plausible description of the patients' situation.

- In a second step, the activities were weighted. A group of five professionals (two psychiatrists, a social worker, a nurse and a psychologist) were asked to assess for each activity whether a psychotic patient would need care, other services, special motivation, special (communal) infrastructures and the like when he/she performed this activity. Further, the activities were evaluated in terms of role completion, passivity, routine activity, intellectual activity, physical activity, durability, social contacts, and communication. Some methodological problems emerged in this step of the operationalization. More important, the perspective of the professionals was more strongly oriented towards individual patients and cases than to a fictitious 'model' patient. Given the small number of group members and their heterogeneity, some inconsistencies were likely to occur. Omitting such methodological constraints, results showed that providing incentives ranked clearly before supplying services and staff care in respect to the necessity of different types of care for the patients. While for inpatients and outpatients this ranking order remained unchanged, exogenous contributions were rated as necessary more often for outpatients than for inpatients. The classification of the activities themselves into the enumerated dimensions revealed no similar ranking order, but underlined former results with more role completion-oriented activities for outpatients and more passivity for inpatients.
- With respect to costs, resource consumption for direct staff care was calculated both for inpatient and outpatient therapeutic care. Doctors', nurses' and therapists' working times were aggregated across patients and weighted monetarily with average salaries. The cost volume for this type of direct care (excluding other costs) was about five times higher for the inpatients of the study than for the others. A controlling estimate calculated for inpatients only (based on the average percentage of the share for the respective staff cost from per diem rates – see Table 1) revealed, in addition to the above calculated costs of direct staff care, an overhead of just about one third, which seems quite low (even though the per diems are not controlled for hospital case mix).

In summary, these examples show how, by assessing time and other resources (the quantities of which are given by the empirical results), essential elements of resource consumption can be analyzed in different scenarios, e.g. comparison of inpatients and outpatients, but also for different groups of patients who are not defined institutionally (e.g., singles without any family care, 'active' patients).

Conclusions

Our study can be looked upon as the empirically supported endeavour to develop institutionally or culturally flexible tools which could be useful for describing and comparing the treatment and care of chronic (psychotic) patients. Statistical analyses of the data were not intended in this pilot phase of the study; its aim was to explore some relevant dimensions of costs and indicators for functional health, rather than to measure accurately the cost-effectiveness of alternative types of care in predefined dimensions. Even within one type of care, a considerable amount of variation in costs and functional health status was found; this fact alone suggests that multiple approaches must be used to identify costs and effects and to assess them in comparative analyses.

As it is not tied to (the measurement of) institutional costs only, our multi-instrument approach seems to be well suited for exploring differences of the patients' resource consumption in alternative patterns of care. It also permits different types of cost analyses: it can be restricted, for example, to a comparison of the (direct) costs of care by staff. Comprehensive analysis, however, might also provide the framework for a more complete evaluation of (social) costs, based on individual units of observation rather than on institutional costs. Additional data sources, however, could supplement information about institutional or even system-wide costs.

The definition of effects to which costs are attributed is crucial to any analysis of cost-effectiveness. Because of its comprehensive coverage of the patient's (daily) life, the information from time-budget analyses might be suitable to reflect a comprehensive picture of the patient's functional capacities in daily life.

Costs that are not related to the time consumption of the patient are identified but not directly measured; this may cause problems with the adequate attribution of those costs to individuals or just the perception of this resource consumption. This is particularly true for all types of overhead costs. Cost elements linked to the individual time consumption can also lead to methodological problems: When measuring the staff time used for patient care, it is not clear how the doctor's counseling of ten patients in a group meeting that lasts half an hour should be counted: 3 (physician) min per patient, or 30 (physician) min, or even 300 (group-member) min? Thus, different scenarios with alternative assumptions have to be considered. While it is clear that the valuation of costs can influence the results of comparative cost analyses, it can be looked upon as a problem secondary to the exploration of cost categories. Other problems can emerge when income and expenditures, reported for households with more than one person, are to be attributed to a patient or when the expenditures, as reported by the patient and also by relatives, are to be interpreted; for an accurate handling of both problems the questionnaire has to be revised for future applications.

It has been stressed that the analysis of the cost-effectiveness of patterns of care for chronic psychotic patients should include different approaches for measuring and computing elements from different points of view. In this respect, the patient-oriented approach and time-budget analyses - supplemented by other data sources - seem to be appropriate to reveal, integrate and measure analytical categories.

Our study attempted to develop tools for a comparative analysis of patients with different treatments and in different types and patterns of care, living in different environments. This very difficult task, however, is a theoretically most simple prerequisite to cost-effectiveness analyses. But even if we should fail in this respect, a systematic description and interpretation of the different ways that chronic (psychotic) patients live in different settings of care seems to be an important starting point for further research on cost and effectiveness of mental health programs.

Appendix A
Cost-categories used for some cost-effectiveness analyses of mental health services

1. *Weisbrod et al. (1980)*
Direct treatment costs
Indirect treatment costs
– Social service agencies (other hospitals, sheltered workshops, other community agencies)
– Private medical providers
Law enforcement costs
– Overnights in jail
– Court contacts
– Probation and parole
– Police contacts
Maintenance costs
– Cash payments (governmental, private, institutional, patient payments)
– In-kind food and lodging costs
– Family burden costs
– Lost earnings due to patient
– Number of families reporting physical illness due to patient
– Percent of family members experiencing emotional strain due to patient
Burden to other people (e.g. neighbours, co-workers)
Illegal activity costs
– Number of arrests
– Number of arrests for felony
Patient mortality costs
– Suicide
– Natural causes

2. *Müller and Caton (1983)*
Wage loss
Imputed value of homemaker services

3. *Rubin (1982)*
Cost of hospital care
Cost of non-hospital care
Comprehensive community care

4. *Wagner (1977)*
Investment and operation costs
Costs for therapeutic personnel
Costs for lodging (hotel services)
Medical material
Overhead costs
Travel costs

5. *Singer and Bloom (1977)*
Costs for public budgets
Capital costs
Custody costs
Treatment costs
Earnings forgone

6. *Brand et al. (1975)*
Drug costs
Treatment costs
Benefit of therapy substitution
Benefit of reduced hospitalization
Benefit due to increased productivity

7. *Leu (1978)*
Costs of damages
External costs of damages
Costs of health care
None-internalized workload for sickness funds, insurance companies
Costs of illness or accident
Income-maintenance payments in case of illness or accident
Costs of premature death
None-internalized pension payments
Intangible external costs

8. *Fenton et al. (1982)*
Costs of treatment
- Social
  - Manpower and operating costs of treatment
  - Psychotropic drug cost defrayed by hospital
  - Psychotropic drug cost defrayed by social welfare
  - Psychiatrist's cost defrayed by health insurance
- Private
  - Psychotropic drug cost defrayed by patient or patient's spouse or parent
  - Psychotropic drug cost defrayed by other relative or friend
  - Transportation cost defrayed by family
Costs of consequences of illness
- Social
  - Patient's lost salary replaced by social welfare
  - Patient's lost salary replaced by unemployment insurance
  - Number of working days lost by patient
  - Number of working days lost by family
- Private
  - Money given or lent to patient by family
  - Patient's lost salary replaced by family
- Social and private
  - Cost of housekeeper defrayed by family and by social welfare

9. *Ginsberg and Marks (1977)*
Intangible benefits
- Reduction in psychopathological symptoms
- Increase in leisure activity
Tangible benefits
- Reduced use of health services (inpatient and day-patient facilities, other health resources)
- Reduced expenses incurred by patients
- Work (work ability, amount of housework, quality of work, reduced patients' time off work, reduced relatives' time off work, earnings)
Costs
- Cost of hospital visits (travel, work and leisure missed)
- Capital
- Running costs
- Other costs

10. *McCaffree (1969)*
Length of hospitalization
Daily maintenance and treatment costs
Direct budgeted cost of maintenance and treatment
Implicit state capital carrying and depreciation costs
Total of state (public) costs
Loss of income (private)
Emergency family expenditures

Total private costs
Grand total, state and private costs
Transfer (welfare) payments

11. *Hertzman (1983)*
Direct costs
– Inpatient care
– Outpatient care
– Drugs
Indirect costs
– Short-term illness
– Permanent disability
– Premature mortality

Appendix B

'Time-behaviour units' (actons) derived from diaries

Time-behaviour atoms (actons)	Inpatients									Outpatients								
	A	B	C	D	E	M	N	P	Q	F	G	H	I	J	K	L	O	R
waking up, getting up	X	X		X	X	X	X		X	X	X	X		X			X	X
washing, shaving	X		X	X	X			X	X	X			X	X	X	X		X
waiting	X																	
breakfast	X	X	X	X	X	X		X	X	X	X	X	X	X		X	X	X
balneal therapy	X						X											
occupational therapy	X			X	X		X		X									
sleeping after lunch	X	X	X	X	X	X		X	X	X	X	X	X					X
travelling	X																	
lunch	X	X	X	X		X	X	X	X	X	X	X		X		X	X	X
dinner	X	X	X	X	X	X	X	X	X		X	X	X	X	X	X		X
sitting around	X																	
watching television	X	X	X	X	X			X	X	X	X	X	X	X	X	X		X
talking with patients	X		X	X	X			X										
sleeping (evening/night)	X	X	X	X	X	X	X	X	X	X	X	X	X	X	X	X	X	X
taking a shower		X																
listening to music, radio	X	X						X		X		X	X				X	X
tidying up	X											X	X	X	X	X		
visit by the doctor	X	X	X	X			N	X	X									
walking around (indoors)	X	X	X															
doing housework										X	X		X	X			X	
reading in books, Bible	X		X		X	X					X					X	X	
smoking		X	X	X				X	X									
drinking coffee (indoors)		X	X					X		X				X				X
talking with nurses		X																
playing games		X			X													
working in the kitchen				X			N	X										
going shopping			X	X							X	X		X	X			X
drowsing				X														
having a rest				X														
going downtown								X		X								
going for a walk								X		X		X					X	X
cooking a meal											X	X	X	X	X	X		
talking with a relative, friend											X		X		X			
doing the dishes											X	X		X		X		
making a visit (friends)												X				X	X	X
reading the newspaper													X		X	X		
brooding, thinking						X							X	X	X	X		
calling at authorities													X					
washing clothes													X					
taking a course (adult education)													X					
receiving relatives, friends							X								X			
returning home (by public transport)																X		
drinking coffee (outdoors)																X		
playing piano				X														
music therapy							X											

Appendix C
Activities of patients during the month prior to interview

Activities last month	Inpatients									Outpatients								
	A	B	C	D	E[a]	M	N	P	Q	F	G	H	I	J	K	L	O	R
doing tasks	X		X	X					X	X		X		X	X	X	X	
shopping	X	X	X	X		X		X	X	X	X	X	X	X	X	X		X
going for a walk	X		X	X		X				X		X		X	X	X	X	X
riding a bicycle										X	X							
swimming	X														X	X		
making visits										X		X		X	X	X	X	X
going to church						X					X							
going to meetings															X			
going to discos, dancing															X			
bowling																		
going to a pub	X			X						X		X		X	X			
attending a family party																		
making an excursion											X	X	X	X	X			
taking a bus trip											X		X					
tidying up						X	X			X	X	X	X	X	X	X	X	X
cooking										X	X	X	X	X	X	X	X	
doing other housework								X		X	X	X		X	X	X	X	X
knitting											X	X			X		X	
doing handicrafts										X								
repairing things																		
hobbying																		
fulfilling job duties											X			X	X			
interacting with family		X	X								X			X	X			X
playing games	X					X								X				
having a visitor			X	X		X	X	X	X		X	X		X	X	X	X	X
reading				X		X	X			X	X	X	X	X	X	X		
listening to radio		X	X			X				X	X	X	X	X	X	X	X	X
watching television	X	X	X			X				X	X	X	X	X	X	X		
practising sports						X	X			X								
taking part in adult education																		
painting, photographing															X			
following a secondary occupation																		
gardening																		
camping							X				X							

[a] No information

References

As D (1982) Measuring the use of time. In: OECD (ed) The social indicator development programme, Special Study No 7. OECD, Paris, pp 87–114

Brand M, Escher M, Menzl A, Horisberger B (1975) Kosten-Nutzen-Analyse Antidepressiva. Springer, Berlin Heidelberg New York

Fenton FR, Tessier L, Contandrioupoulos AP, Nguyen H, Struening EL (1982) A comparative trial of home and hospital psychiatric treatment: financial costs. Can J Psychiatry 27 (3): 177–187

Frank R (1981) Cost-benefit analysis in mental health services: a review of the literature. Admin Ment Health 8 (3): 161–176

Ginsberg G, Marks I (1977) Cost and benefit of behavioural psychotherapy: a pilot study of neu-rotics treated by nurse-therapists. Psychol Med 7: 685–700

Harvey AS, Szalai A, Elliott DH et al. (1984) Time-budget research. Campus, Frankfurt

Hertzmann P (1983) The economic costs of mental illness in Sweden 1975. Acta Psychiatr Scand 68: 359–367

Leu R (1978) Nutzen-Kosten-Analyse der Behandlung von Alkoholkranken. Wirtschaft Recht 30: 377–399

Mangen SP (ed) (1985) Mental health care in the European Community. Croom Helm, London

McCaffree K (1969) The cost of mental health care under changing treatment methods. In: Schulenberg et al. (eds) Program evaluation in the health fields. Behavioral Publications, New York, pp 452–471

Müller CF, Caton CLM (1983) Economic costs of schizophrenia: a postdischarge study. Med Care 21 (1): 92–104

Rubin J (1982) Cost measurement and cost data in mental health settings. Hosp Community Psychiatry 33 (9): 750–754

Singer NM, Bloom HS (1977) A cost-effectiveness analysis of Patuxent Institution. Bull Am Acad Psychiatry Law 5 (2): 161–170

Wagner M (1977) Kosten-Nutzen-Rechnung zu den Reform-Empfehlungen der Psychiatrie-Enquête-Kommission. (Überarbeiteter Beitrag zur WHO-Tagung in den Haag, Juni 1976: Kosten-Nutzen-Analyse in der Psychiatrie). Soz Fortschr 26 (1): 9–18

Weisbrod BA, Test MA, Stein LI (1980) Alternative to mental hospital treatment. II. Economic benefit-cost analysis. Arch Gen Psychiatry 37 (4): 400–405

Health Systems Research

W. v. Eimeren, B. Horisberger (Eds.)

Socioeconomic Evaluation of Drug Therapy

1988. 52 figures. XV, 244 pages.
ISBN 3-540-18662-X

Modern drugs are invented according to medical needs, making use of the latest innovations in technology. They are sophisticated, efficacious, and costly, but are they effective?
The book describes the environmental situation in the United States and in Europe in which pharmaceutical development takes place it also explores the grounds for agreement as well as disagreement between the social and the economic evaluations of progress. It tackles the problem of outcome measurements, patients' behavior, quality of life, and individual value judgments and describes methodological boundaries in the socioeconomic evaluation of drugs.

D. Schwefel (Ed.)

Indicators and Trends in Health and Health Care

1987. 7 figures. VIII, 131 pages.
ISBN 3-540-16998-9

Several examples of regional and national sets of indicator systems which could be used for regular reporting on health and health care are given in the book. It also discusses a variety of possibilities for discerning and estimating trends; these include mathematical and statistical methods, critical analysis, imagination, and morale. The book, thus, contributes to establishing a link between the development of indicator systems for today's health situation and the exploration of the future.

F. F. H. Rutten, S. J. Reiser (Eds.)

The Economics of Medical Technology

Proceedings of an International Conference on Economics of Medical Technology

1987. 8 figures. VIII, 140 pages.
ISBN 3-540-17984-4

In this volume the development and diffusion of medical technologies are described as well as the policy questions arising from technological development. A large section of the book is devoted to the methodology of technology assessment as a discipline, and outlines are given for methodological challenges to be tackled in the future. Finally, the book provides an evaluation of the role of ethics and of economics training in relation to the rational use of medical technology.

Springer-Verlag
Berlin Heidelberg New York
London Paris Tokyo

Springer

Health Systems Research

D. Schwefel, P.-G. Svensson, H. Zöllner (Eds.)

Unemployment, Social Vulnerability, and Health in Europe

1987. 30 figures, 40 tables. XII, 325 pages. ISBN 3-540-17867-8

This book considers the theoretical, methodological, empirical and political questions on the relationship between unemployment and health. Social and psychological aspects are given particular attention. The main part of the book deals with empirical research from nine European countries. Analyses from Eastern Europe are compared with corresponding studies from the West. Youth and long-term unemployment, and the psychological effects of unemployment are important issues discussed, as are the political conclusions drawn by the Council of Europe and the WHO.

W. v. Eimeren, R. Engelbrecht, C. D. Flagle (Eds.)

Third International Conference on System Science in Health Care

Troisième Conférence Internationale sur la Science des Systèmes dans le Domaine de la Santé

1984. XXXIII, 1,451 pages. ISBN 3-540-13692-4

The contributions to the Third International Conference on System Science in Health Care, which are presented here, all concern the development of health resources in a broad systemic context. Emphasis is placed on three major concerns: first, a major health problem, such as cardiovascular disease, or an important segment of the population at particular risk, such as the elderly, children or industrial workers; second, some generic aspects of organization and decision making, including the trial and evaluation of innovative health strategies; and third, the methodology of research and analysis in the health service system.

Springer-Verlag
Berlin Heidelberg New York
London Paris Tokyo

Springer